Alphabet SOUP

A Recipe for Spiritual Fulfillment

Alphabet SOUP

A Recipe for Spiritual Fulfillment

MICHAEL GAFA

Printed in the United States of America

Packaged by WinePress Publishing, PO Box 428, Enumclaw, WA 98022. The views expressed or implied in this work do not necessarily reflect those of WinePress Publishing. Ultimate design, content, and editorial accuracy of this work are the responsibilities of the author.

ISBN 1-57921-513-0
Library of Congress Catalog Card Number: 2002114597

Dedicated to my wife, Pamela; my son, Spencer; and my son, Trevor. May all of your days be filled with joy and fulfillment through Jesus Christ.

With Gratitude . . .

The best chapters in this book are the ones edited by Tamara. Her insight and encouragement were invaluable.

Lamont helped me to locate "the leader within," and taught me much about what it means to live as a beloved child of God.

My mother, Angie, and my dearly departed father, Alex, lie very much at my heart. My parents taught me how to live and how to love. I am so blessed to be their son.

My sister, Denise, and my brother, Tom, are the world's greatest siblings! Our bond runs deep, as does our love toward one another. I am grateful to be their brother.

My grandmother, Agnes, and dearly departed grandfather, Sam, exemplify unconditional love. How fortunate I am to have inherited such loving grandparents!

My dearly departed grandmother, Mary, and dearly departed grandfather, Emmanuel, taught me much about love for God and love for family. Their lessons have never left me.

My mother-in-law, Elaine, and stepfather-in-law, Bob, have treated me as one of their own from day one. I have felt loved and cherished by them for over eighteen years (and counting), and for that I am absolutely thankful.

My father-in-law, Darrell, and stepmother-in-law, Doreen, have made me feel welcome and loved since we first met. What a joy and privilege it is to be their son-in-law!

My dearly departed grandparents-in-law—Henry, Lorina, Andrew, and Audrey—left a legacy of love for family and for God. Their legacy is one I treasure and hope to pass on to my children.

My brothers and sisters in law—Dave, Lisa, J.P., Naomi, Cindy, Joe, Andy, Kirsten, Heather, and Mike (almost!)—are all wonderful, loving people who have spoiled me much more than I deserve! I am richly blessed to be their brother.

My nieces and nephews—Elissa, Lauren, Kiran, Karis, Ariel, Alysia, Olivia, Kameron, and Connor, are all special. What an honor and privilege it is to be their uncle! I love each one of them very much.

My aunts and uncles, and aunts and uncles in-law—Joe, Patrina, Carmen, John, Chris, Karen, Pat, Mario, Barb, Mike, Beverly, Blaine (you da man!), Robb, Carole, JoAnn, Roger, Linda, Roger, Pete, Pat, Marlene, David, Ken, Donna, Elaine, Art, Sharon, and Ed—along with all of my cousins and cousins-in-law, are near and dear to my heart. I give thanks for their love and affection over the years.

I have been richly blessed with a plethora of wonderful friends. I have friends from many places and from many different backgrounds. I have known some for many years and others for just a few months. Regardless of where they live or how long we have been friends, I treasure each one of them. I am blessed to have so many *true* friends.

My children, Spencer and Trevor, are a continual source of amazement and delight! My constant companions never fail to put a smile on my face. I give thanks to God for giving me the privilege of fathering two wonderful, loving, and very special children.

With Gratitude . . .

My wife, Pamela, has been the love of my life since the day we met. I am forever grateful for her unending encouragement, generosity and affection, and for being an absolutely incredible mother to our children. My wife completes me. I am the luckiest man in the world.

Ingredients

Introduction

During the spring and summer of 2001 I felt that God was calling me to write a book about . . . something. But on most days I neither acknowledged nor contemplated God's will, choosing instead to define my own path instead of following His preordained path for me. Yet as the days went by that summer I felt the Lord's call go from subtle to unmistakable, and eventually I decided to honor God's will. At first I had no idea what I was called to write *about,* and was in fact rather befuddled as to why the Lord would have me write a book at all! I can claim neither an impressive array of published writings nor any formal theological training; in fact, the only "credentials" I can justifiably claim are a strong desire to grow in faith, knowledge, and discipleship in the Lord Jesus Christ, and an *untapped* ability to string sentences together. Thus it is in the absence of any false modesty whatsoever that I truthfully tell you that I lacked "proper" credentials to write *any* book, particularly one that would delve into several complex facets of Christianity.

But as God's will was more powerful than my insecurity, I persistently and prayerfully began to discern what He would have me write about. Eventually I settled on the topic of genuine spiritual fulfillment, which originates through initial acceptance of Jesus Christ as Lord and Savior, but is sustained only through actively *embracing* the rewards that salvation offers.

While initially discerning how to go about writing the book, I quickly came to understand that I didn't need to rely on myself—that I *couldn't* rely on myself-for the book to be filled with truth and integrity. I desperately needed Jesus to be, in a very real sense, my Co-author. Thus I began my "research" in the only manner possible: prayer, prayer, and more prayer, in parallel with considerable study of God's Word.

I determined that taking an "A to Z" approach for identifying "ingredients" of spiritual fulfillment would force me to look beyond the obvious and to rely on the Lord for clarity and guidance. Much to my delight, I found that this approach yielded an integral and rather comprehensive list of ingredients for genuine, sustainable spiritual fulfillment.

Writing this book has brought me closer to the Source of spiritual fulfillment than I have ever been in my life. And while I am convinced that the words contained herein will aid considerably in allowing you to unlock the door to fulfillment, I am even more convinced that the key to the door resides *solely* with Jesus Christ. My simple hope is that "Alphabet Soup" brings you closer to Jesus' saving grace and loving arms, for ultimately that is where you will find spiritual fulfillment.

Alignment

What are your foundational beliefs? What is the *basis* for your beliefs? How negotiable are your beliefs? Do your beliefs consistently govern your thoughts, words, and actions? If you introspectively answer these questions with absolute honesty you will increase your understanding of what beliefs govern you, why they govern you, and whether or not you are *truly* committed to living according to what you most ardently believe. No one can experience genuine and sustainable spiritual fulfillment without first being so convicted in their foundational beliefs that they fervently desire to live according to them.

All Beliefs Are Not Equal

It is rather apparent that our beliefs evolve over time. When we are first born, basic human needs such as nourishment, shelter, and security are our primary focus, but over time we learn from many different sources and are often overwhelmed with inputs. We process those inputs and then either consciously or subconsciously categorize them (acceptance, rejection, curiosity, amusement, delight, anger, etc.).

As we change and evolve, the same inputs are often categorized differently. For example, when I was four years old and heard stories about Santa Claus giving presents to children scattered all over the world, I believed in him wholeheartedly; but when I was eight years old and heard the same stories, I processed them with considerably more doubt.

A distinction must be made between negotiable and non-negotiable beliefs. When we believe in something yet remain purposefully open to being swayed by other viewpoints, we possess a negotiable belief; but when we fervently believe in something such that we cannot be swayed whatsoever, we possess a non-negotiable belief. Non-negotiable beliefs can be equated to *foundational* beliefs, for in essence they define who we are and what we stand for.

To illustrate the point, my belief in Jesus Christ as Lord and Savior is not up for negotiation, but my belief that George W. Bush is best qualified to lead our nation certainly is. Why? Because the *basis* for the two beliefs are markedly different. My belief in Jesus as Lord and Savior stems from a combination of upbringing, personal experiences during which I have felt His presence, and, most importantly, the absolute and irrefutable Truth of God's Holy Word—the Bible. My belief in George W. Bush as a highly commendable United States President is based on his stated and demonstrated political ideology, handling of foreign affairs, compassion for others, and *apparent* love for God and family. However, if his actions and/or words don't align with his stated political ideology, or with his apparent love of God and family, I will re-examine my belief that he is best qualified to lead our nation.

The process of determining foundational beliefs starts at an early age. We model parents, uncles, aunts, grandparents, teachers, pastors, etc. Ultimately, who we are largely reflects the people who have most influenced us on a long-term basis. While I am not like my father in many respects, my sense of humor and love of sports are very much taken from him. The empathy I have toward people reflects behavior that was taught and modeled by my mother. The patience I have developed of late is largely attributable to learning from my wife. And my decision to write this book stems from the influence provided to me by my friend and Leadership Coach, Lamont Moon.

It is worth noting that all of our beliefs, even those that are foundational, evolve over time and create new challenges. We must choose between embracing or denying those additional challenges. If we embrace them, short-term pain most often turns into long-term gain, which in turn leads to personal and spiritual growth; but if we deny them, complacency sets in and spiritual growth is stagnant.

Deepening the Roots of Foundational Beliefs

I have been increasingly convinced that the Lord desires to play an active role in my life. He has been knocking on my door for many years, and I have started to open the door wider and wider. The results are always fruitful and at times astonishing, and my faith in Jesus Christ has become unshakable.

In many respects, having faith so deeply rooted has made living according to my belief in God (and by extension God's Word) easier, but in other respects alignment has actually become more difficult. The easy part is that my conviction is unwavering, and there is significant intrinsic joy in serving God. The difficult part is that I still get frustrated with my inability to *consistently* embody my beliefs through corresponding thoughts, words, and actions. My spiritual "bar" has been raised, but I am unable to consistently clear it. Yet despite my shortcomings, I continue to grow spiritually. An increased reliance on God gives me an inner strength that can only be realized through human weakness.

The apostle Peter was the rock that the Christian church was built on, yet even he didn't *fully* align his actions with a belief in Jesus as Lord until after Jesus' resurrection. Peter had a foundational belief in Jesus, but his belief wasn't rooted enough for him to acknowledge an association with the Lord when confronted during Jesus'trial. Later, Peter's belief in Jesus as Lord and Savior was so deeply rooted that it allowed him to be the rock that Jesus said he would be.

Indeed, when beliefs aren't deeply rooted, we must search for truth and meaning, which will yield either deeper roots or a change to our beliefs. Regardless of which occurs, the process of understanding and seeking to deepen the roots of our beliefs is vital to achieving healthy alignment.

Assessing Alignment

In terms of assessing whether your thoughts, words, and actions are properly aligned with your beliefs, it is my opinion that only you can make that determination. To be of value, this assessment requires honesty and vulnerability. Ask for open, honest feedback from people with whom you are most intimate—spouses, children, parents, siblings, friends, etc. If you approach them with an attitude of *wanting* to know the truth, you will genuinely factor their input into your self-assessment; but if you approach them in a manner not conducive to getting honest feedback, it's not worth taking the time.

Beyond soliciting feedback from family and friends, you should find one person to be an accountability partner. Ideally, this person isn't a family member, but rather a friend who shares many common interests, as well as general concurrence with your worldview. The relationship with this person should be based on mutual trust, respect, and desire for self-accountability. In order to maintain continuity, regular meetings should take place. I have been blessed in abundance with many dear family members and friends, but in terms of having one accountability partner, my good friend Jack has been instrumental in helping me define and adhere to a set of beliefs based on sound Biblical principles.

A weekly self-assessment, which ought to take no more than fifteen minutes, helps considerably in maintaining proper alignment, and provides both a historical record and current "snapshot" showing beliefs we are properly aligned with and out of alignment with.

As shown below, my approach is simple and straightforward: foundational beliefs in the left-hand column, assessment dates on the top row, and designations for the assessment itself (● for unsuccessful, **?** for somewhat successful, and ✔ for successful):

	DATES:			
FOUNDATIONAL BELIEF	JAN. 1	JAN.8	JAN.15	. . . etc.
Alignment	✔	✔	✔	
Balance		✔	**?**	✔
Christianity		**?**	✔	✔
Discernment		✔	✔	●
. . . etc.				

When my thoughts, words, or actions are not properly aligned with a foundational belief(s), my initial focus is to attempt to understand why, then to make the necessary adjustments. Oftentimes having a greater sense of awareness and increased focus is enough to temporarily remedy the problem. But striving for proper alignment is a continuous challenge, for our thoughts, words, and actions are *never* perfectly aligned with our beliefs.

Empowerment through Grace

While we are all sinful beings, the sacrifice and grace extended through Jesus Christ sufficiently cleanses us if we believe accordingly:

> *For all have sinned and fall short of the glory of God, and are justified freely by his grace through the redemption that came by Christ Jesus.*
> *(Romans 3:23–24)*

It is through acceptance of Jesus Christ as my Lord and Savior that I can *strive* to reach optimal alignment, knowing full well that I will never actually realize it. Recognizing that we all fall short in this endeavor, it is still of the utmost importance to strive for absolute accordance between what we think, say, and do with what we most ardently believe.

Even the Apostle Paul, who brought so many to Christ and whose unshakable faith in God while facing intense persecution is well noted, had his struggle in this area:

> *I know that nothing good lives in me, that is, in my sinful nature. For I have the desire to do what is good, but I cannot carry it out. For what I do is not the good I want to do; no, the evil I do not want to do—this I keep on doing. Now if I do what I do not want to do, it is no longer I who do it, but it is sin living in me that does it.*
> *(Romans 7:18–20)*

Despite Paul's trials and tribulations, he sought perfect alignment, which for him meant living up to what God created him for:

> *Not that I have already obtained all this, or have already been made perfect, but I press on to take hold of that for which Christ Jesus took hold of me. Brothers, I do not consider myself yet to have taken hold of it. But one thing I do: Forgetting what is behind and straining toward what is ahead, I press on toward the goal to win the prize for which God has called me heavenward in Christ Jesus.*
> *(Philippians 3:12–14)*

Striving for perfect alignment is an unattainable challenge. Yet as Paul demonstrates, what's most important is not how you start the race, nor that you run a perfect race, but that you consistently strive to do the best you can.

Take solace in knowing that when you stumble, which you most certainly will, Jesus will carry you if only you ask Him. The choice is yours.

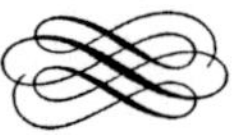

A Hard Lesson in Alignment

I have been blessed with parents who taught me the difference between right and wrong, and the importance of following God's commandments. Their lessons were instrumental in shaping my character and beliefs, despite the fact that I failed to heed their advice all too frequently while growing up.

One day, when I was 12 years old, a friend and I rode our bikes to a store. I only went along for the ride, for I didn't have any money and wasn't looking to buy anything.

Soon after we entered the store, my friend put a cassette tape under his jacket! I had never stolen anything in my life, and immediately started to sweat profusely. My anxiety increased even more when he told me that I should put a record album under my coat, since there was "no way" I could be caught. I found myself tempted by his argument, thinking that I might like listening to a record album I didn't even have to pay for! On the other hand, I knew that stealing was wrong.

While thinking about what to do, I felt surprised as I started to tuck the record underneath my coat. My sweat quotient increased even more as I inched closer to the store exit. By the time I walked out the door, I was scared to death! I already regretted stealing the record ... then I *really* regretted stealing the record when I was grabbed by the store security guard.

We were pulled into a room and had to listen to the security guard call our parents. That phone call is one I'll never forget.

After signing some papers, we biked home, all the while dreading what our parents would say and do to us. Finally, we arrived home and it was time to face the consequences of our actions.

My mom and dad said all the requisite things that parents normally say in these situations: that they had raised me better than this and that just because one person does something wrong doesn't mean I should follow his lead. But what hurt most was that I had let down the people I loved most in the world.

Since that day I have never stolen anything, nor have I even been tempted to steal anything. I give glory and thanks to God for changing alignment from a lightly held belief into a tightly held foundational belief.

Balance

While recognizing that life balance is all-encompassing, for the purpose of tying balance to spiritual fulfillment I have narrowed it to two primary categories: Emotional balance and Activity balance. *Emotional balance* pertains to managing our emotions, while *Activity balance* pertains to optimal utilization of our time. Both are essential in order to become all that God calls us to be.

Emotional Balance

Maintaining healthy emotional balance has always been a struggle for me. I have been guilty since I can remember of mistaking *controlling* emotion for *managing* emotion. Only within the past few years have I understood how errant my approach has been.

Emotions such as unbridled joy, intense sadness, and deep love have been frequently repressed during my adult life. Interestingly, many people have expressed admiration for my ability to remain on an even keel during difficult situations. And while I appreciate (and to some extent agree with) their sentiments, more often than not my ability to remain calm during a crisis simply stems from *denying* feelings and emotions.

The Battle between Logic and Emotion

Imagine for a moment that there are two of you: a "logical" self and an "emotional" self. Every situation in your life would be processed through both of you. Your logical self sees the bigger picture, is often geared toward crisis avoidance, and seeks to rationalize things in order to achieve a desirable outcome. Your emotional self is much quicker to react, doesn't seek specific outcomes to situations, and is highly instinctive.

Ask yourself these questions:

1. Which do you like best—your logical self or your emotional self? *Why?*
2. Do you intentionally suppress either "self" on occasion?
3. Do you *unintentionally* suppress either "self" on occasion?
4. If you answered "yes" to either 2 or 3 above, do you find yourself frustrated by this at times?
5. Again, thinking of both your logical self as well as your emotional self, how would each respond to the following situations and which would be more prevalent?
    a. Your manager has just given you an unfavorable performance evaluation, which in your opinion does not accurately reflect your job performance.
    b. You are listening to a thought-provoking sermon at church, one that prompts you to reflect on your relationship with God.
    c. Someone in your immediate family has passed away.
    d. You have just witnessed the birth of a child.
    e. A co-worker seems to be having a difficult time dealing with a situation, even though that person hasn't said anything about it to you.

I am guessing that if you put ample thought and complete honesty into answering these questions, then this exercise reinforced in your mind the chronic challenge faced in balancing emotions. I believe that most of us lean *instinctively* toward either logic or emotion, with relatively few people able to stay optimally (and consistently) balanced between the two. As stated earlier, my instinct is to gravitate toward logic, though it is increasingly apparent to me that in order to find healthy emotional balance I must *allow* emotion to surface more frequently.

Suppressing versus Channeling Anger

There are some situations in which emotion can and should be controlled. For example, succumbing to hostility certainly isn't healthy; in fact, where there is raw anger involved, our best approach is to suppress it to whatever extent possible.

The exception to suppressing anger occurs when our non-negotiable beliefs are blatantly compromised, and our best approach becomes constructively *channeling* anger. In these situations, not only is channeling anger acceptable, it is often the only *viable* option. For example, the civil rights movement was born from years of slavery and persecution, from which anger was a natural byproduct. The anger held by so many people was frequently, and *necessarily,* repressed, yet it was never extinguished and eventually led to reform.

Even our Lord righteously channeled anger so as to avoid compromising a non-negotiable truth:

Jesus entered the temple area and drove out all who were buying and selling there. He overturned the tables of the moneychangers and the benches of those selling doves. "It is written," he said to them, "'My house will be called a house of prayer,' but you are making it a 'den of robbers.'"
(Matthew 21:12–13)

Do We Feel Emotions As Jesus Did?

Jesus experienced intense emotion, including sorrow and anguish:

When Jesus saw her weeping, and the Jews who had come along with her also weeping, he was deeply moved in spirit and troubled. "Where have you laid him?" he asked. "Come and see, Lord," they replied. Jesus wept.
(John 11:33–35)

"My soul is overwhelmed with sorrow to the point of death," he said to them. "Stay here and keep watch."
(Mark 14:34)

While Jesus allowed Himself to experience intense emotion on numerous occasions, many of us find it difficult to follow His lead. I believe the main reason we repress emotion is to camouflage our own insecurities. We learn from a young age that "boys don't cry," that we should have "thick skin" and that "only the strong survive." And though we frequently mistake outward displays of emotion for weakness, Jesus' anger, sadness, and grief not only didn't weaken Him, it strengthened Him. In His human condition, God's Son placed *absolute* faith in the Father, knowing that God *is* strength, and that God would be with Him at all times.

As for myself, I have recognized the need to stop blatantly controlling emotions at the expense of not *managing* them. I believe the difference is in having a better understanding of when to knowingly repress emotion and when to *embrace* emotion. Two relatively recent situations have opened my eyes considerably.

Life and Death

Pam and I had been married for around three years when we decided to try for children. After trying unsuccessfully for six years we were both tested, during which time we discovered that Pam needed surgery for endometriosis. Shortly after the surgery, Pam was prescribed fertility medication, and one month later she was pregnant. During those years both she and I were at times distraught, yet didn't talk much about it. I especially was in emotional denial! Logic circumvented emotion as I was determined to happily accept whatever the outcome would be.

After finding out that Pam was pregnant, I cried tears of joy. This genuinely surprised me! I couldn't remember the last time I cried about anything, yet my tears acknowledged that having children was more important to me than I had allowed myself to believe it was.

After Pam had been on bed rest for several weeks, and after many close calls of premature delivery, we welcomed our children into the world on March 27, 1996. Again I was overcome emotionally, and yet felt perfectly comfortable being in that state. Needless to say, I love my wife and children more than anything in this world and treasure my time with them. I have an emotional attachment to Pam and the boys that is deeply satisfying and, based on my history of suppressing emotion, occasionally surprising.

The other situation was at the opposite end of the spectrum. My father passed away from liver cancer on February 10, 2000, after battling deteriorating health on and off for several years. I had previously lost both of my grandfathers and one of my grandmothers, but had never lost anyone this close to me.

Leading up to my father's death, there were many days spent at the hospital. During this time, despite doing my best to keep my logical self at the forefront, my emotional self often prevailed. I felt my father's pain. I felt his concern for my mother and for everyone in our family. And I felt his self-assurance that he would soon be with the Lord. Each visit was followed by intense examination of self and of the relationships in my life. Even in devastating loss, I was able to experience gain: my father demonstrated faith, grace, and love throughout the worst circumstances imaginable, leaving an imprint on me that will never be forgotten.

It may seem rather foreign to think that anyone would be surprised at being highly emotional during the birth and death of a beloved family member, but I can only tell you that it's not a conscious choice to suppress emotions, it's a result of long-standing habits. Sometimes extreme situations wake us up to the fact that everything we need to know about life is given to us through God's Word. I am continuing to grow in the area of emotional balance and by the grace of God will find optimal balance during my lifetime.

Activity Balance

While activity balance is very different from emotional balance, it too is vitally important. Each of us has twenty-four hours in a day and a degree of freedom in how we spend that time. Should we work extra hours? Watch television? Exercise? Read Scripture?

As a general rule, I believe that activity balance is easier achieved than emotional balance, simply because it's more conducive to planning and discipline, as opposed to emotional balance which is based largely on instincts that are difficult to change. I would further suggest that improvement in one's activity balance will *directly* improve one's emotional balance. How we spend our time heavily influences how we balance emotions.

Optimal activity balance can be equated with spending time in direct support of foundational beliefs. That doesn't mean that every minute of every day should directly support foundational beliefs, but rather that we consciously focus on making sure we spend *enough* time, with enough *focus*, on the things we have determined are most important to us.

Free Time and Required Time

Think carefully when making the distinction between activities that are required versus those that are free (i.e., of our own choosing). Would you categorize the activities that follow as "free" or "required"?

1. Watching television.
2. Visiting relatives.
3. Voting in elections.
4. Going to church on Sunday morning.
5. Volunteering to help at church.
6. Spending time with your family.
7. Community service.
8. Reading and studying from the Bible.
9. Home repairs.
10. Pursuing further education.

I would submit that *none* of these activities are required. I would further submit that, excepting rare cases, the *only* time "required" of us is to sleep and, for some, to work. That leaves a lot of available time!

You may believe that some of the activities on the list (such as going to church, spending time with family, and Bible study) are required, but we *choose* to go to church, spend time with family, and study God's Word. We choose everything we do! Hopefully our choices support our beliefs, and our beliefs are aligned with God's Word, but in the free world, if we abide by societal laws, we are not punished in an earthly sense for how we spend our time.

All this freedom sounds pretty good, doesn't it? Well, freedom is certainly something to cherish, but it carries great responsibility too. Unlike some other cultures (and faiths) that require time to be spent in more regimented fashion, we in the free world choose how to spend our time, and our choices in large part define our very being.

Optimal versus Healthy Activity Balance

It is widely believed that optimal balance is achieved through some combination of social, physical, mental, and spiritual activity. But we need to recognize that our activity will never be equally apportioned in each element, and that individuals invariably prefer certain elements to others. I myself am naturally inclined toward the mental and spiritual, which necessitates effective *planning* in order to achieve a healthy balance in the physical and social elements.

Indeed, the best approach for ensuring healthy activity balance on an ongoing basis is through a combination of planning and self-accountability. Each week, I set goals (actions) for the physical, mental, spiritual, and social areas of my life, as well as for several of my "roles" (parent, spouse, Christian, employee). I also review the preceding week, using a red-yellow-green system (red for goals missed, yellow for goals somewhat completed, and green for goals successfully completed). I focus on each area to ensure that I am doing *something*, as well as making sure that I am not missing the same things repeatedly. If bad habits start to develop, I begin scheduling those activities.

For me, a "typical" week includes *some* mixture of the following: Attend and volunteer at church, exercise, Bible study, write, read, family activities, time with friends, prayer, and work. I am usually successful at doing all of these each week, yet I am careful to remember that the goal is not finding perfect balance, but finding healthy balance.

Spiritual Balance

I strongly believe that people share a universal desire to unlock life's secrets. What leads to fulfillment? How did the world come about? What happens after we die?

We share a spiritual "thirst" that needs to be quenched, though we often rationalize our *unquenched* thirst as "good enough." It's not enough to simply believe in Jesus; we need to *act* on our belief in Him! Involvement in church, fellowship, and Bible study are tremendously important, but an even better test of how we are doing spiritually comes when we are not in a place of worship or studying the Word, but when we are at work, or having lunch with a friend, or facing a moral dilemma. Do you feel *perpetually* connected with Jesus? Do you consistently embody your belief in Him?

The starting point for perpetual connection with Jesus is developing regular habits, which include but are not limited to Bible reading, devotions, prayer, and church participation/fellowship. Our spiritual habits shape us and lead us closer to the Lord. A strong connection with Jesus becomes ever present, and the satisfaction gained from it immense.

Mental Balance

The wise person makes learning a joy; fools spout only foolishness.
(Proverbs 15:2)

Interaction with others is essential for learning. Do you engage in challenging discussion with those around you? Are you open to people who hold opposing viewpoints? Engaging others contributes to our own learning tremendously! If we internalize knowledge too much, we're fooling ourselves; nobody is the expert on all things.

Reading is not only enjoyable, it's a vital component for learning. We absorb more than we realize while reading. Its effects are different than other mediums such as television or radio where there's more "interference" to distract us. Be selective when determining what to read, seeking material that will expand your knowledge.

One important aspect of pursuing mental challenges is to simply recognize their availability. Look around-we have television, talk radio, people from all walks of life, classes, books, Internet sites, seminars, opportunities at work, church programs, etc. All of these (and more) represent opportunities to stretch our mental capacity! Take advantage of God's gift to grow through learning.

Lastly, consider teaching or mentoring others in some capacity. There is no better way to grow than through helping others. If you allow your knowledge and gifts to benefit other people, you will also benefit. And do not underestimate what you can offer others—we all have something to contribute.

Physical Balance

This area is difficult, and unfortunately does not get easier with age!

Nevertheless, we are called to nourish and take care of our bodies, for a healthy, active body helps maintain a healthy, active mind.

Getting the "right" amount of exercise is highly subjective and varies by individual. Some people crave exercise (and competition) and are incomplete without it. Others loath exercise, preferring to focus their energies on other areas. In any case, challenge yourself as to what's best for you, then hold yourself accountable. Avoid falling into bad habits, and if it becomes necessary, schedule time to exercise. Keep in mind that whether you run marathons or walk in a shopping mall, you benefit from physical exertion.

Social Balance

Whether you are naturally outgoing or naturally shy, social interaction is one of life's necessities. We are put on this earth to commune with and enjoy one another. Evenings out, family vacations, and dinner parties give us necessary relief against the daily rigors of life. Jesus knew His destiny well, yet still took the time to be social:

> *On the third day a wedding took place at Cana in Galilee. Jesus' mother was there, and Jesus and his disciples had also been invited to the wedding.*
>
> *(John 2:1–2).*

Healthy social interaction shouldn't be limited to a select group of like-minded people. Yes, we *need* an inner-circle consisting of close friends and family members, but we also need to reach out to others who *aren't* like-minded, and who in fact may hold opposing viewpoints.

I am not suggesting that we accept viewpoints that contradict our own, but rather that we *respect* the beliefs held by others, just as we want them to respect ours. There is no better way to tear down barriers than by engaging other people whom we do not see eye to eye with.

Jesus teaches us not to conceal, but to reveal our beliefs:

> *"You are the salt of the earth. But if the salt loses its saltiness, how can it be made salty again? It is no longer good for anything, except to be thrown out and trampled by men. You are the light of the world. A city on a hill cannot be hidden. Neither do people light a lamp and put it under a bowl. Instead they put it on its stand, and it gives light to everyone in the house. In the same way, let your light shine before men, that they may see your good deeds and praise your Father in heaven."*
>
> *(Matthew 5:13–16)*

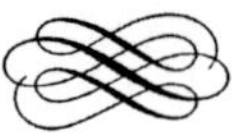

A Matter of Balance

By the time I was thirty-five years old, I had achieved, by most standards, a degree of success. I held a managerial position at a solid international company, I was well paid, and I was happily married with two precious baby boys. Yet in spite of feeling more secure than ever, I felt increasingly unbalanced and unfulfilled. My career occupied more and more of my attention, to the point where my definition of "success," which had historically revolved around faith and family, now revolved around career aspirations.

Making matters worse, while the company I worked for was both sizable and successful, the plant I worked out of was, at that time, characterized by intolerance, intra and inter-departmental friction, and finger pointing en masse.

One day I stood by as a key quality requirement was circumvented in order to attain a highly sought after certification. I had a chance to voice my disagreement but failed to, a choice that would haunt me afterwards since it went against everything I claimed to stand for.

Slowly but surely, I bent my will to suit my employer's. In the workplace, I had always prided myself on being an agent for positive change and for helping other people, but during that time I did neither, choosing instead to take a "safe" (i.e., politically correct) position on most issues. And in my personal life I wasn't doing much better: long hours at work left little or no time for physical, social, or spiritual pursuits. I lacked healthy activity balance, and my emotional balance wasn't good either!

Out of desperation I began to pray that God would lead me down the right path, whatever that path might be. Shortly thereafter I received a call from a recruiter representing a company in Holland, Michigan. I had received many calls from recruiters over the years and had always told them I wasn't interested in moving, but when she mentioned that her client placed a huge emphasis on people, culture, and ethics, I was intrigued. The more she talked, the more I listened. Over the next several weeks, Pam and I prayed for discernment of God's will.

Finally, after interviewing with what seemed like a hundred people, and after accepting a cut in pay, I went to work for the company in Holland. That move was the best one I have ever made. Pam and I have never been happier. We live in a wonderful, Christian community, in close proximity to Lake Michigan's sandy beaches. I have healthier life balance than ever before, something that I will never again compromise for a healthier paycheck. Finally, *real* success.

Christianity

That I have a foundational belief in Christianity is undeniable, but how I define and translate the depth of my belief into words is a daunting task. I believe that the large majority of people who feel closely connected to Jesus would find it difficult to accurately explain the *depth* of their connection.

God's Love Is Pure

It is of great comfort to know that God loves us, as we are, *all the time.* He desires that we obey His commands and honor Him through godly living, yet even when falling well short of His desires, God loves us.

Although we cannot begin to fathom the depth of God's love for us, a comparison (however feeble) can be made with the love we have for our own children. When we truly love our children unconditionally it produces an intense sense of connection, one that's difficult to describe but absolutely real. Interestingly, during times of deep connection with our children, we may initially feel more insignificant than before due to feeling ill equipped to raise our children in accordance with God's will; *How can we, with our sinful ways, raise our children to be godly?*

But when we step back and recall that our God is one of grace, kindness, and love, our sense of significance reaches unparalleled heights. We realize that we have been entrusted by the Lord to raise *His* children, and that He is with us every step of the way.

Similarly, when we are open to our heavenly Father's presence in our lives, we experience new feelings of significance through increased awareness that, as His beloved children, God's love for us is perfect *and* unconditional. The incredible feeling of being connected to God is available to all of us, *all the time*, if we choose to seek it.

I have not always allowed myself to be fully open to Jesus' love. My faith journey has had many twists and turns, and more than a few forks in the road, but lately I have sought His presence as never before. And as I *allow* myself to feel God's presence, I feel a deeply gratifying connection with the Lord.

The Spiritual Journey

All of us are on some kind of spiritual journey, even if we don't know it. As mentioned briefly in the chapter on *Balance*, I believe that we are "wired" to search for truth and meaning in our lives. Some of us look for answers all the time, some look for answers some of the time, and others decide that the journey is too taxing and abdicate at some point. Jesus wants all of us, even those who already ardently believe, to *grow* in faith in order to optimally experience His love:

> *"You did not choose me, but I chose you and appointed you to go and bear fruit-fruit that will last. Then the Father will give you whatever you ask in my name."*
>
> *(John 15:16)*

Are you listening for His calling? Are you *willing* to be blessed?

Whether you are in the beginning, middle, or maturity stage of your spiritual journey, we all start at the same place: inheritance.

Inheritance and Compliance

We *inherit* initial beliefs from our parents or whoever raises us. Since my parents were both Catholic, I was baptized and raised according to *their* beliefs.

Closely following inheritance is *compliance.* When we lack the confidence or ability to discern truth, we generally comply with inherited beliefs. This is an appropriate course of action during the beginning stages of one's spiritual journey, and can in fact be extremely positive if we *inherit* Truth (hence the importance of leaving a legacy). However, if we inherit false beliefs, our spiritual journey will very likely be more challenging. Yet while it may appear that some people have an easier road to salvation than others, God ensures that all people are given equal opportunity to have eternal life:

> *For God does not show favoritism.*
>
> *(Romans 2:11)*

How long we stay in compliance varies widely. Some will be compliant their entire lives, others only briefly. For Christians, a common scenario for remaining compliant is to simply place absolute faith in inherited beliefs. I only partially agree with such an approach; while there is no debating that faith is vital for maintaining a strong belief in God, to have *absolute* faith we need to better understand *why* we have placed our faith in Jesus. It is not enough to be baptized, go to church, and profess a belief in Christ, simply because that's what we have inherited. To have lasting, unshakable faith, we need to *seek* the Lord earnestly:

> *I sought the Lord, and he answered me; he delivered me from all my fears. Those who look to him are radiant; their faces are never covered with shame.*
>
> *(Psalms 34:4–5)*

The Search for Truth and Meaning

During the time that we begin replacing compliance with *searching*, we may experience emptiness never felt before. It comes from craving fulfillment but looking in all the wrong places. Instead of seeking God, we often look inward, believing that if we can just improve some aspect or facet of ourselves, we will be fulfilled. But any "fulfillment" we find solely through ourselves, or for that matter from any worldly source, will be fleeting. That is not to say that we shouldn't seek to improve ourselves, but rather that genuine, *lasting* fulfillment can only be found when we allow God's love to permeate us.

Reaching that point is difficult. God gives us freewill to carve our own destiny, but because we possess a sinful nature, we often stray from His grace and protection. This tendency is compounded by the wickedness of the world in general, and runs counter to God's will. The Psalmist was intimately familiar with man's wicked ways:

> *Be merciful to me, O God, for men hotly pursue me; all day long they press their attack. My slanderers pursue me all day long; many are attacking me in their pride.*
>
> (*Psalm 56:1–2*)

Yet even in turmoil, the Psalmist rarely strayed from God's grace and protection. In fact, after lamenting man's persecution, he immediately follows with a pledge of trust in the Lord:

> *When I am afraid, I will trust in you. In God, whose word I praise, In God I trust; I will not be afraid. What can mortal man do to me?*
>
> (*Psalm 56:3–4*)

David knew that God's love is unwavering, regardless of whatever evil was done unto him, or for that matter whatever evil he did unto others. All God asks is that we repent and accept Jesus as our Lord and Savior. His grace is sufficient to cleanse us from sin. That sounds simple, and indeed it is simple, but often the problem is in recognizing the *need* to repent.

The dilemma is this: God calls us to be humble, to love one another, and to worship Him with all of our heart, soul, and might. But in movies, television, sports, etc., the public figures most admired are those who are unabashedly bold, selfish, and independent. In western culture we have elevated actors, rock stars, and athletes to role model status, supplementing (and in some cases replacing) traditional role models such as parents, grandparents, pastors, and teachers. What is there to repent from if society condones just about everything?

The answer is, of course, that we have much to repent for. But in order to feel a need for repentance, we must first understand the differences between our world and God's will:

> *Do not love the world or anything in the world. If anyone loves the world, the love of the Father is not in him. For everything in the world—the cravings of sinful man, the lust of his eyes and the boasting of what he has*

and does—comes not from the Father but from the world. The world and its desires pass away, but the man who does the will of God lives forever.
(1 John 2:15–17)

The Ten Commandments serve to further illustrate the chasm between our world and God's will (ref. Exodus 20:3–17):

- You shall have no other gods before me.
- You shall have no false idols.
- You shall not misuse the name of the Lord in vain.
- Keep holy the Sabbath day.
- Honor your father and mother.
- You shall not murder.
- You shall not commit adultery.
- You shall not steal.
- You shall not give false testimony against your neighbor.
- You shall not covet your neighbor's wife.

At a macro level, our society rarely heeds God's commandments. His commandments were a gift, yet rather than cherish them we tend to obey only those that *we* agree with. And God's commandments were not intended to define the limits of our faith; they were set forth as *minimum requirements.*

Becoming Obedient to God

In order to be godly, we must become *obedient.* It is important to note that even as we become increasingly obedient to God, we continue to search. We are no longer searching for truth because we have already discerned that Jesus is Truth, but we still search for meaning. How do I glorify the Lord? What are my spiritual gifts and how should I use them? How can I feel connected to Jesus every minute of every hour? Am I capable of bringing others to Christ? These are questions that require introspective, thoughtful answers as we mature in faith.

You may be thinking that the *obedience* stage isn't much different than the *compliance* stage. I would argue that it is dramatically different. When in *com-*

pliance to inherited beliefs, we're on automatic pilot, simply acting on what we inherit. But when we begin to search earnestly on our own accord, and when our search yields the truth that Jesus is our Lord and Savior, we become *obedient* to His will, not out of compliance but *desire*. Our obedience reflects our love for the Lord.

And make no mistake: obedience leads to increased spiritual connection with the Lord. If we study and obey the Word, ask forgiveness, and offer thanks and praise to Jesus, obedience will allow us to bear more fruit. Obedience is not restrictive; it's liberating. And it is essential for finding optimal connection with the Lord: *abiding* in Him.

Abiding in Jesus

In the Merriam-Webster Collegiate Dictionary, the word "abide" is defined as follows: 1. to wait for. 2a. to endure without yielding. 2b. To bear patiently. 3. to accept without objection. Intransitive senses: 1. to remain stable or fixed in a state. 2. to continue in a place.

When abiding in the Lord, we fully turn our attention to understanding His will for us and acting accordingly. Our spiritual gifts are easily discerned and consistently put to good use. We truly grasp the significance of Jesus' death and resurrection and are reborn as His disciples.

As mentioned earlier, I have not always been fully open to receiving God's love. I have accepted Jesus as my Lord and Savior, and I purposefully strive to do His will, but to abide in Jesus is to be *perpetually* in step with Him, and that is something I have not yet done. I believe that God is leading me toward that place, and I pray that my heart will be open to His invitation.

The Road to Redemption

Recognizing that each of us has taken a unique path to wherever we are today, I believe that most who come to Christ follow these steps:

1. *Inheritance of beliefs*
2. *Compliance to inherited beliefs*
3. *Search for truth and meaning*
4. *Acceptance of Jesus Christ as Lord and Savior*

5. *Obedience to God*
6. *Search for meaning*
7. *Abiding in God's love*

My Spiritual Journey

My own spiritual journey certainly follows the path above. With God's grace, I am confident that I will reside in step number seven sooner than later. Following are some key points from my spiritual journey that reflect where I have been and where I am today.

1966–1977: Being born into the Catholic faith, I attended Catechism. I found the experience to be a mixed blessing; I learned a lot about the Holy Trinity, the Blessed Mother and the importance of discipline, yet there was a noteworthy lack of passion from the priests who taught Catechism at our church. I am not suggesting by any means that it reflected on the Catholic Church as a whole, but rather on this particular church during this particular time. And again, that is simply my opinion—take it as such.

1969: First communion. This was a proud day. I was seven years old and still remember that day fondly. This was a true rite of passage and I felt privileged to partake in the Lord's supper.

1972: Around this time, I suffered from a rather severe case of psoriasis of the scalp. Psoriasis is a disease that effects around 2% of the population, and its effects can range from mild to severe. It results in red lesions on the skin, which multiply and scale over with silvery patches. The treatment I was prescribed involved a daily application of a type of cream, which made for extremely greasy, unsightly hair. Not an ideal situation for a 10-year old with low self-esteem! As the health.medscape.com web site says, "There is no cure for psoriasis, and most people who develop it have it for life. It may improve at times and worsen at others, but generally it never goes away."

My mother earnestly prayed for me, and urged me to do the same, which I did. She was also active in a "charismatic" movement at that time within the Catholic Church, and one evening invited me to attend a Prayer Meeting with her at a local church. A group of people laid hands on me, and within a few weeks I was healed. That was twenty-nine years ago, and I have yet to see any additional trace of psoriasis. And I never will.

1979–1984; 1994–1998: These are times when I did not attend church. The 1979 to 1984 period covered my last few years of high school, and through college. Although this was a shortsighted time in my life, I learned a lot about responsibility, the pursuit of truth, and what really matters in life. I did not realize it at the time, but God was at work in my life. As for the 1994 to 1998 time period, this was a time when Pam and I had moved from Hoopeston, Illinois, where we were very active in our church, to St. Joseph, Michigan. We decided to take a "break" from church, citing burnout; in reality, we were deceiving ourselves. Our "break" lasted four years, yet we both continued to search for meaning in our lives. This is not a time that I am particularly proud of, but as an integral part of my overall faith journey I value it.

2000: When my father died, a part of me died too. Yet the memories and lessons my dad provided helped to offset the grief felt with his passing. I miss him every day, but his legacy is very much alive and well. He was a remarkable man who did much during his time on earth.

1998–present: This has been a time of understanding the depth of God's glory. I am consistently awestruck by His goodness and humbled by His grace.

Why Can't We All Just Get Along?

One aspect of Christianity that I wish to briefly touch on is that of denominational disagreements. As people of God, we are guilty of excessive focus on the differences we have with other Christian denominations, at the expense of diminishing God's kingdom.

Whether you are part of the Protestant, Catholic, Baptist, Evangelical, or any other arm of the *Christian* Church, do not lose sight of the fact that you are first and foremost a member of the *united* Body of Christ:

> *Just as each of us has one body with many members, and these members do not all have the same function, so in Christ we who are many form one body, and each member belongs to all the others.*
>
> *(Romans 12:4–5)*

When we dwell on our differences while ignoring the Source of our beliefs, we only serve to reinforce the notion held by non-believers that the Christian church lacks solidarity. This is a serious issue that needs correction, and it starts with us individually. I may not agree (nor should I be expected to agree) with everything that other Christian denominations practice, but if the *foundation* is Jesus Christ and the theology comes from God's Word, that's good enough for me.

I am not suggesting that we stop challenging one another (that would be disastrous), but rather that we stop obsessing over details while missing the big picture. How strong would the Christian Church be if we came together as a united Body?

While my hope is that this book will capture the essence of my unwavering and absolute belief in Jesus Christ as Lord and Savior, I recognize that there are many others much better equipped than I to make an airtight case for Christianity. If you are unsure of whether or not Christianity is Truth, there are a number of options available for you to investigate, including but not limited to religious leaders (Pastors, Priests, etc.) and various books. There are a plethora of books written about Christianity, but two of my personal favorites are *"Mere Christianity"* by C.S. Lewis, and *"How Now Shall We Live?"* by Charles Colson and Nancy Pearcey.

Closing Comments about Christianity

There are many elements of Christianity that I have not touched on in this chapter. The reason is simple: Christianity is all encompassing. Every chapter in this book, which in sum represents my belief system, is rooted in Christianity. My goal for this chapter was to simply touch on connection to God, the spiritual journey and its stages, and the need to become a united Body of Christ.

Let us never lose sight of the fact that God sent his only begotten Son so that we could have abundant life in Him. This is a gift that should not be taken lightly. Little is required of us except that we believe, repent, and follow the Lord:

> *For God so loved the world that he gave his one and only Son, that whoever believes in him shall not perish but have eternal life.*
>
> *(John 3:16)*

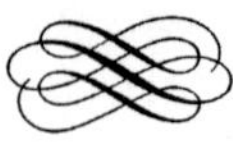

You Just Never Know!

In September 2000 an announcement was made at our church that we were short several Youth Leaders for the coming year. A meeting would be held on the coming Monday for people to help fill the void.

I felt that God was calling me to be among that group. Several years earlier we had attended a Methodist church in Warren, Michigan, and I helped lead a Junior High youth group, and later was Sunday school superintendent. I remembered that I often felt overwhelmed by the responsibility of mentoring kids, but that it was extremely gratifying to see the kids grow in faith and understanding. I looked forward to teaching children again, and leaned toward teaching younger children this time around.

Several people were at the Monday meeting. It was apparent that many others had heeded God's call as well. I listened as Shelley explained that leaders were needed for classes that took place during the Church Service, and on Wednesday evenings for the "Ministry In Motion" program. She also mentioned that we would be starting "Caraway Street" (a puppet ministry for young children) and needed puppeteers.

I began to process the situation, thinking to myself: I have two four-year old children who will be excited about attending Caraway Street; I have always been good with voice impersonations; and I love being with kids.

I decided to be a puppeteer for Caraway Street. What a joy it has been! The children learn from the interaction between the actors, puppets, and themselves. They memorize books of the Bible as well as selected verses, and there are plenty of lessons learned each week on "the street."

I did not expect that God would lead me to be a puppeteer for Him, but my spiritual gifts are such that it's a perfect fit. I am truly blessed to have been part of our church's puppet ministry. Anything is possible when you're open to God's calling . . . you just never know!

Discernment

From a Biblical perspective, discernment entails deciphering God's will. Discernment is a gift from God, and grows through obedience, prayer, and the study of Scriptures:

> *I have more insight than all my teachers, for I meditate on your statutes.*
> *(Psalm 119:99)*

Obedience, Prayer, and Scripture Lead to Discernment

Obedience is a critical element of discernment in that it produces habits that lead toward consistency of character and actions. In large part, those habits define who we are. Obedience is to be done out of desire—not obligation—and will lead to better alignment with foundational beliefs. Conversely, when we are not obedient in daily living, foundational beliefs become watered down. How can our beliefs mean much if we lack the obedience necessary to ensure that our actions align accordingly? If we are only willing to follow our beliefs when it is convenient to do so, we will never be the discerning people God calls us to be.

Prayer is closely connected to obedience and is a vitally important tool for ensuring that our decisions are in support of God's will:

Watch and pray so that you will not fall into temptation. The spirit is willing, but the body is weak.

(*Matthew 26:41*)

The Bible gives the answers to any situation we encounter. It is the ultimate reference Book! But before we can apply its teachings, we must understand them. Anyone who can discern God's will has invested time and effort in studying the Scriptures:

All Scripture is God-breathed and is useful for teaching, rebuking, correcting and training in righteousness, so that the man of God may be thoroughly equipped for every good work.

(*2 Timothy 3:16–17*)

What We Need to Discern and Why Discernment Is Critical

While a combination of obedience, prayer, and the study of Scripture are the keys to discerning God's will, we must also understand *what* needs to be discerned and *why* discernment is so important.

What needs to be discerned is . . . *everything!* Every minute of every waking hour we make decisions. Think about the decisions you make during the course of any given day, and the ramifications thereof. It boggles the mind when trying to project the overall effect of our decisions.

For example, my commute to work is around eight miles each way. During the course of my drive, I make six turns and pass through seven stoplights. I adjust my speed based on road conditions, traffic, and posted speed limits. But if I mistake a red light for green, my actions will result in some type of negative situation, ranging from minor inconvenience to loss of life. Though I am the only person in my car during my commute, my decisions effect many others. If I obey traffic laws and drive at reasonable speeds, I increase the probability that others driving in close proximity will safely reach their destinations. If I fail to drive responsibly, I *decrease* the probability of myself and others arriving safely.

That is just one example of why the decisions we make are so important. This applies to every aspect of our lives: work, family, friends, church, community, and so on. *All* of our decisions have ramifications, and it is important to try to understand what they are in advance.

I challenge you to think about and write down five decisions you make during each of the next three days. Also write down *why* you made the decisions, and the impact of your decisions. I think you will be surprised when taking stock of the effects your decisions have.

When we step back for a moment to recognize the volume and impact of decisions we make in our daily lives, we more clearly understand that our belief system is well defined and includes many societal paradigms passed on from generation to generation. We have learned that when the traffic light is red we stop, and when it's green we go. And while the great majority of laws that govern society are just that simple, what are we to do about societal paradigms (including some government laws) that are not aligned with God's commandments? Are we comfortable with what we hear on radio and watch on television? Are we alarmed when we hear that over forty percent of American marriages end up in divorce? Does legalized abortion represent progress? It is obvious that we live in a world that for the most part does not honor God's commandments.

If one out of every twenty people driving on our roads decides that a better approach is to stop when a traffic light is green, and go when it's red, we would have chaos. Traffic accidents would skyrocket, automobile insurance would be unaffordable, and people would avoid driving. And most of us would be left shaking our heads trying to understand how so many people could choose to ignore such a simple, straightforward law.

I wonder if God sees us in a similar way. His commandments are clear, but we consistently and knowingly break them. He commands us to have no false gods, but instead of looking for the one true God, many look elsewhere. He commands us to have no idols, but we promote "celebrities" to a higher status. He commands us not to steal, yet many people are overjoyed while shopping when discovering that an item has been incorrectly tagged at a lower price. He commanded us not to give false testimony against one another, yet even in our own churches there is gossip and pettiness.

The examples above illustrate *why* we need to discern God's will. We have been given freedom of choice, but with it comes human weakness. Temptation exists in many forms and presents itself frequently. If not properly armed to fight against temptation, we will succumb to it.

Fighting Against Temptation

Fortunately, we can successfully fight against temptation through three intertwined approaches: finding strength through Scripture; "filtering" temptations through our belief system; and praying for Jesus to shield us from and keep us strong when encountering temptation.

The first approach for fighting temptation shapes the second. When we allow God's Word to become us, we become it. Our beliefs reflect His Word and strengthen our resolve. We are able to filter temptation through a strong belief system and make decisions according to God's will.

Developing a strong belief system is fundamental to avoid acting on temptations. We need to seek the Lord's counsel to know what to believe. He gives us the answers provided that we are willing to invest time and energy in search of Truth:

> *"Ask and it will be given to you; seek and you will find; knock and the door will be opened to you. For everyone who asks receives; he who seeks finds; and to him who knocks, the door will be opened."*
>
> *(Matthew 7:7–8)*

The answers God gives define our foundational beliefs, and serve to tear down some prior beliefs that are not aligned with His Word. I find that as God's Truth is revealed to me, I thirst for more knowledge. It is not good enough anymore to just go through the motions of attending church and occasionally reading the Bible. I have developed a desire to be in regular communion with Jesus, spending more time studying and applying the Word, as well as in prayer. My eyes have been opened and what was blurry is becoming increasingly clear.

During this time of spiritual awakening, my ability to properly discern has increased dramatically. Yet I fully realize that danger lurks around the corner—many Christians have given in to temptation even after reaching spiritual maturity, mainly because of a false sense of security. In truth, Satan knows all of our weaknesses and takes great pleasure when a person of faith acts in opposition to their beliefs. Remember that Satan chose to tempt Jesus at a time when Jesus *might* have been physically and spiritually challenged:

> *Then Jesus was led by the Spirit into the desert to be tempted by the devil. After fasting forty days and forty nights, he was hungry. The tempter came to him and said, "If you are the Son of God, tell these stones to become bread." Jesus answered, "It is written: 'Man does not live on bread alone, but on every word that comes from the mouth of God.'" Then the devil took him to the holy city and had him stand on the highest point of the temple. "If you are the Son of God," he said, "throw yourself down. For it is written: 'He will command his angels concerning you, and they will lift you up in their hands, so that you will not strike your foot against a stone.'" Jesus answered him, "It is also written: 'Do not put the Lord your God to the test.'" Again, the devil took him to a very high mountain and showed him all the kingdoms of the world and their splendor. "All this I will give you," he said, "if you will bow down and worship me." Jesus said to him, "Away from me, Satan! For it is written: 'Worship the Lord your God, and serve him only.'" Then the devil left him, and angels came and attended him.*
>
> (Matthew 4:1–11)

Jesus example is one we need to follow. When undergoing the ultimate temptation at a time of *potential* vulnerability, Jesus rebuked Satan out of an absolute belief and understanding of Scripture, which allowed Him to clearly process the situation. We too need to learn and apply Scripture, letting it shape our beliefs so that it serves as a filter against temptation.

Up to this point, as far as the study of Scripture and prayer are concerned, I have primarily focused on how they shape our beliefs and filter out temptation. But while these aspects are crucial to discerning God's will, a strong belief system by and in itself is not enough to consistently ward off temptation.

The third approach is our ultimate triumph card against temptation. When we pray for Jesus to *shelter* us from evil, and to take control when we are tempted, we are able to do His will. This requires that we surrender our will to His, which is extremely difficult. I struggle with this frequently, even as I know that failure to surrender my will to His only cheats myself. Even the most ardent believer is vulnerable to acting on temptation without the Lord's protection. Our human condition is one of sin, and as such we need Jesus' divine intervention to live godly lives.

For clarification, though we are to surrender our will to the Lord, we are *not* to stop using our minds. Too many Christians wait for the proverbial "tap on the shoulder" when it comes to discerning God's will. Earnestly ask God to lead you, then listen to your heart, but do not remove your mind from the equation. God gifts us with intellect for a reason. Spiritual paralysis comes about when mistaking passivity for patience. Prayerfully discern God's calling, but do it *actively*.

How else can we fight temptation? God teaches believers to lean on each other for strength:

> *Brothers, if someone is caught in a sin, you who are spiritual should restore him gently. But watch yourself, or you also may be tempted. Carry each other's burdens, and in this way you will fulfill the law of Christ.*
> *(Galatians 6:1–2)*

I have many family members and friends that I confide in frequently, all of whom help me through hard times and in staying on a path toward righteousness.

Advancing God's Kingdom

Scripture. Belief. Obedience. Prayer. Fellowship. All are necessary ingredients to become discerning Christians, but to experience God's blessings for us on a whole new level, we need to take an additional step: advancing His kingdom.

Think about a basketball player who learns his craft, works hard, believes in himself, and makes it to the highest level—the NBA. Is he a successful athlete? Absolutely! Talent, hard work, and dedication have allowed him to reach the upper echelon of his sport. But if he has a burning desire to be a *champion*, he will develop a clear understanding of what his role should be in order for the team to succeed as a whole. Maybe he will sacrifice offense in order to improve defensively. Or perhaps he is more valuable coming off the bench than being in the starting lineup. It may even be that he is the team's best scorer, and must step up to the task. Whatever the case, to achieve true greatness he must understand how to best contribute to overall team success. And he must help ensure that his teammates are successful in their respective roles too.

Just as being a championship basketball team requires each player to understand and apply their gifts for overall team success, so does being a champion for God. Each of us has unique spiritual gifts designed to advance God's kingdom. We can read the Bible, pray regularly, and live obediently for Christ, but if we fail to advance God's kingdom than we have not done everything we are called to do. Being a discerning Christian *always* involves advancing the Lord's kingdom. How we do it varies widely, but that we do it is not up for debate:

> *Then Jesus came to them and said, "All authority in heaven and on earth has been given to me. Therefore go and make disciples of all nations, baptizing them in the name of the Father and of the Son and of the Holy Spirit, and teaching them to obey everything I have commanded you. And surely I am with you always, to the very end of the age."*
>
> *(Matthew 28:18–20)*

Evangelism is an area that many Christians, myself included, struggle with. We become so inwardly focused that we don't heed Jesus' call to share the Good News with others. It is humbling to think of the sacrifices made throughout history by people who have proclaimed the Gospel Truth of Jesus Christ. From the earliest days of the church and through modern times, there has always been widespread persecution of Christians. Yet we can draw strength from knowing that when we suffer while advancing the kingdom, we are rewarded accordingly:

> *Dear friends, do not be surprised at the painful trial you are suffering, as though something strange were happening to you. But rejoice that you participate in the sufferings of Christ, so that you may be overjoyed when his glory is revealed.*
>
> *(1 Peter 4:12–13)*

Nothing Ventured, Nothing Gained!

The old adage "nothing ventured, nothing gained" is especially applicable to our faith journey. We are to be assertive in proclaiming that eternal life is available only through acceptance of Jesus Christ as Lord and Savior. And while not everyone is a gifted speaker or able to do missionary work, everyone *is* capable of applying God-given spiritual gifts to advance the kingdom.

A few years back, during a planned shutdown, a small group of managers from our operations team went on an outing. Initially, we were unaware of what we would be doing, but upon arriving learned that we would be parasailing. If you are not familiar with parasailing, it basically entails soaring in a parachute at about three hundred feet in the air for fifteen minutes while being pulled by a boat. For those who are adverse to heights and like to feel in control, parasailing presents a challenge to one's will.

Our instructor demonstrated how to correctly use the equipment, assuring us that it was unfailingly reliable. This helped calm my nerves a bit, though I was still plenty nervous. As the first two people on our team took to the air, it became apparent that their anxiety turned to enjoyment after a few minutes, which helped to further calm my nerves. Finally it was my turn. Still feeling some anxiety, I said a quick, silent prayer. The prayer helped—at least initially! During those first few minutes, while climbing toward three hundred feet altitude, anxiety quickly returned. But after settling in, a wonderful sense of calm and awe took over. Viewing Lake Michigan and its surroundings while three hundred feet in the air is an incredible experience! When my turn was over I was ready to do it again.

My experience with parasailing is similar to what happens when we step out of our comfort zone to promote God's offer of salvation. Fear and apprehension begin to subside when we utilize the "equipment" He gives us: His Holy Word. We are further strengthened by remembering those who have gone before us and basked in God's glory as a result. Prayer gives us additional strength to do God's will. More often than not we *still* feel some anxiety and must decide whether our commitment to Christ entails this level of sacrifice. But when we finally step out and leave our comfort zone, we experience the fullness of Christ, and we desire to hold on to that fullness at whatever cost. Our resolve may even surprise us at times, but we are wise to remember that the only reason we can advance God's kingdom is because of faith in Jesus Christ:

I can do all things through Christ who strengthens me.
(Philippians 4:13)

Follow God's Calling

Pray earnestly for God to reveal your unique spiritual gifts. Be open to His calling. Let Him lead you in different and wonderful directions. Pray for discernment when you feel you are being led. Talk to others, and have them pray for you as well. Be open to the challenges you may face along the way, knowing that the reward is eternal life.

I often think of God's will as a magnet. Sometimes I feel Him taking me in a definite direction, while other times it's not clear where He is taking me. Too often, pride and uncertainty cause me to resist His will. But during those times when I fully submit my will to His, and do my best to discern what He would have me do, I am fulfilled in His name.

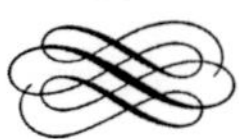

A Different Tune

During my late teens and early twenties, I wrote song lyrics for my very good friend Keith. Keith's ability to bring the words I wrote on paper to life through music and voice never failed to amaze me!

While the lyrics I wrote during that time reflected how I felt, I know that if I wrote them today they would be different. One of the lyrics I wrote then was called "*The Balance.*" What follows is the original version wrote nineteen years ago, and an updated version written in February 2002.

<u>The Balance (circa 1983)</u>

Many people cannot comprehend that where there's good, there's often bad

Many people cannot understand that for every beginning there must be an end

But why the confusion with man's persecution? Look to yourself—you're the solution

Chorus
Just keep the balance
Hold on to the balance
Live for the balance
Life is balance

You're down and out (or so it seems)—if you look beneath the surface you might see

That even in the very worst of times, you can make it—just hold on to your pride

So why the illusion? Why the delusion? Look to yourself—you're the solution

Chorus

The Challenge (February 1, 2002)

Many people do not comprehend that where there's good, there's often bad

Many people do not understand that for every beginning there can be an end

So why the confusion with man's persecution? Look to the Lord—He's the solution

Chorus

Just heed the challenge
Hold on to the challenge
Live for the challenge
Life is the challenge

You're down and out (or so it seems)—if you look beneath the surface you might see

That even in the very worst of times, you can make it—just seek the living Christ

So why the illusion? Why the delusion? Look to the Lord—He's the solution

Chorus

Empathy

"You have heard that it was said, 'Love your neighbor and hate your enemy.' But I tell you: Love your enemies and pray for those who persecute you, that you may be sons of your Father in heaven. He causes his sun to rise on the evil and the good, and sends rain on the righteous and the unrighteous. If you love those who love you, what reward will you get? Are not even the tax collectors doing that? And if you greet only your brothers, what are you doing more than others? Do not even pagans do that? Be perfect, therefore, as your heavenly Father is perfect."

(Matthew 5:43–48)

Jesus' words are timeless. To love one another unconditionally is a radical departure from our human nature. Throughout history men have hated their enemies, and those they perceived as enemies. Yet Jesus teaches us not to hate one another, but to love one another. To do as the Lord teaches us, we *must* become empathetic.

What restricts us from Empathy?

On the most simplistic level, the importance of having empathy for one another is obvious: It is in our *collective* best interest to peacefully co-exist. So why is it that history continues to repeat itself through conflicts, ranging from bitter family disputes to nations at war?

The answer is found in the origins of mankind. When Adam and Eve succumbed to temptation, harmony was replaced with chaos. An ordered society characterized by love and obedience was replaced with a disordered society where mistrust, greed, and selfishness became the rule. Our sinful nature is inherent yet does *not* excuse us from following God's commandments.

Think of the most pressing issues facing our world today—famine, war, and human rights, among others. Would any of these exist if we collectively heeded Jesus' command to love one another? No! Nearly all the world's problems can be attributed to placing the interests of self ahead of others. We have enough food, natural resources, and technology to ensure that *everyone* in the world could live hunger-free, and with relative health and security. But that won't happen because of selfishness.

The devastating effects of selfishness are evidenced in the war against terrorism that the United States and its allies are presently fighting. The war was brought on by vicious and hateful attacks levied against the United States on September 11, 2001 by Osama bin Laden and his al-Qaeda terrorist network. Thousands of innocent people died when hijackers flew commercial airplanes directly into the World Trade Center in New York City and the Pentagon building in Washington. Many more died on the same day after heroic passengers wrestled control of Flight 93 to prevent the plane from crashing into a populated area. Incredibly, the stated rationale for the attacks was a desire to obey God. But what "god" condones murdering innocent people? And is such a "god" worthy of our praise?

The one True God, the God of the Bible, condones no such actions, for He is a God of love. Indeed, the rationale for what took place on September 11, 2001 is derived not from godliness, but from selfishness. A small number of influential men persuaded several other men that killing "infidels" is part of God's plan. They are using the holy name of God to further a personal agenda of hate and exclusion. How tragic it is when men place selfishness ahead of genuine godliness.

The situation in the Middle East is incredibly precarious. The prevailing viewpoints are so diametrically opposed that one cannot help wonder if we are *ever* going to progress toward peace. Yet where does peace start? Perhaps with an honest look at what lies within.

Consider for a moment that hunger and poverty have long been a problem in Afghanistan. Part of America's post-September 11 strategy had been to distribute food rations via air to the Afghani people. Reports quickly filtered in of Taliban officials and al-Qaeda terrorists intercepting and destroying food rations. On the surface it is difficult to fathom how people could be so evil as to knowingly starve their own countrymen out of hatred for a sworn enemy. But through *honestly* assessing the situation with an open mind, we are able to dig deeper in an attempt to better understand *why* they felt compelled to act in this manner.

It is quite possible that if we were born into their culture and taught from an early age that the Jihad (Holy war) was God's will, our actions would match theirs. People are heavily influenced by what they perceive to be truth. Those who are passionate about their beliefs will always align their actions accordingly. This in itself is not a problem, but when man misinterprets or rejects God's commands, the result is always hatred. Sometimes hatred is dressed up as obedience, or even as holiness, but without heeding Jesus' command to love one another, hatred invariably lies beneath the exterior.

Even in America, the "melting pot" where opportunities abound, racism has long been an issue; in fact, slavery was *legal* in our country for decades. The mistreatment of blacks and other minorities throughout our history has been well chronicled. Racism exists in many forms, some obvious and some discreet, and continues to plague our nation more than 200 years after its birth. It serves as living proof that even in America, where wars have been fought in the name of freedom and equality, we too are guilty of hatred toward one another.

The Empathy Test

Understand that in comparing American citizens to Taliban officials and al-Qaeda terrorists, I am in no way condoning their actions, which are abhorrent. But there are similarities between us, as illustrated through honest answers to the following questions:

1. Have you ever judged another person before even speaking to them?
2. Have you ever followed a leader without completely agreeing with their viewpoint?
3. Have you ever wondered what your worldview might be like if you were born into a different family or culture?

We have all judged others without speaking to them first, consistently categorizing people based on outward appearance. If I see a middle-aged woman in Saks Fifth Avenue dressed to the nines and wearing fine jewelry, I will likely assume that she is wealthy and able to afford pretty much whatever she wants. If I see a young man covered with tattoos and body piercings, I will likely assume that he has grown up in a rough neighborhood and faces a difficult future. My impressions of both people have been formed with no direct communication whatsoever! What if the woman I saw is actually a person of modest means who suffers from low self-esteem, which she camouflages through her appearance? Perhaps she has a debt problem that keeps her awake at night. And what if the young man I saw is actually an honors student who was recently awarded a scholarship to a prestigious university? Talk about an error in judgement!

I know that I am not alone in labeling people prematurely; we all do it. But it is only when we begin to *recognize and acknowledge* our built-in prejudices that we will be able to set them aside in favor of seeking to understand others rather than rushing to judgement:

> *"Do not judge, or you too will be judged. For in the same way you judge others, you will be judged, and with the measure you use, it will be measured to you."*
>
> *(Matthew 7:1–2)*

Before I move to the second question, I wish to make an important point. From the 1960's and through today, there has been an increased movement for equality. In its purest form, this has been a welcome and long needed development. But many people who are active in this pursuit fail to realize that they are guilty of the very thing they are so adamantly against! Think of the various special interest groups that are prevalent in our culture—The National Association for the Advancement of Colored People (NAACP) and The National Organization for Women (NOW), among others. These groups and many others have the *best* of intentions: equal rights and equal opportunity for all people. But frustration over the slow pace of change often results in failed attempts at *overcorrecting* injustice by tipping the scales too much. Helping one "group" at the expense of another creates mistrust and animosity, and works against societal harmony. We are wise to understand that equal rights and equal opportunity are essential to democracy, and worth fighting for, but that equality in its purest form will never exist in our world. We *are* different, and our differences should serve to unite us; not divide us. Though we can never fully appreciate another person's worldview without ever having walked in their shoes, we should be open to understanding their experiences and viewpoints to the best of our ability, remembering that none of us is more important than all of us. We are different in many respects, but one thing we have in common is that we are all beloved children of God. And that is the only place where equality will ever exist: in God's eyes.

The second question asks if you have ever followed a leader without completely agreeing with their viewpoint. The answer to this question can only be "yes." In the workplace, if you value your employment, you learn quickly to comply with *most* things you are asked to do, even if you disagree to some extent. Think also of your own childhood, during which you undoubtedly had many disagreements with a parent, but more often than not did what they told you to do. Following direction from authority figures while not totally concurring with their viewpoint is perfectly acceptable, provided that your actions don't violate foundational beliefs.

Unfortunately, many people follow leaders whose foundational beliefs do not align with their own. The reasons are many, but by far the most prevalent is fear of persecution. All the world's dictatorships were established from a base of fear, with none surviving for a sustained period of time. People who are repressed naturally look for alternatives, and eventually another person or group topples the previous regime. And because absolute power corrupts, the cycle continues. Even in our free society, greed and selfishness can overcome upstanding people. Leaders—in business, government, school, and even churches—can and should be held to the highest standards of moral and ethical behavior. At my place of employment we call that "leadership worth following." It is worth noting that many of the Taliban fighters in Afghanistan switched their allegiance to the opposing Northern Alliance during the war. Their actions remind us that most people are only *truly* loyal to causes they strongly believe in. The Taliban ruled through intimidation and repression, neither of which can stand the test of time.

The third question regards what our worldview might be if we were born into a different family or culture. This is a question I have often pondered, but cannot begin to answer. In the "*Christianity*" chapter, I mentioned that we inherit beliefs from birth, and eventually need to search for truth and meaning to define deeply rooted foundational beliefs. But what if you were born in communist China? Or Africa? Or war torn Afghanistan? We can't assume that our worldview would be the same as the one we hold today. I have no idea what my beliefs and actions would be if I had been told from early childhood that western society stood for evil, and that sacrificing "infidels" is part of God's plan. I would like to think that I would see through this flawed logic, but I will never really know.

What Empathy Isn't

Before proceeding further, I wish to make clear my position on what empathy *isn't*. Regardless of the circumstances we are born into and the beliefs that we inherit, there are basic rules that govern mankind. Acts of senseless violence and terror have no place in any corner of the world and must be dealt with accordingly, including through use of military force when diplomacy fails. Furthermore, beliefs and actions that run contrary to our own are not to be blindly accepted. Having empathy for others does not mean we are to condone wrongful beliefs and actions, but that we are to seek a better understanding of individual and cultural beliefs, and corresponding actions. Blind acceptance leads to moral decay, but developing a better understanding of other people leads to finding common ground, which opens the door to change.

The Importance of Finding Common Ground

Discovering common ground is the single most important step toward becoming a person of empathy. The human mind is incredibly complex, but I believe our similarities far outweigh our differences. One universal desire we share is a craving for acceptance. Regardless of whether it comes from parents, friends, family, or even God, we all crave acceptance.

I read an article in this morning's *USA Today* newspaper titled "*Enemies play in peace.*" This intriguing, inspiring story tells of a group of Israeli and Palestinian men brought together for one week to play basketball together at the University of Vermont. The trip was sponsored by the University of Vermont and the Israel-based Peres Center For Peace, which attempts to build trust through various projects.

I was deeply moved by this wonderful example of people developing empathy for one another under difficult circumstances. Following are a few excerpts:

> *"At first the chill in the air at that meeting—not helped by an Arabic-Hebrew language barrier-worried organizers as the two groups sat sepa-*

rately. Then a warmth spread as basketball and America dominated the talk. Israelis and Palestinians agreed to speak English."

"Sports is a language everyone understands', said Galily, who would have played as a professional had he not had to enter the army at age 18. 'Now it is not us and them here, it is just us. It is just a small step, but in the journey it is an important one.'"

"This trip has let me see such wonderful guys here' Kotto, 25, said, sweeping his hand around the lunch table. 'I encourage everyone to understand the other side of things. They are guys just like me.'"

These sworn enemies found that they were not so different after all. But to get to that point they had to be find *common ground.* What they found is that they all had a love for basketball and could all speak English. That was their starting point, which enabled them to remove barriers that divided them. There was no mention of politics or religious beliefs discussed between the men, but they have developed a level of trust that may well open the door for such discussions later.

A Roadmap for Evoking Change

Sadly, most people who have opposing viewpoints are not as willing to engage one another as these men were. We erect barriers that, regardless of whatever evidence others present, are difficult to remove. And while it is difficult to convince someone to change when they are not interested in changing, there is a logical approach that requires following these steps:

- At least one person must show a willingness to communicate, with an emphasis on listening. Approachability is essential.
- Establish common ground. This is the key to beginning an interactive dialogue.
- Build trust through clarity and purpose of words.
- Listen intently for opportunities to teach.
- Be patient ... sometimes change is worth waiting for.

Jesus' provided this model while traveling through Samaria, where He encountered a woman who had been living in sin:

Soon a Samaritan woman came to draw water, and Jesus said to her, "please give me a drink." He was alone at that time because his disciples had gone into the village to buy some food. The woman was surprised, for Jews refuse to have anything to do with Samaritans. She said to Jesus, "You are a Jew, and I am a Samaritan woman. Why are you asking me for a drink?" Jesus replied, "If you only knew the gift God has for you and who I am, you would ask me, and I would give you living water." "But sir, you don't have a rope or a bucket", she said, "and this is a very deep well. Where would you get this living water? And besides, are you greater than our ancestor Jacob who gave us this well? How can you offer better water than he and his sons and his cattle enjoyed?" Jesus replied, "People soon become thirsty again after drinking this water. But the water I give them takes away thirst altogether. It becomes a perpetual spring within them, giving them eternal life." "Please sir", the woman said, "give me some of that water! Then I'll never be thirsty again, and I won't have to come here to haul water." "Go and get your husband", Jesus told her. "I don't have a husband", the woman replied. Jesus said, "You're right! You don't have a husband—for you have had five husbands and you aren't even married to the man you're living with now." "Sir", the woman said, "you must be a prophet. So tell me, why is it that you Jews insist that Jerusalem is the only place of worship, while we Samaritans claim it is here at Mount Gerizim, where our ancestors worshiped?" Jesus replied, "Believe me, the time is coming when it will no longer matter whether you worship the father here or in Jerusalem. You Samaritans know so little about the one you worship, while we Jews know all about him, for salvation comes through the Jews. But the time is coming and is already here when true worshipers will worship the Father in spirit and in truth. The Father is looking for anyone who will worship him that way. For God is Spirit, so those who worship him must worship in spirit and in truth." The woman said, "I know the messiah will come—the one who is called Christ. When he comes, he will explain everything to us." Then Jesus told her, "I am the Messiah!"

(John 4:7–26)

Immediately after her encounter with Jesus, the Samaritan woman went back to her village and told others about her experience. She and many in her village believed that He was the Messiah. When we examine this story in detail, we find that before Jesus told the Samaritan woman that He was indeed the Messiah, He went through the five steps outlined previously. Repeated below are the steps for evoking change in others, with key points from Jesus' lesson included:

1. ***At least one person must show a willingness to communicate, with an emphasis on listening. Approachability is essential.***

   As a mixed race, Samaritans were hated and considered impure by the Jews, who did all they could to avoid traveling through Samaria. Yet Jesus not only traveled through Samaria, He stopped to converse in a public place with a woman who was living a life of sin. This in itself is astonishing! The woman was clearly surprised by Jesus' overture, which opened the door to step two.

2. ***Establish common ground.***

   Getting water from a well was hard work! The wells were normally located outside the city along the main road, and woman would typically go for water twice each day, morning and evening. It was especially difficult for this woman, who, because of her reputation, came at noon to avoid other people who might know her. Jesus' offered her "living water" that would take away one's thirst forever and give eternal life. The woman interpreted His offer to mean that she would never have to come to the well again, which held obvious appeal. Her desire for lasting improvement provided common ground between Jesus' and the Samaritan woman.

3. ***Build trust through clarity and purpose of words.***

   After the woman expressed a desire to drink the living water that Jesus offered her, Jesus instructed her to go and get her husband, knowing that she had already had five husbands and was currently living with a man she wasn't married to. She believed Jesus to be a prophet, and tried to change the subject by questioning Him on why Jews and Samaritans worshiped at different places. Jesus then explained that the time is upon us when all believers will worship God with spirit and truth as one Body.

4. ***Listen intently for opportunities to teach.***

   The woman responded by stating her belief that the Messiah will come and explain everything. Finally, having gained her trust after initiating conversation, establishing common ground, and providing clarity in his message, Jesus simply says "I am the Messiah." By this time, that's all she needed to hear in order to believe!

5. *Be patient . . . change is worth waiting for.*

   This is a critical element that is often overlooked in our culture. Jesus could have walked up to the Samaritan woman and said something like "I am the Messiah. Please give me a drink." Isn't that the approach we tend to take when trying to change something? Our tendency is to state our desire, then expect immediate results. But Jesus demonstrates that before we can expect change, we must first establish trust and understanding, which takes time.

Ignorance Inhibits Empathy

Beyond selfishness, ignorance is a major obstacle to developing the empathetic mindset necessary to love others unconditionally. This is exemplified by what we see in young children.

My children, Trevor and Spencer, are six year-old twin boys. They have had limited experience in understanding the ways of the world, which is one of many reasons I am so captivated by them. They demonstrate openness and acceptance for all people, regardless of appearance or manner of speech. My children are not unique in that regard—all children have the same approach *until they learn otherwise.* How they learn, and by whom they are taught, varies widely, but there is no question that children become increasingly closed-minded over time.

This is a paradox of sorts-on the one hand, children are constantly gaining knowledge and understanding, implying that they become less ignorant as they learn; but on the other hand, ignorance takes many forms, and what we learn comes from what we hear and observe. If I use profanity, my children will do the same. If I am abusive toward my wife, my children will assume that abuse toward women is acceptable. However, if I read Bible stories to them and pray with them, they will develop a better understanding of Christianity and be better positioned to live for God. Nevertheless, we should not lose sight of the fact that kids learn from many sources, all of whom influence them for better or worse.

When it comes to understanding how ignorance holds us back from developing empathy for others, there is a distinction to be made between ignorance of man's prejudices and ignorance of knowing and applying God's Truth. The "ignorance" we see in children is of the first variety, which allows them to see the world without a jaded point-of-view. As for the rest of us, we become ignorant when we replace God's Laws with our own, which prevent us from having empathy for others.

Mission Possible

In the summer of 1998 our Focus Factory leadership team embarked on a "team building" trip. Other than being told that we would be staying one night in Chicago, we knew little except to pack lightly and meet at the Holland, Michigan Amtrak station in the morning.

After Amtrak carried us from Holland to Chicago, we hopped on the subway, then took a bus to a neighborhood in south Chicago. From there, we made our way to a Homeless shelter sponsored by a local church. That's where we met Pastor Eddie, who explained to us that he had helped set up our outing in conjunction with our employer. He also mentioned that we would be spending that evening and part of the next day doing some badly needed home repairs at a house around the corner, and that we would be eating dinner and sleeping at the shelter.

We proceeded to the house, where we were greeted warmly by the owners. After getting the necessary supplies, we worked until late evening.

We walked back to the shelter to have dinner with the other "guests." We sat at different tables in order to converse with different people. I had an engaging conversation with a gentleman who was reading from a worn out paperback book about civil rights. What this man lacked in the way of formal education, he more than made up for with intuition and insight. I had little to offer him while he had much to offer me. He talked passionately and optimistically of a day when maybe, just maybe, people of all races could set aside prejudice and hatred in favor of unity and respect.

After dinner we went back to the house and worked until around 10:00 p.m. From there we met once again with Pastor Eddie. Having now been exposed firsthand to people not nearly as fortunate as ourselves, we were sufficiently ready for Pastor Eddie's lesson on empathy: *"People are people. And all people deserve to live with dignity." "We ought to treat people as Jesus did." "Look beyond the exterior to see a person's inside." "I'm here because I've been called here. This is where I belong."*

The passion this man had for the Lord and for his fellow man was evident. The shelter he runs helps others not only to find a place to eat and sleep, but to give them *hope* through Jesus Christ. Pastor Eddie taught us that unconditional love doesn't make exceptions. His lesson is one I treasure, and it serves as a vivid reminder that having empathy toward others is essential for godliness and spiritual fulfillment.

Faith

This chapter was written shortly after a time of dealing with work related issues that alternately shook my confidence, strengthened my resolve, and called my faith in God into question. Beyond dealing with several minor issues that contributed to my overall situation, one issue was particularly challenging, and ultimately resulted in a very irate customer. What's worse is that I personally (and inadvertently) sparked the issue in the first place.

Throughout the ordeal, I wondered why during a time when I was growing in my walk with Christ, I was suddenly confronted with a challenge to my faith in Him.

After doing much soul searching and praying, as well as tapping into family members and friends for advice, prayer, and support, I came to three conclusions: First, that God called me to write about faith (originally this chapter was to be "Family/Friends"). Secondly, that in order for me to write *earnestly* about faith, I needed a firsthand reminder that remaining faithful is not easy during tough times. And thirdly, that when one remains faithful in God, one is properly positioned to bear fruit for Him, which in turn brings forth spiritual fulfillment *in abundance.*

> *"I am the vine; you are the branches. If a man remains in me and I in him, he will bear much fruit; apart from me you can do nothing."*
> *(John 15:5)*

In the *"Christianity"* chapter, I wrote that initial compliance to inherited beliefs was like being on automatic pilot, but that after we discover the Truth of Jesus Christ we become obedient not out of compliance, but love and desire. Faith works the same way; initially our faith is derived from blind acceptance of inherited beliefs, but as we mature our beliefs are substantiated by in-depth understanding and a strong desire to discern absolute truth. And when we do place *absolute* faith in something, we are absolutely certain of the outcome. For Christians, when we repent of our sins and accept Jesus as Lord and Savior, and when we *strive* to live according to God's Word, we are assured eternal life. When taking time to step back from our daily struggles, this truth becomes crystal clear. The problem is that we do not step back nearly enough. Most people tend to live in the moment, during which we essentially, and unknowingly, categorize circumstances as good or bad. It presents a tremendous challenge to live in faith when our desired outcomes fail to match what actually takes place!

Learning to Trust God

During my recent struggles at work, I frequently lamented my situation: *Why is God allowing this to happen? How could I make such a careless mistake in judgement? What can I do to get out of this predicament? Can I effect the outcome so that it feels "right" to me?*

Gradually, I discovered some truths about where my faith in God was, and where it needed to be. I prayed frequently during that time, but mostly for protection, which is fine only as a *component* of prayer. What I did not do enough of, at least initially, was *praise* God for placing me in a situation that required my heart to be laid open in order that my faith in Him could grow.

Placing absolute trust and faith in the Lord goes against human inclination. From a worldly standpoint, self-reliance is an admired and cherished trait; but from a Biblical standpoint, if God isn't part of the equation, self-reliance is just another word for selfishness.

When it comes to work, I have always taken pride in being forthright and honest when in the wrong about something. Rarely do I cover up mistakes or deflect blame upon others. I am my own worst critic, and tend to internalize mistakes. And while my approach to work is seemingly commendable, in truth I sometimes fail to see the bigger picture because I am overly consumed with pursuing unattainable perfection. This was especially true during my struggles at work. My eyes are open now, but had they been opened earlier, I would have taken solace in knowing that purity of purpose far outweighs errors in judgement. And rather than being overly harsh on myself, I would have taken comfort in knowing that all is forgiven for those who believe in the saving grace of Jesus Christ. Indeed, while I found it difficult to forgive myself, Jesus forgives us of sins much more heinous than what I had done. Selfishness prevented me—at least temporarily—from accepting His grace.

Moreover, while being completely immersed in my own troubles, I forgot to count my blessings. I failed to fully appreciate my family and close friends who love me unconditionally. I did not bask in the comfort of knowing that others were praying for my well being. And I did not act on the *acknowledgement* from God that I didn't have to deal with these challenges by myself—I could give them to Him. In retrospect, I would have had a much easier time dealing with stress had I immediately given my problems—all of them, in their entirety—to God.

As stated previously, having faith can be difficult during tough times. But aren't those the times when we should be strongest in faith? God certainly doesn't abandon us during our lowest moments, but we often abandon Him during those times. When faced with a crisis, our tendency is to immediately work on resolving it *our* way. We may augment this approach with prayer, but even during prayer we often think of what *we* need to do to resolve the crisis. How much better off would we be if we truly gave our troubles to the Lord?

> *"Come to me, all you who are weary and burdened, and I will give you rest. Take my yoke upon you and learn from me, for I am gentle and humble in heart, and you will find rest for your souls. For my yoke is easy and my burden is light."*
>
> *(Matthew 11:28–30)*

To give our troubles to the Lord, to *really* give them to the Lord, is a huge leap of faith. As with many aspects of my life, faith is an area in which I have become increasingly mature, yet have not completely developed *perpetual* faith: trusting the Lord at all times.

Walking In Step with Jesus

I decided to follow Jesus many years ago, recognizing that His path is the path of righteousness. I sometimes visualize Him walking ahead, waiting for me to catch up so that I can be in lockstep with Him. But I persist in walking at varying paces, sometimes with the Lord, sometimes behind Him, and sometimes in a different direction altogether. When I am not walking with Him, He encourages me to catch up. He calls me through a sermon, Scriptures, prayer, my wife and children, and just about every means imaginable. *If* I am open to His calling, I catch up and walk with Him. But I don't seem to stay with Him very long, even though His path is straight and His pace unchanging. He is always there, inviting me, encouraging me, helping me. He never abandons me, but I frequently abandon Him.

I believe there is a direct correlation between being out of step with Jesus and being weak of faith. And I further believe that there is a direct correlation between weakness of faith and excessive self-reliance.

When faith in God is at its lowest, we are unable to abide in Him, and therefore unable to bear more fruit. Even as God calls us to be *strengthened* by our faith in Him, we are weakened due to lack of faith. We become further weakened when we increasingly try to fight our way through struggles without seeking the Lord's help. Contrast the differences between strength in God versus strength in self:

> *He gives strength to the weary and increases the power of the weak. Even youths grow tired and weary, and young men stumble and fall; but those who hope in the Lord will renew their strength. They will soar on wings like eagles; they will run and not grow weary, they will walk and not be faint.*
>
> *(Isaiah 40:29–31)*

> *He who trusts in himself is a fool, but he who walks in wisdom is kept safe.*
>
> *(Proverbs 28:26)*

God calls us to trust Him, not ourselves. The "wisdom" Solomon refers to is not of this earth, but comes from seeking, listening, obeying, and remaining faithful to God. When allowing God to dwell in us, we are strengthened by Him.

Each day is different from the last, with new circumstances challenging our faith, but we can always take refuge in knowing that God's Word is both absolute and eternal. In good times and bad, God is there for us.

Assessing the Quality of Our Lives

I have created two mathematical equations that illustrate the contrast between how people tend to define the quality of life, and how God teaches us to define the quality of life:

> <u>*Our Human Tendency:*</u>
>
> *(EARTHLY BLESSINGS / EARTHLY PROBLEMS) * SELF-SUFFI CIENCY * FAITH IN GOD * DEEDS = QUALITY OF LIFE*
>
> <u>*God's Equation:*</u>
>
> *BLESSINGS + EARTHLY PROBLEMS * FAITH IN GOD * DEEDS * GRACE = QUALITY OF LIFE*

The two equations may at first appear similar, but in reality they are markedly different. The first equation represents our tendency to live in the moment, categorizing circumstances as blessings or problems and placing them *opposite* one another. We look to create positive outcomes by doing whatever possible to have blessings outweigh problems. Many factor in faith in God, but because we are pre-occupied with charting our own course, faith isn't a constant, it's a variable. Many also factor in deeds, and then proceed to *informally* assess their quality of life.

Before you dismiss the first equation as overly simplistic or generalized, ask yourself which aspects would be included in an overall assessment of the quality of your life. Would you include your family situation? Wealth? Education? Friendships? Freedom? Grace? Faith? Eternal life?

How we arrive at an overall assessment of life varies by individual, but I am convinced that even those who are strong in faith consistently, and often inadvertently, assess life according to worldly criteria. We may factor in faith, grace, and salvation, but rarely do we give the eternal aspects of our lives their proper consideration. If we believe that the *only* thing truly lasting in our world is eternal life through acceptance of Jesus Christ, then why are we so consumed with money, cars, houses, appearances, and other worldly things?

When we look at the second equation, which is *derived* from Scripture, we see that God desires us to live not for today, but for eternity. When we follow this equation, we find that earthly blessings are *supplemented* by blessings from the Holy Spirit. Our problems are no longer at odds with our blessings because we understand that God often calls us to grow in faith during times of hardship. Our *absolute* faith in the Lord results in little or no variability of faith—it becomes constant! Deeds are still important, but when we inevitably stumble, we don't lose sight of God's saving grace. The end result is a life lived for God, one filled with joy, human suffering, passion, purpose, and most of all, the promise of *eternal life.*

Selfishness and Insecurity Inhibit Faith

Two primary reasons for why we often find ourselves walking behind Jesus instead of in step with Him are selfishness and insecurity.

Selfishness is inherent and keeps us from fully opening our hearts to accept God's gifts. Insecurity, as it relates to faith, stems primarily from placing too much credibility in worldly standards. As a Body, Christians have become far too insulated. And while I am humbled when thinking of the many missionaries who have inconvenienced themselves (including taking physical risk) to advance the Good News, I nevertheless feel justified in raising the issue that the greater Christian community has become unhealthily passive.

Should we be surprised that people search for truth and meaning in other places? What are we doing, individually and as a Body, to bring the message of salvation to all people? If we believe that confessing Jesus as Lord and Savior leads to eternal life, then we should actively seek to expand the kingdom by sharing the Good News:

> *I urge you then, first of all, that requests, prayers, intercession and thanksgiving be made for everyone—for kings and all those in authority, that we may live peaceful and quiet lives in all godliness and holiness. This is good, and pleases God our Savior, who wants all men to be saved and to come to a knowledge of the truth.*
>
> *(1Timothy 2:1–4)*

When was the last time you prayed for an enemy to be saved through faith in Christ? Speaking for myself, that is not something I do instinctively. I fall well short of God's expectation to pray for all people, including those who I may consider unworthy. And yet in truth, without grace I myself am unworthy to be called a Christian.

Insecurity effects faith in that not only does the world condone behavior contrary to God's teachings, but as Christians we are not doing enough to evoke individual and societal change. This leads to resignation and insulation within the Christian community, with the end result being a world that continues to slide into turmoil and moral decay.

Our challenge is to first develop faith, then to exercise it, just as we condition our bodies through exercise. From there we are to share our faith with others, seizing opportunities and consistently demonstrating passion and compassion.

We have been given the ultimate tool for developing faith. What the Scriptures contain is timeless, and when viewed objectively, indisputable. Many prophecies from the Old Testament have been fulfilled with Jesus birth, life, death, and resurrection, and many more are being fulfilled even today. The Bible contains absolute Truth.

Yet because we live in a world that values self-sufficiency, political correctness, and compromise, the teachings of the Bible are considered by many to be antiquated or useless. On the contrary, the Word of God has always been, and will always be, essential. Even though we might *think* we are in control of our destiny, apart from God we most certainly are not. Virtually every region in the world (some more than others) is experiencing turmoil. Violence, prejudice, and hatred dominate the headlines in our newspapers every day. Even those who live in the relative serenity of suburban America are not exempt, as gangs, drugs, teen pregnancies, and domestic violence are ever present. Meanwhile, in the Middle East, violence continues to escalate over differences between ethnic groups and religious beliefs. People search for truth and believe they find it from men who mold "truth" to fit personal agendas.

Placing Faith in the One True God

Far from advocating that we harm one another, the one True God commands us to extend grace, love, and prayer for our enemies. The hatred and violence we experience in life is not because God doesn't care, but because He lovingly made us to have free will. Contrary to God distancing Himself from man, man's sinful ways have wrought a world in which people have distanced themselves from God.

The *only* source of absolute Truth in the world is God. Study His Word and vigorously apply it to everyday life so that you can effectively advance

God's kingdom. God's Word is never out of date, and is in fact chronically powerful and perfectly relevant:

> *For the word of God is living and active. Sharper than any double-edged sword, it penetrates even to dividing soul and spirit, joints and marrow; it judges the thoughts and attitudes of the heart.*
>
> (Hebrews 4:12)

While the Scriptures are essential for developing faith, we are also wise to seek other believers, and to be tuned in to God's Truth everywhere we go. Even as we grow in faith, we must be on guard from Satan's attacks, which take the form of distraction and rationalization. Satan's approach is to twist the Truth just enough so that we end up with something less than absolute. He has used this approach since Adam and Eve, and is both incredibly predictable and incredibly cunning, but rest assured that when we dwell in God's Word we are capable of seeing through Satan's lies.

Exercise Your Faith

While developing faith, we must also continuously exercise it. Setting aside quiet time each day for reading Scripture and journaling thoughts is a great way to exercise faith. Time spent alone with God, in prayer and in reading the Word, will increasingly convict us in faith. Of course the opposite is also true—if we fail to spend time with God, we are more susceptible to Satan's temptations, which though often subtle serve in totality to disconnect us from the Lord.

The importance of exercising faith through quiet time with God is illustrated by an example of a well-conditioned athlete. Even the most gifted athletes recognize the need to stay in top physical condition in order to do their best. But if an athlete starts skipping practices on a regular basis, thinking he can simply show up and win when it really counts, he will fail. The same thing is true of our faith journey. God teaches us to dwell in His Word and to live accordingly:

> *Anyone who listens to the word but does not do what it says is like a man who looks at his face in a mirror and, after looking at himself, goes away and immediately forgets what he looks like. But the man who looks intently into the perfect law that gives freedom, and continues to do this, not*

forgetting what he has heard, but doing it—he will be blessed in what he does.

(*James 1:23–25*)

Applying the word of God is an important aspect of faith. Knowing God's Word but not applying it is like a painter who has artistic vision and ability, and the finest equipment available, but works on amateurish paint-by-number pieces. The artist may take enormous pride in knowing that she is *capable* of producing marvelous works of art, but how empty she must feel deep inside knowing that she has never actually done so.

Applying our faith requires that we step out and be bold, knowing that it is Christ who strengthens us. If the world is our canvas, then we are to use faith, knowledge, and insight to paint the world in bright, bold colors that signify Truth. If we do not step out and boldly proclaim God's message of salvation, others will paint our world using a paint-by-number approach, wherein the world has already decided what is acceptable and what is not.

I mentioned earlier that we are to share our faith with passion and compassion. If we believe God's message of salvation—if we *truly* believe with our heart, soul, and mind—then we have no choice but to be passionate about sharing it with others! Yet we also need to show compassion, recognizing that every person has been placed in circumstances removed from our own. Avoid judging others and focus instead on the purity of God's Word.

Remaining Faithful

While developing faith, exercising faith, sharing faith, and living according to faith lead to a healthy relationship with God, *remaining* in faith is always challenging during difficult times, for our human tendency is to doubt God's commitment during those times. Doubt is often compounded by temptation and the ever-widening chasm between God's Word and carte blanche societal acceptance of almost everything. Scripture gives us the "armor" we need to remain in faith:

Put on the full armor of God so that you can take your stand against the devil's schemes. For our struggle is not against flesh and blood, but against the rulers, against the authorities, against the powers of this dark world and against the spiritual forces of evil in the heavenly realms. Therefore put on the full armor of God, so that when the day of evil comes, you may be able to stand your ground, and after you have done everything, to stand. Stand firm then, with the belt of truth buckled around your waist, with the breastplate of righteousness in place, and with your feet fitted with the readiness that comes from the gospel of peace. In addition to all this, take up the shield of faith, with which you can extinguish all the flaming arrows of the evil one. Take the helmet of salvation and the sword of the Spirit, which is the word of God. And pray in the Spirit on all occasions with all kinds of prayers and requests. With this in mind, be alert and always keep on praying for all the saints.

(Ephesians 6:11–18)

Truth. Righteousness. The Gospel of Jesus Christ. Faith. Salvation. Prayer. If we arm ourselves with these things we will be strong, and our faith unwavering. All the answers we need are given to us, and all we have to do is equip ourselves accordingly.

The next time I am confronted with an issue that threatens to weaken my faith, I will not wait to hand my struggles over to the Lord. I will replace worry with prayers of protection and thanksgiving, and I will rejoice in knowing that the Lord is with me at all times:

For our light and momentary troubles are achieving for us an eternal glory that far outweighs them all. So we fix our eyes not on what is seen, but on what is unseen. For what is seen is temporary, but what is unseen is eternal.

(2 Corinthians 4:17–18)

I see Jesus walking ahead of me, always at the same pace and always on the path of righteousness. He invites me to walk with Him. Today I accept His invitation. I pray that tomorrow I will do the same. The choice is mine.

A Leap of Faith

In the summer of 1992 I was asked by my employer to lead a project with a cross-functional team of nine people. Emphasizing quality and reliability, we were to do a thorough situation analysis, then recommend and implement changes to many current processes. There were two additional teams focusing on other areas of the operation, and visibility would be high at both a plant and corporate level.

I was excited and proud to be asked to lead the team. At that time I had no prior formal leadership experience, thus I was flattered that others saw potential in me. I was also rather nervous! This was a union plant that had been operating for over 100 years with very low employee turnover, and a general resistance to change. In addition, with the exception of one person, everyone on the team was at least ten years my senior.

While encouraged after meeting with Stan (a corporate Quality Director assigned to mentor me), I also began to better understand the magnitude of the project and felt somewhat overwhelmed. Yet I worked diligently and persistently toward desirable outcomes, even while encountering resistance from management and some employees. I felt like I was in the middle of a crossfire between people who didn't desire change at all, and people who desired change just for the sake of change.

The project seemed too big, and I felt ill equipped to lead it. Stan helped move things along at times, but he wasn't there often, and in reality the burden of advancing the project was squarely on my shoulders.

I began praying for God to take the project over and ease the stress I was feeling. Sure enough, even though the assignment remained stressful at times, things began to fall into place and the team accomplished several objectives during the time we were together. In the end, even though we didn't realize all of our objectives, we came together as a team and showed what could happen when people set aside individual biases in favor of working toward a common goal.

I found that when I gave my struggles to the Lord I became confident and assertive. That lesson was instrumental in preparing me for future leadership roles, and more importantly as a person of faith.

Grace

We are all unworthy to receive God's grace. With one very notable exception, anyone who has ever walked the earth has sinned against God and is therefore unworthy to receive grace. Of course, the lone exception is God's only begotten Son, the Lord Jesus Christ. Jesus lived on earth as a man, was subjected to temptation, ridicule, and intense physical abuse, but never sinned. And despite the evil done unto Him, Jesus' suffering, death, and resurrection gave all who believe in and follow Him the greatest gift imaginable: eternal life in the kingdom of heaven. This gift is offered to us not because we deserve it, but because of God's incredible sacrifice, which cleanses us from sin when we accept it:

> *To the praise of his glorious grace, which he has freely given us in the One he loves. In him we have redemption through his blood, the forgiveness of sins, in accordance with the riches of God's grace.*
>
> *(Ephesians 1:6–7)*

Does Anyone Deserve Grace?

It is impossible to fathom the depth of God's grace. It enters into a realm that cannot be understood until the day we stand in judgement and receive God's eternal promise. And though we cannot fully understand or appreciate the grace extended to us from God, simply to ponder it is to be awestruck.

Think of a day—any day—in your life. Think of the people you came in contact with, as well as the people you may have read about in the newspaper or saw on television. Think also of your own actions throughout that day and of any judgments you rendered (consciously or subconsciously) on others. Try to recollect, to quantify in some way, the sins you committed that day, as well as the sins committed by people you encountered throughout that day. Is *anybody* you're thinking of worthy to receive God's grace? Is anybody *worthy* to dwell with the Lord in heaven?

Thinking of the same day, imagine now that *you* are the one who determines the fate of every person you talked to, read about, or saw on television. Their eternal fate is determined by your judgement. But before rendering judgement, there is one other aspect you will need to consider: not only are you able to accurately recall every word and action of those you came in contact with, you are also able to read their every thought. Their innermost desires, dreams, and fears are laid open for you to see. Some have committed heinous sins and are only now asking for your forgiveness, while others have *appeared* to be righteous but harbored wickedness in their hearts. Again, your judgement determines whether anyone you're thinking of, *including yourself*, deserves grace and the right to live in eternal paradise.

Finally, imagine the same scenario, except this time you're not rendering judgment, Jesus is. He knows our words, actions, and deepest secrets. Nothing is hidden from Him. He has lived amongst men and been murdered by men, yet never sinned. His standard of goodness is untouchable. Why should Jesus allow the likes of us to dwell with Him in eternal bliss? Have we followed His commandments and teachings each and every day? Do we *deserve* eternal life?

Without God's grace, the answer can only be a resounding "no"! But with God's grace, combined with acceptance of Jesus as Lord and Savior and a renewable commitment to *try* to live according to His Word, the answer is an even more resounding "yes"!

Grace is the ultimate gift. We should treasure it, vehemently praise God for it, and do our best to extend it to others. If God in His infinite power and wisdom gifts us with grace through Jesus Christ, then who are we to deny grace to our fellow man?

Two criminals flanked the Lord as He hung near death on the cross. One of the two showed no fear or remorse for his actions, but the other did. After being beaten, abused, and left to die a most painful death, Jesus still forgave a condemned man:

> *One of the criminals who hung there hurled insults at him: "Aren't you the Christ? Save yourself and us!" But the other criminal rebuked him. "Don't you fear God," he said, "since you are under the same sentence? We are punished justly, for we are getting what our deeds deserve. But this man has done nothing wrong." Then he said, "Jesus, remember me when you come into your kingdom." Jesus answered him, "I tell you the truth, today you will be with me in paradise."*
>
> (*Luke* 23:39–43)

The Complexity and Simplicity of Grace

I am intrigued by the paradox between the complexity of God's grace and the utter simplicity required of us to receive His grace.

The complexity lies in God's willingness to allow His only begotten Son to live with us, be tortured by us, and be killed by us, so that *we* may be forgiven of our sins. It is especially difficult to understand why God would allow this to happen when thinking about how frequently we turn away from Him. What does God see that makes us worthy of receiving His grace and redemption? I am unable to come up with an answer, but I take great comfort in knowing that God promises grace to those who believe in and follow Jesus. And God's promises are absolute and eternally binding.

Therein lies the simplicity of God's grace—there are no strings attached. Our past sins are wiped away and a new covenant is formed, and all we have to do is confess Jesus as Lord and Savior and strive to live as Jesus did. How much simpler can it get?

Although our human weakness never leaves us, we find a reservoir of strength when seeking Jesus. Our lives are significantly enhanced, with lasting fulfillment found through living for Christ. And the cost is free, because Jesus already paid the price for us. Still, because of our sinful nature, many struggle with acceptance of grace.

For some, God's gift of grace still sits in wrapping paper, having never been opened. Others view grace as a sort of "Get Out of Jail Free" card. And still others have difficulty accepting that God's grace is available to everyone, not just a select few.

Hardened Hearts Prevent Acceptance of Grace

People who have never opened the gift of grace share a common characteristic: hardened hearts. The reasons are many, but the bottom line is that they are not open to accepting God's grace. In many cases, people who grow up in difficult circumstances struggle with acceptance of grace. Studies throughout the years have shown that people who were subjected to dysfunctional behaviors and/or environments as children often themselves exhibit the same behaviors in adulthood. They may loathe their actions, but because they have never been exposed to (or accepted) Jesus' love and mercy, they perpetuate destructive behavior. This isn't merely opinion; sexual abuse, teen pregnancies and abortions, drug and alcohol abuse, domestic violence, etc., are problems that affect one generation after another in many families. Without the hope given by the one True God, it is to be expected that people who grow up in dire circumstances will have hardened hearts.

It is also to be expected that people who inherit religious beliefs that preclude grace will be less inclined to accept the Truth of Jesus Christ. The only faith in the world that allows for eternal life to be available to *all* people who believe that God sacrificed Himself in order to cleanse us from sin is Christianity. All other religions have conditions and spiritual interpretations of law established by *people*. The Word of God is the only Law that matters when it comes to Christianity. The Scriptures contain everything we need, and all we have to do is live by the Word and bring it to others.

Contrast Christianity with other religions that promote vengeance and exclusion. If a person is led to believe that God has placed one group of people above another, should we be surprised at their unwillingness to promote peace? People who inherit false beliefs have hardened their hearts from the day they were born. Just as abuse and misbehavior tend to perpetuate from generation to generation—often worsening over time—so do false beliefs. In order to avoid confronting truth, many adopt increasingly extreme beliefs and actions based out of man's sinful nature, not God's love and compassion.

We can learn from the story of King Solomon, who for all his wisdom was also weak of the flesh. The Lord instructed him not to intermarry with women from certain nations because they would lead him to worship false gods. But because his love for women was stronger than his love for the Lord, Solomon married many foreign women. Eventually Solomon began worshiping other gods instead of the one true God. Solomon was a brilliant man, but his heart was hardened when he placed his desire over God's desire for him:

> *The Lord became angry with Solomon because his heart had turned away from the Lord, the God of Israel, who had appeared to him twice. Although He had forbidden Solomon to follow other gods, Solomon did not keep the Lord's command.*
>
> *(1 Kings 11:9–10)*

I don't know how to soften the hearts of non-believers other than to follow what Scripture teaches us. We are to love and pray for all people, and bring others to Christ whenever possible. We are to defend our faith with all our might, even if it requires giving our lives in the process. And we are to remember that we are *never* alone when doing our best to bring Truth to others:

> *Then Jesus came to them and said, "All authority in heaven and on earth has been given to me. Therefore go and make disciples of all nations, baptizing them in the name of the Father and of the Son and of the Holy Spirit, and teaching them to obey everything I have commanded you. And surely I am with you always, to the very end of the age."*
>
> *(Matthew 28:18–20)*

Some View Grace as a Get-Out-Of-Jail Free Card

At the opposite spectrum from those whose hearts have been hardened are those who consider grace to be a "Get Out of Jail Free" card. These are people who likely have accepted Jesus as Lord and Savior and are open to receiving his grace, but are not willing to turn away from sin. God's Word tells us that when we accept Jesus into our lives we must accept His grace *while* ridding ourselves of sin:

> *What shall we say, then? Shall we go on sinning so that grace may increase? By no means! We died to sin; how can we live in it any longer? Or*

don't you know that all of us who were baptized into Christ Jesus were baptized into his death? We were therefore buried with him through baptism into death in order that, just as Christ was raised from the dead through the glory of the Father, we too may live a new life.

(Romans 6:1–4)

Simply put, we can't have it both ways! We cannot believe in salvation through Jesus Christ, yet allow our daily lives to be governed by worldly standards of right and wrong. What are we afraid of? We should be empowered in knowing that even as we will never be worthy to receive God's grace, when we *strive* to live like Jesus, He gives it to us regardless.

One way to live according to God's will is to fight against nonchalance when it comes to our faith. If we attend church strictly out of compliance, if we knowingly indulge in sinful practices, if we discard our Christianity when entering the workplace, we lose our connection with God. *Initial* freedom comes through acceptance of Jesus as Lord and Savior (finding Christ is incredibly powerful and liberating), but without an ongoing commitment, spiritual fulfillment cannot be sustained. *Lasting* fulfillment comes from replacing our past with a desire to follow Jesus *all* of our days:

Those who belong to Christ have nailed the passions and desires of their sinful nature to his cross and crucified them there.

(Galatians 5:24)

While many struggle with accepting God's grace because of hardened hearts, and others see grace as a "Get Out of Jail Free" card, still others see grace as being available only to a select few.

God's Grace Doesn't Discriminate

God's Word makes it clear that grace is extended to all people who are open to receiving it through faith in Jesus Christ:

For there is one God and one mediator between God and men, the man Jesus Christ, who gave himself as a ransom for all men—the testimony given in its proper time.

(1 Timothy 2:5–6)

How can we be blind to the fact that God shows no favoritism? His word clearly states His love for all people, and yet *we* tend to label people as either worthy or unworthy. He calls us to make disciples of all people in all nations (ref. Matthew 28:19–20), yet even in our own churches we hesitate to reach out to people in need or who we don't see eye-to-eye with.

Oftentimes we unknowingly take an elitist approach with regard to worthiness in God's eyes. It is easy to get caught up in thinking that the people worthy of God's grace are those who think and act as we do. Personal prejudice clouds the ability to understand the purity of God's grace. What do we see when we look at a picture of a convicted criminal in the newspaper? Most of us instinctively look at that person with disdain, seeing him as inherently evil, and in contrast to our inherent goodness. We overlook that we are all children of God, and as such are precious to Him. We decide that the criminal deserves his punishment, while conveniently forgetting that it is only through discovering, accepting, and living for Christ that *we* are forgiven of our own sins. Rather than considering the convicted criminal a waste of life, we should take pity on him, and pray that he comes to know the saving power of Jesus Christ. Indeed, the criminal deserves his earthly punishment, but he also deserves our eternal prayers.

As God gives us grace, we are to extend grace to our fellow man. This is shown through the story of Joseph, son of Jacob. As a young man, Joseph's jealous brothers betrayed him and left him for dead. Many years later, when Joseph was in a position to judge them, he extended grace rather than punishment:

> *When Joseph's brothers saw that their father was dead, they said, "What if Joseph holds a grudge against us and pays us back for all the wrongs we did to him?" So they sent word to Joseph, saying, "Your father left these instructions before he died: 'This is what you are to say to Joseph: I ask you to forgive your brothers the sins and the wrongs they committed in treating you so badly.' Now please forgive the sins of the servants of the God of your father.'" When their message came to him, Joseph wept. His brothers then came and threw themselves down before him. "We are your slaves," they said. But Joseph said to them, "Don't be afraid. Am I in the place of God? You intended to harm me, but God intended it for good to accomplish what is now being done, the saving of many lives. So then, don't be afraid. I will provide for you and your children." And he reassured them and spoke kindly to them.*
>
> (Genesis: 50:15–21)

The Golden Rule

I have always tried (and often failed) to live by the golden rule: treat others as I want to be treated. While this approach is supported Biblically, it does not in itself address how to react when people fail to reciprocate in the same manner. That's where grace comes in. When others treat us badly, are we willing to forgive as Joseph was? Joseph saw the good in his brothers and therefore extended grace to them. Finding goodness in people is often a vital step toward extending grace.

Anyone who has remained in a healthy marriage will tell you that one of the keys to happiness and longevity is to focus on what's *good* about your spouse. This would seem self-evident, but many marriages have dissolved due to one or both spouses dwelling on what they perceive to be annoying habits and irreconcilable differences in viewpoints. While some married couples are legitimately incompatible, most marital problems result from one or both people consuming themselves with negative aspects of their spouse, which inhibit them from absolute appreciation for that person. And without true appreciation for a person, extending sincere grace to them is next to impossible.

In the movie "*Good Will Hunting,*" Robin Williams played the part of Sean, a Psychologist who helps Will Hunting (Matt Damon) remove the emotional barriers that prevent Will from experiencing deep love. A turning point occurs when Will tells Sean that the reason he's not calling up a girl he recently met is that "*Right now she's perfect, I don't want to ruin that.*" Sean replies, "*My wife used to turn the alarm clock off in her sleep. I was late for work all the time because in the middle of the night she'd roll over and turn the damn thing off. Eventually I got a second clock and put it under my side of the bed, but it got to where she was getting to that one too. She was afraid of the dark, so the closet light was on all night. Thing kept me up half the night. Eventually I'd fall asleep, out of sheer exhaustion, and not wake up when I was supposed to because she'd have already gotten to my alarms. My wife's been dead two years, Will. And when I think about her, those are the things I think about most. Little idiosyncrasies that only I knew about. Those made her my wife. And she had the goods on me too. Little things I do out of habit. People call these things imperfections Will. It's just who we are. And we get to choose who we're going to let into our weird little worlds. You're not perfect. And let me save you the suspense, this girl you met isn't either.*"

Whether it's your spouse or your worst enemy, learn to appreciate others. Nobody is perfect, and when we are overly critical of people we create divisiveness. We are *not* to embrace everything people say and do, but are to set aside personal prejudices in order to see people as God sees them.

And remember that grace from God is the ultimate gift—a gift that keeps on giving.

When Losing is Winning

Paul was one of my best friends while growing up. We had known each other since first grade, and when I was eleven our friendship was at its strongest. That summer we saw each other nearly every day.

But when school started that year, something changed. An older kid named Jim began to have an influence on me. I started hanging around him and ignored the fact that he and Paul did not particularly care for one another. Paul could see that I was beginning to change—hanging out with a "tougher" crowd, swearing a lot, and not being as friendly as I used to be.

Eventually, Jim and Paul got into a fight and I felt I had to choose one side or the other. By this time, I knew that Paul was my real friend, and that Jim was not, but I was afraid of what Jim might do if I took Paul's side. So I abandoned my childhood friend for a kid who was bigger and meaner, and not nearly as fun to be around.

I drifted away from Jim, yet did not feel comfortable knocking on Paul's door. Late in the school year, I ran into Paul and he invited me to his house to play APBA baseball, a simulated baseball game played with dice and cards for each major league player. I nervously went to his house, feeling unworthy of being his friend. What kind of person abandons a friend for no good reason?

Within minutes, it was like old times. We laughed, played air guitar, and decided that playing APBA baseball was a great way to spend our days. For the next three years, when I wasn't playing baseball, football, street hockey, or basketball with Paul, we could usually be found at his house playing APBA baseball. Paul's team was the Tri-City Aces and mine was the Greenfield Thunder. My team lost more games than it won, but I still felt like a winner for having regained a valued friendship.

Although Paul and I have not kept in contact during the past several years, I still cherish the gift of grace he gave me at a time when I really needed it.

PS—I enjoyed playing APBA baseball with Paul so much that I ended up buying one for myself when I was fifteen years old! The game is currently stored in my basement, but in a few years, when my children are older, the Greenfield Thunder will once again square off against the Tri-City Aces. And both teams will win.

Humility

When he had finished washing their feet, he put on his clothes and returned to his place. "Do you understand what I have done for you?" he asked them. "You call me 'Teacher' and 'Lord,' and rightly so, for that is what I am. Now that I, your Lord and Teacher, have washed your feet, you also should wash one another's feet. I have set you an example that you should do as I have done for you. I tell you the truth, no servant is greater than his master, nor is a messenger greater than the one who sent him. Now that you know these things, you will be blessed if you do them."

(John 13:12–17)

Everything we need to know about humility is contained in this passage. Jesus' words and actions teach more about humility than a million books on the subject ever could! God's Son lived as a man, suffered as no one ever had (or ever will), and was killed by people . . . and willingly served people. Jesus exemplifies servant leadership, of which humility is the first and most vital ingredient.

Servant Leadership

I believe that *true* servant leaders are in short supply. I am talking about people who are willing to discard pride, prestige, and position to help others. While humility is a virtue almost universally admired, most of us will only humble ourselves on *our own* terms. I can't think of many people who are anxious to experience Christ—like humility, which requires submitting our will to His in totality.

Effectiveness as a servant leader is determined in large part by how willing we are to be genuinely humble. Living in true humility is extremely difficult because it requires personal sacrifice without *obvious* benefit. And oftentimes behavior in opposition to humility is mistaken for humility.

I am convinced that people are either naturally *self-limiting* or naturally *self-serving*, both of which are derivations of selfishness. To be self-limiting is to allow human insecurity to define the scope of your life. To be self-serving is to routinely place your interests above the interests of others. Many people remain either self-limiting or self-serving their entire lives, but those who willingly replace their natural tendencies with an overriding desire to serve God and people eventually move toward being *selfless,* which equates to true humility.

People who are Self-limiting

Self-limiting people generally lack confidence in themselves, yet do not seek (or accept) strength through the Lord. Rarely do they stray from their comfort zones. Begrudging acceptance of circumstances, which are often dire, becomes their mindset. Some look to Christ for hope and inspiration, but their search is done half-heartedly. In reality, because they have resigned themselves to accepting what they perceive to be their pre-determined lot in life, they are not fully open to experiencing strength through God.

People who are self-limiting are like a carpenter who persists in using old, worn out tools, even though he could make his job easier by using new and better tools. Maybe he has asked for and received new tools, and perhaps he has even used them on occasion, but he feels more *comfortable* using his old tools. So on he goes struggling with antiquated, worn out tools, while new top-of-the-line tools are available to make his job easier. When asked why he doesn't use the new tools, he humbly replies, *"the old tools are just fine for a fellow like me. Let others use new tools. I'll just muddle along with what I've always had."*

On the surface, it appears that the carpenter indeed models the kind of humility that Jesus taught. But in reality, he is not so much humble as he is reluctant to give up a status quo. His old tools may be antiquated, but they are also predictable. He knows how to handle them and what results they will bring. The new tools seem promising, and he is fairly certain that they would represent a positive change, but he is paralyzed by insecurity and therefore lives in a state of perpetual indecision. He masks insecurity with false humility, and since so many people believe him to be genuinely humble, he begins to believe it himself. Yet the moment he confuses his insecurity for humility, he resigns himself to being something less than what God made him to be.

The carpenter does not step beyond his comfort zone because he is in over his head. On his own, he does not have the will or conviction to enhance his life by using the new tools. But a Carpenter who walked the earth over 2,000 years ago will help if only we ask. When we seek Jesus, two seemingly paradoxical things happen: we are strengthened *through* humility:

> *Humble yourselves before the Lord, and He will lift you up.*
> *(James 4:10)*

When thinking about King David, many instinctively associate him with courage and charisma, a man who was unafraid of confronting difficult challenges head on. But David placed *absolute* reliance on God as his source of strength:

> *As for God, his way is perfect; the word of the Lord is flawless. He is a shield for all who take refuge in him. For who is God besides the Lord? And who is the Rock except our God? It is God who arms me with strength and makes my way perfect. He makes my feet like the feet of a deer; he enables me to stand on the heights. He trains my hands for battle; my arms can bend a bow of bronze. You give me your shield of victory, and your right hand sustains me; you stoop down to make me great. You broaden the path beneath me, so that my ankles do not turn.*
> *(Psalm 18:30–36)*

People who are Self-serving

Self-serving people are almost always overly confident of *their own* skills, abilities, or appearance, without a real and ongoing appreciation for the source of their attributes. Self-serving people tend to develop a sense of arrogance and/or entitlement, and while many are *seemingly* interested in the welfare of others, deep rooted arrogance often holds them back from being true servant leaders.

Just as insecurity coupled with not seeking strength through Christ is a problem, so is having too much self-confidence without seeking Christ. Things often come too easy for self-serving people, and they are lulled into a false sense of security. Whether they acknowledge their elitist attitude or not, it becomes ingrained in them unless they are willing to humble themselves before God, and ask for God's help in keeping them humble *by any means necessary*. But how many self-serving people are willing to give up their worldly position to better serve God and people? How difficult it must be to have a contrite heart when society places a premium on people who achieve "success" through self-reliance!

I am convinced that self-serving people face the hardest challenge in finding true humility. Interestingly, many self-serving people hold positions of influence in our culture, and often their words and actions *seem* to reflect genuine humility. And indeed, while many in this group attempt to live humbly, most define humility on their own terms. By society's standards they may be considered humble, but Biblically speaking they likely lack true humility.

For example, it is common knowledge that most corporations give a lot of money to charity. But one wonders whether their *motivation* is in the giving itself, or if tax laws and shareholder perception are the driving forces behind their gifts. And many public figures contribute to fundraisers and charities, mostly with good intentions, but it would be naive to deny that in some cases their motivation is simply to benefit from positive public relations.

During the formative years in our nation's history, government officials were regarded as larger than life figures, worthy of being held in high esteem. But over the course of many years, a pattern of lesser standards for intellectual, legal, and moral conduct has produced many government officials who are more interested in serving themselves than their constituency. The only reason for government to exist is to serve its citizens. And while many politicians are still committed to this basic tenet, there are those who are more loyal to themselves and their political party than to the citizens they are sworn to serve and protect. I am convinced that if an alien from a distant planet were to visit earth and listen only to the words *publicly* spoken by our Politicians, he would most assuredly report back to his fellow aliens that the most humble beings in the universe can be found on planet earth!

Jesus gave a parable that warns of the danger of being overly self-serving:

"Two men went up to the temple to pray, one a Pharisee and the other a tax collector. The Pharisee stood up and prayed about himself: `God, I thank you that I am not like other men-robbers, evildoers, adulterers-or even like this tax collector. I fast twice a week and give a tenth of all I get."" 'But the tax collector stood at a distance. He would not even look up to heaven, but beat his breast and said, `God, have mercy on me, a sinner.'" 'I tell you that this man, rather than the other, went home justified before God. For everyone who exalts himself will be humbled, and he who humbles himself will be exalted.'"

(Luke 18:10–14)

The Secret to Finding True Humility

People who seek God's help in becoming genuinely humble will become increasingly selfless, developing real, lasting humility. Anyone who is genuinely humble was first either self-limiting or self-serving, but in seeking Christ has traded indecision, selfishness, and human weakness for boldness, humility, and inner strength.

Humble people understand that by earnestly attempting to live according to God's Word, they become comfortably confident while remaining humble. They are strengthened by God, knowing that all things are possible through Him, and they are humbled in knowing that everything they have is a gift from God.

They are the "carpenters" who have put away their old tools in order to experience a greater sense of accomplishment and happiness through using new and better tools. They are the "politicians" who have relegated re-election as secondary to helping others.

My Journey toward Humility

My journey toward true humility has been difficult to say the least. I am one of those people who tend to rationalize self-limitation as humility. During the first thirty years of my life, I rarely took chances, preferring instead to remain entrenched in my personal comfort zone. I sounded contrite and humble—and often was—but in reality much of my behavior stemmed from insecurity. I have recognized over time that God has gifted me in many areas, yet so many times during my life I was the carpenter who refused to replace old tools with new tools.

When I was in 7th grade, I was sure my career would be in Journalism. I was a gifted writer, able to quickly detect pertinent information, but never bothered to get involved with the school newspaper or yearbook.

In 10th grade, I became interested in radio, did a few guest newscasts on the station located across town, had a smooth delivery and good "radio voice," but didn't bother to enroll in Broadcasting class the next year because it required giving up an Accounting class.

In college, I became enamored with advertising and eventually graduated with a Bachelor's degree in Marketing, with Advertising as an area of specialization. I was engaged to marry Pam shortly after graduation, and had student loans to repay, so I decided that getting into advertising at ground floor wages was not in my best interests.

And on it went until around ten years ago when I realized that my supposed humility was just another word for self-limitation. Other people saw potential in me that I often didn't see in myself. Yet even after coming to grips with insecurities, I still lacked *lasting* confidence that comes through Jesus Christ. Only during the past few years, as I've sought the Lord as never before, have I begun to understand how powerful and liberating true humility is.

I have no desire to dwell in the past, or, rhetorically speaking, to go back in time and do things differently. Who I am is largely attributable to my cumulative life experiences. Though I see things differently now than in my younger days, I would not trade my life with anyone. When I think of my past, it is with a combination of thankfulness and a strong desire to learn from it in order to be better in the future. But old habits die hard, and without awareness and vigilance, backsliding is inevitable.

The Challenge of Remaining Humble

Just as getting to true humility is a difficult yet rewarding journey, *remaining* humble is also difficult and rewarding. There is an old adage that says, "once you've reached the mountaintop, the only way to go is down." In terms of humility, that's *almost* true. After we have lived in genuine humility through submission to Jesus Christ, there is a very real danger of losing perspective at some point down the road. We can become overly comfortable maintaining a Christian *appearance*, but be lacking in Christian humility.

Think about a football team that just defeated its bitter cross-town rival. The players and coaches are confident, capable, and motivated, but if they go through the motions at practice, or gloss over scouting reports of their next opponent, they'll be in trouble. Their confidence will be based on a *false* belief in themselves rather than the coaching, dedication, and personal sacrifice that brought them there. On the other hand, if their confidence comes from staying the course, taking *every* opponent seriously, and maintaining a collective sense of purpose, they will likely experience further success.

That's what it takes to remain humble. Fight against complacency, remembering that God is the source of our strength. When our focus is on ourselves first, we lose perspective. If we attend church only out of obligation, pray only out of habit, and read the Word yet fail to apply it, we become like the self-serving Pharisee that Jesus spoke of in Luke 18:10–14.

God instructs us to be humble toward Him and to one another, so that we experience the richness of His presence in our lives:

> *All of you, clothe yourselves with humility toward one another, because, "God opposes the proud but gives grace to the humble." Humble yourselves, therefore, under God's mighty hand, that he may lift you up in due time. Cast all your anxiety on him because he cares for you. Be self-controlled and alert. Your enemy the devil prowls around like a roaring lion looking for someone to devour. Resist him, standing firm in the faith, because you know that your brothers throughout the world are undergoing the same kind of sufferings. And the God of all grace, who called you to his eternal glory in Christ, after you have suffered a little while, will himself restore you and make you strong, firm and steadfast. To him be the power for ever and ever. Amen.*
>
> *(1 Peter 5:5b–11)*

Humility Triumphs Pride!

At the opposite spectrum from humility is pride. All of us experience proud moments in life, and to deny pride is to deny a basic human emotion. But when pride overrides humility, the result is selfish behavior. Conversely, when humility overrides pride, the result is a move toward selflessness.

Beyond the untouchable example of humility demonstrated by Christ, there are many other people who have shown how transforming it is when the needs of others are placed above the needs of self.

Mother Teresa dedicated her life to helping others, doing so with genuine humility and compassion. Although she went to be with her Lord in 1997, she remains one of the most beloved people in history. In 1979 she won the Nobel Peace Prize and remarked in her acceptance speech, *"I choose the poverty of our poor people. But I am grateful to receive (the Nobel) in the name of the hungry, the naked, the homeless, of the crippled, of the blind, of the lepers, of all those people who feel unwanted, unloved, uncared—for throughout society, people that have become a burden to the society and are shunned by everyone."*

Compare Mother Teresa's humble, selfless approach to life with the misguided, selfish approach exemplified by so many others. Throughout the history of the world there is a consistent, predictable pattern of decay when corrupt, selfish individuals govern nations. And when the welfare of citizens is secondary to a leader's personal agenda, there will always be hardship. Even the United States, with a Constitution containing checks and balances designed to protect its citizens, has gone through periods of decay due to selfishness. In the years leading up to 1861, selfishness led to greed, greed to slavery, and slavery to civil war.

Think about great leaders from any sector of society—business, community, government, church, etc. I believe that any leader in any organization who desires to make a *lasting* contribution must first possess genuine humility. Leaders who are humble are much more likely to inspire trust, and people who inspire trust foster environments that open doors to lasting reform.

To illustrate, in December 1999 C-SPAN surveyed ninety top Historians regarding top American Presidents. Overall and in descending order, the Historians ranked Abraham Lincoln, Franklin Roosevelt, George Washington, and Theodore Roosevelt as the top four Presidents in United States history. In addition to the overall ranking, the Historians ranked American presidents in ten sub-categories, including "*Moral Authority,*" a category that would seemingly reflect the ability of a President to act in a manner more selfless than selfish. In "*Moral Authority,*" the Historians rated Washington, Lincoln, Theodore Roosevelt, and Franklin Roosevelt as the top four of all time. Thus, although the exact order differed, the Historians considered our best presidents to also be our most moral presidents.

Each of these men held the highest office in the land during a bygone era, yet their accomplishments shaped our society then as they do now. Democracy, Equality, Environmentalism, Security—all cornerstones of American culture—were shaped in a major way by these four men. I am absolutely convinced that what each of them accomplished was in large part attributable to having strong moral character, including personal humility. All had different approaches, and some—particularly Theodore Roosevelt—were more headstrong than others, but each of them frequently suppressed their personal desires in order to abide by the opinions held by trusted advisers and/or their constituency. And it goes without saying that being humble while entrusted with the highest office in the land would present a great challenge! These four Presidents achieved greatness by focusing primarily on the betterment of the nation and its citizens, demonstrating that when the interests of others are placed ahead of the interests of self, good things happen.

As a side note, while the Historians ranked Bill Clinton last in the *"Moral Authority"* category, they ranked him a very respectable eleventh in the "*Public Persuasion*" category. Is it possible in modern America for a leader to be highly persuasive while morally lacking?

Encouragement from Paul

In his letter to the Philippians, the Apostle Paul reminds us that following Jesus requires Christ-like humility:

> *If you have any encouragement from being united with Christ, if any comfort from his love, if any fellowship with the Spirit, if any tenderness and compassion, then make my joy complete by being like-minded, having the same love, being one in spirit and purpose. Do nothing out of selfish ambition or vain conceit, but in humility consider others better than yourselves. Each of you should look not only to your own interests, but also to the interests of others. Your attitude should be the same as that of Christ Jesus: Who, being in very nature God, did not consider equality with God something to be grasped, but made himself nothing, taking the very nature of a servant, being made in human likeness. And being found in appearance as a man, he humbled himself and became obedient to death—even death on a cross! Therefore God exalted him to the highest place and gave him the name that is above every name, that at the name of Jesus every knee should bow, in heaven and on earth and under the earth,*

and every tongue confess that Jesus Christ is Lord, to the glory of God the Father.

(Philippians 2:1–11)

Amen? Amen.

A Life Well Lived

My grandmother was a remarkable person. Mary Gafa was born and raised in Malta, moved with her husband and two children to the United States in 1947, and lived through the great depression, World War II, and Vietnam. But that only begins to tell her story.

Over 25 years, starting in 1939, Grandma gave birth to eight children! She died in 1993 and was survived by all eight children, twelve grandchildren, two great granddaughters, and a list of friends too long to count.

When my grandfather, Emmanuel Gafa, went to fight in World War II, my grandmother was pregnant with her first child. I cannot imagine the turmoil and apprehension she must have felt at that time. After she had the baby (my dad), she raised him for three years by herself. My grandfather did not see his firstborn child until three years after his birth.

Grandma was a woman of faith, a devout Catholic. Even while raising eight children, she found time to regularly help out her church. She prayed every day, said the rosary with passion, and always placed the needs of others ahead of her own.

In 1974, Grandpa died of liver cancer. Grandma was a young widow with children still living at home. Robb, the youngest, was only nine years old at the time.

Grandma was never bitter over the difficult circumstances she faced. She raised her children with discipline, love, and obedience to the Lord. And rather than bemoan having to raise a child on her own at an advanced age, Grandma showered Robb with love, affection, and adoration.

Toward the end, Grandma knew she was close to death. But rather than wait passively, she took control. She arranged many details of her visitation and funeral! At the visitation, I witnessed the greatest tribute to a life well lived that I could imagine. At precisely 2:00 p.m. a large group of parishioners from her church collectively and passionately said the rosary, just as Grandma had requested. And in heaven, I am certain that Jesus told her "*Well done, good and faithful servant.*"

Influence

Everything we think, say, and do stems from what we have been influenced by. The power of influence is not to be underestimated. Whether short-term or long-term, subtle or bold, negligible or life changing, influences permeate us for better or worse *every single day*.

We reflect what we learn, and over the course of time develop foundational beliefs based on a variety of influences. A level of "mental maturity" is found when replacing adolescent thought with adult logic and reasoning. And for those who search earnestly for life's deeper meanings, "*spiritual maturity*" is achieved through absolute acceptance of Jesus as Lord and Savior, and a strong desire to live according to His Word.

Influence Changes Over Time

During our infant and toddler years, we are almost completely dependent on other people. What we see and hear defines our world, and we adapt through imitation. Parents are often amused when toddlers say the same things they do, but they should be careful to consistently speak and act in support of their beliefs. Knowingly or unknowingly, parents define initial standards of conduct for their children, as kids are quick to imitate words and even quicker to imitate behavior.

Between toddler and teenage years, we are influenced by an ever-increasing array of sources, including but not limited to friends, teachers, television shows, church leaders, movies, and books. Children are in discovery mode during these years, with their minds like sponges soaking up everything around them. This is an opportune time for parents to mold their children into people of God. Work diligently to be a positive influence. Model love and compassion. Be available. Bring Bible stories to life through creativity and imagery.

Teenage years are a time of transition. Teenagers are not children anymore, but they are not yet adults either. A desire for acceptance and affirmation is especially strong at this time, particularly from peers. As many teens succumb to pressure while seeking to fit into a particular social circle, it becomes imperative that positive influences offset the many negative influences teens' face. Unfortunately, many parents become one-dimensional during these years, equating parenthood with either supervision or friendship. The underlying goal of parenthood must always be to nurture children to be responsible, godly adults:

> *Train a child in the way he should go, and when he is old he will not turn from it.*
>
> *(Proverbs 22:6)*

Depending on the situation, a parent must alternately be a friend, counselor, teacher, disciplinarian, etc.—whatever it takes to help the child develop into a responsible adult.

As we grow into adulthood, we are still influenced by a wide variety of sources, but are better equipped to filter influences through an evolving belief system. Over time, we tend to become increasingly convicted in our beliefs and able to influence people beyond our immediate peer group.

To grow in knowledge, develop healthy habits and beliefs, and discern our purpose in life, we must exercise patience. No one has had a more profound or lasting influence on humankind than Jesus, yet His ministry didn't begin until he was around thirty years old. Not much is known about the Lord between His birth and baptism, but we can surmise that Jesus sought a full understanding of knowledge and purpose *before* embarking on His mission:

Every year his parents went to Jerusalem for the Feast of the Passover. When he was twelve years old, they went up to the Feast, according to the custom. After the Feast was over, while his parents were returning home, the boy Jesus stayed behind in Jerusalem, but they were unaware of it. Thinking he was in their company, they traveled on for a day. Then they began looking for him among their relatives and friends. When they did not find him, they went back to Jerusalem to look for him. After three days they found him in the temple courts, sitting among the teachers, listening to them and asking them questions. Everyone who heard him was amazed at his understanding and his answers. When his parents saw him, they were astonished. His mother said to him, "Son, why have you treated us like this? Your father and I have been anxiously searching for you." "Why were you searching for me?" he asked. "Didn't you know I had to be in my Father's house?" But they did not understand what he was saying to them. Then he went down to Nazareth with them and was obedient to them. But his mother treasured all these things in her heart. And Jesus grew in wisdom and stature, and in favor with God and men.

(Luke 2:41–52)

Influence Isn't A Choice

Former NBA all-star Charles Barkley once did a commercial for Nike in which he stated "I am not a role model. I am paid to wreak havoc on a basketball court. Your parents and your teachers are your role models."

Barkley challenged parents to raise their children so that their role models would be moms, dads, and teachers—not athletes. His comments were controversial yet refreshing in an age of political correctness, and I agree with him that parents carry the bulk of the responsibility for positively influencing their children. Yet at the same time the inevitable influence emanating from a multitude of other people and sources cannot be ignored.

Whether we acknowledge it or not, we live in a world where influences abound and shape our thinking. The food we eat, the clothes we wear, the church we attend, our political affiliation—all are influenced by a variety of sources. With respect to Mr. Barkley, while *he* may not consider himself to be a role model, in reality he has no choice. Regardless of his worthiness, the fact is that he does influence others, particularly kids who are in the early stages of defining and solidifying foundational beliefs.

The ancient African proverb "It Takes A Village to Raise a Child" still applies, only the village is a lot bigger than it used to be! We live in a real time, information-laden world where influences vary like never before. Books, magazines, and music are accessed through the Internet. News is reported *as it occurs*. Polls are conducted electronically with immediate results following. The influx of information is staggering and unprecedented. I am convinced that making sense of what we see, hear, and observe is more challenging today than ever.

Imagine if Jesus first walked the earth in our present age. Would His miracles be broadcast on television? Would there be editorials and on-line polls about what should be done with Him? Would His message of salvation carry any weight in our culture of instant gratification? We can only speculate on the answers to these questions, but one thing for certain is that for many people, His recognized *worldly* "position" would directly determine His scope of influence. Much has changed during the past 2,000 years, but human nature hasn't.

Don't Equate Influence with Position

Individually and as a society, we consistently equate influence with position, placing inordinate trust in people based solely on their position. Business leaders, professors, politicians, doctors, etc. are deemed credible even though many lack practical knowledge and/or moral standards. There is a need to seek advice and services from accredited sources, but problems occur when we blindly equate a person's credibility with their position.

Until recently, Enron Corporation was one of the world's leading energy providers and listed as the world's seventh largest company. In September 2000, Enron's stock was trading at around $90 per share. On September 26, 2001, its stock had fallen to around $25 per share. On the same day, in an email conference with concerned employees, Enron Chairman Kenneth L. Lay called Enron's stock price "an incredible bargain" and said that the third quarter is "looking great." Lay neglected to inform his employees that he had begun selling his own Enron stock the previous month. By October 2001, new information was uncovered indicating that Enron management, in conjunction with its accounting firm (Arthur Anderson), had long engaged in deceiving investors, analysts, and its own employees by grossly inflating the value of the company. Finally, on December 2, 2001, Enron filed for bankruptcy, and its stock tumbled to a meager $0.26 per share.

It is extremely disconcerting to think that a $100 billion company could operate for extended periods of time in blatantly deceptive fashion. I don't fault the many people who were victimized by Enron and/or Arthur Anderson, because they justifiably believed that the company was healthy. But the Enron situation served as a wake-up call. In business, as in life, we should never place *blind* trust in people or institutions based on their prestige or position. Even normally reliable sources require ongoing scrutiny in order to sustain credibility. The excerpt that follows, from a February 2001 press release, reinforces the fact that position and prestige do not necessarily equate to accuracy:

> *ENRON NAMED MOST INNOVATIVE FOR SIXTH YEAR*
> *FOR IMMEDIATE RELEASE: Tuesday, February 6, 2001*
>
> *HOUSTON—Enron Corp. was named today the "Most Innovative Company in America" for the sixth consecutive year by Fortune magazine. "Our world-class employees and their commitment to innovative ideas continue to drive our success in today's fast-paced business environment," said Kenneth L. Lay, Enron chairman and CEO. "We are proud to receive this accolade for a sixth year. It reflects our corporate culture which is driven by smart employees who continually come up with new ways to grow our business."*

While we tend to overly trust people based solely on their position, we also tend to overly doubt those who don't fit pre-determined standards for credibility. If a janitor offers free advice on where to invest our money, we are likely to ignore his opinion, believing that he lacks the requisite credentials to offer such advice. Yet if a professional investment counselor offered the *same advice*, we would likely accept it with enthusiasm. Too often we confuse the validity of the message with the messenger's position.

I wonder if we are any different from the Jews of Jesus' time. They bore witness to miracles and fulfillment of age-old prophecies, yet would not accept Jesus as the Messiah simply because He didn't conform to their definition of what a Messiah should say and do. Don't we also tend to frequently miss the big picture by letting prejudice get in the way?

The next time Jesus comes, His position and mission will be immediately and abundantly clear:

"Immediately after the distress of those days the sun will be darkened and the moon will not give its light; the stars will fall from the sky, and the heavenly bodies will be shaken. At that time the sign of the Son of Man will appear in the sky, and all the nations of the earth will mourn. They will see the Son of Man coming on the clouds of the sky, with power and great glory. And he will send his angels with a loud trumpet call, and they will gather his elect from the four winds, from one end of the heavens to the other."

(Matthew 24:29–31)

Influence, Attitude, and Character

Just as we reflect the influence of others, so do they reflect our influence. Sometimes we are cognizant of our influence, but on many occasions we are not. During a "typical" day, I don't think many people reflect on the impact they have on others.

When people interact with one another, everything said and done has *some* impact. How do you feel when your spouse seems pre-occupied with her problems and doesn't appear to care about yours? When your boss doesn't acknowledge your presence? When your kids don't help around the house?

Taken individually, perhaps these things don't bother you, but in combination they will likely effect your attitude that day. And if they happen on a regular basis, your character may adversely change to *reflect* your attitude.

I do not claim to know why we are so affected by the people around us. It is obvious that we control our emotions and attitudes, yet because God made us to commune with one another, it's difficult to avoid being influenced by one another. And being influenced doesn't have to be a stigma! When we are influenced in a positive manner, our outlook is enhanced and we grow. But when negative influence sets in, we rationalize our actions and compromise our sense of right and wrong. A fundamental challenge we all face is filtering out negative influences.

I believe that the most effective means of fighting against negative influence is to be so strong in faith that you can't help but be positive! Being a positive person requires hard work and an investment in reflection, discipline, and restraint, but like any worthwhile investment, the returns are enormous. We are spiritually healthy, joyful, and fulfilled when maintaining a positive attitude that flows *naturally* from *living according to God's Word*. And when outwardly reflecting our beliefs, we help bring about positive change in others that we often don't even realize.

There is great power in human kindness. A smile, a thank you, or a word of encouragement carries much weight. Kindness allows us to be a light to other people while keeping negativity at bay in our own lives. And most importantly, when our conduct *consistently* reflects a strong belief in the Lord Jesus Christ, we find favor with Him:

> *Don't have anything to do with foolish and stupid arguments, because you know they produce quarrels. And the Lord's servant must not quarrel; instead, he must be kind to everyone, able to teach, not resentful.*
> (2 Timothy 2:23–24)

Use Your Position to Help Other People

There is an interesting paradox between position and influence. While we should never blindly trust people based solely on their stature or position, we should seek to leverage *our own* position to best influence others.

Leveraging our position in order to be a positive influence on others involves both opportunity and responsibility. People are naturally interested in and influenced by others who hold key positions *relative to themselves*. What we say and do is meaningful to them. That being the case, we must be careful to act in absolute accordance with our beliefs, and we had better make sure that we consistently influence others for good.

I make a point to regularly praise and support Pam in front of our children. I understand that my inherent position, relative to my children, offers great opportunity to influence them for good. But my position with them also entails a heavy responsibility, since everything I say and do is magnified. My hope is that by treating Pam with respect (which she most assuredly deserves), I will influence my children to treat their mother, and everyone else for that matter, with deserved respect.

It is easy to understand the influence we have on our own children (particularly when they're young), but not so easy to understand and appreciate our potential influence in less obvious situations. Opportunities to influence are plentiful, but too often we fail to capitalize on legitimate opportunities, or overextend the boundaries of our influence, and discredit ourselves in the process.

Developing a mindset of *looking* for opportunities to influence others does not happen overnight. Nor should it! Foundational beliefs need to be justified and well anchored, and caution exercised when weighing opportunities to influence. Only after we thoroughly assess both the scope of our influence and our ability to influence—*relative to the other person*—can we justifiably begin to influence that person.

Two questions to ask ourselves in order to understand scope and ability are:

1). *In what particular areas am I credible to this person?*

2). *Am I certain that I will be absolutely credible in what I tell this person?*

The answer to the first question defines the scope of our influence by providing specific areas to focus on. The answer to the second question simply provides a quick check-and-balance to ensure that we *maintain* our credibility with the other person. The second question is especially important because people often mistakenly believe others to be credible in areas where they are not. We help others by being honest about what we know and what we don't know.

For example, I can usually influence my friends about the importance of balance in life. They are aware that I value and strive for balance, which allows me to credibly recommend *general* approaches for achieving healthy balance. But if I try to sell them on the merits of practicing yoga, they will quickly discount my opinion. Having never done yoga, how can I credibly sell anyone on its merits? We need to be careful to not discredit ourselves while trying to influence people. Just because we hold a position of influence to someone does not mean that we are expected to know everything. Understanding the boundaries of our influence, and staying within those boundaries, is essential.

With Position Comes Responsibility

One of the men from our Tuesday Men's Bible Study group recently shared some of his personal experiences. "Sam" was a Christian at an early age and felt strong ties to the church he grew up in. But as a teenager, he began to distance himself from the church while going through some personal challenges. Sam found a healthy outlet for teenage angst by joining a Christian rock band, and actively played at churches and various functions. But the band broke up, leaving Sam somewhat despondent. A short time later, he began dating a girl whom his parents disapproved of. Forced to decide whether to obey his parents or continue seeing the girl, Sam left home and bounced around for a time, usually staying with friends. Nevertheless, he continued to attend church.

One day the Senior Pastor at his church called Sam to "talk." By this time, Sam had let his hair grow long and had several earrings. The Senior Pastor explained that he and the Board of Elders decided it was best for Sam to leave the church. At a time when Sam most needed to be shown Christ-like love and compassion, he was cast aside as unworthy . . . *by the church.*

Sam was at a low point in his life when he turned to alcohol for relief. The results were predictable, and for many years Sam went through turbulent times.

Sam still managed to hold on to courage and conviction, and decided around five years ago to begin attending a different church. This time the Pastor and the greater congregation greeted him as Christ commands—with open arms. A few years ago, after attending church but being "on the fence" a short while, Sam submitted his will to the Lord and has not looked back since. Sam is passionate about Jesus and committed to following Him. Sam teaches our youth on Wednesday evening, and I look forward to the day when my children are part of his group.

In an interesting twist of events, a few months ago Sam was in a building downtown, getting ready to board an elevator. Out of the corner of his eye, Sam spotted his former Senior Pastor-the same person who had removed him from the church many years earlier. Sam calmly assessed the situation, not entirely sure of what he would say or do, then walked up to him and struck up a friendly, forgiving conversation. By that time Sam had decided to be a positive influence on others, and knew that his position relative to his former Pastor was one of empowerment—he had Jesus on his side! One can only hope that the kind words and message of reconciliation from Sam helped to change his former Pastor for the better. I wouldn't bet against it—influence is powerful under any circumstances, but when inspired by God it is *exceedingly* powerful!

The Exponential Effect of Influence

Perhaps you remember the 1970's television commercial in which a woman, delighted with the results from using Faberge shampoo, says *"I told two friends, and they told two friends, and so on, and so on, and so on . . ."*

That's how influence works. Just as you reflect your influences, so do others reflect the influence you have on them. They in turn influence others accordingly and the cycle continues. Influence becomes powerful and increases exponentially, as evidenced by some very telling examples.

According to a 1990 "Addictive Behaviors" study headed by KE Bauman, young people aged 15–19 are nearly twice as likely to smoke if both parents smoke (36% of males; 41% of females) than if neither parent smokes (17% of males and females). It is rather apparent that children emulate their parents.

But the exponential effect of influence extends well beyond mere emulation. In many cases, the behaviors and habits we develop serve as gateways to other similar behaviors and habits. According to a 1991 "National Household Survey on Drug Abuse," conducted by the National Institute on Drug Abuse, children who smoke are *19 times* more likely to use cocaine than nonsmokers. Too often, one negative influence leads to destructive behavior later on.

Thankfully, influence isn't always negative, and positive influence also becomes a gateway to similar behaviors and habits.

In 1965, Millard and Linda Fuller visited a small Christian farming community called Koinonia. Located outside of Americus, Georgia, the community had been founded by farmer and Biblical scholar Clarence Jordan. In 1976, the Millards left their successful business in Montgomery, Alabama, so that they could develop "partnership housing" with Mr. Jordan in Koinonia. The idea was that people in need of adequate shelter would work side by side with volunteers to build simple, decent homes ... *at no profit and with no interest charged.* New homeowners' house payments, donations, and other fundraising activities would cover necessary expenses. Out of this came the model for Habitat for Humanity. By 1973, the Fuller's began to work in developing countries such as Zaire, and in 1976 Habitat for Humanity International (HFHI) was established. In 1984, former United States President Jimmy Carter and his wife Rosalynn became personally involved in Habitat, bringing even more visibility to the cause. Habitat for Humanity has experienced phenomenal growth, and has built more than 100,000 houses sheltering more than 500,000 people in 2,000 communities worldwide.

The positive influence from Mr. Jordan and from the Fuller's took on a life of its own. The results are stunning and serve as a vivid reminder of the power of influence. The best things in life often emerge from humble beginnings. It is up to us to determine how we will influence other people, and perhaps even change the world one person at a time.

John the Janitor

I have always felt that the first day of Kindergarten for any child is marked by a tinge of sadness. Kindergarten represents a transition between a time when children are mostly innocuous, to a time when they begin behaving more like—dare I say—adults.

Children who had been largely naïve to the wickedness of the world begin to experience it firsthand when they start school. Cliques are formed, insults hurled, and informal social classes defined. It starts slowly with Kindergarten, then becomes more pronounced as each year passes. And it continues in other ways throughout adult life.

At my first school, Weber Elementary, there was an informal class structure that consisted of two groups: those who were good kickball players and those who were not. The ability to kick a small burgundy ball a long distance would largely determine one's social position!

When thinking back to elementary school days, I can laugh at the name-calling, the cliques, and the stereotyping, but at the time, those were the things that kept me awake at night. Fortunately for me, and for a lot of kids at our school, there was one person we could always go to for assurance: John the Janitor.

Nobody knew John's last name, but it didn't really matter. *Everyone* knew John. He was a great man in our eyes, a man who knew us by name and always took the time to wave, say hello, or just give a wink and a smile.

John the Janitor was clearly a man of modest means. Uneducated and not terribly articulate, yet full of compassion, John seemed a lot like us. He recognized the class structure at our school, but he didn't acknowledge it: every kid was important to John.

It is amazing to me that one humble, modest man had that much impact on so many young lives. John didn't do anything extraordinary. All he did was ensure that each child knew they had at least one friend they could turn to at any time.

Hmmm . . . maybe John the Janitor *did* do something extraordinary.

Joy

Imagine for a moment that the joy you have experienced throughout your life has been plotted on a graph. Your most joyful days are plotted along the top of the graph, while your least joyful days are plotted along the bottom. I believe that most people, by their own assessment, would end up with a "Joy Graph" similar to the example below:

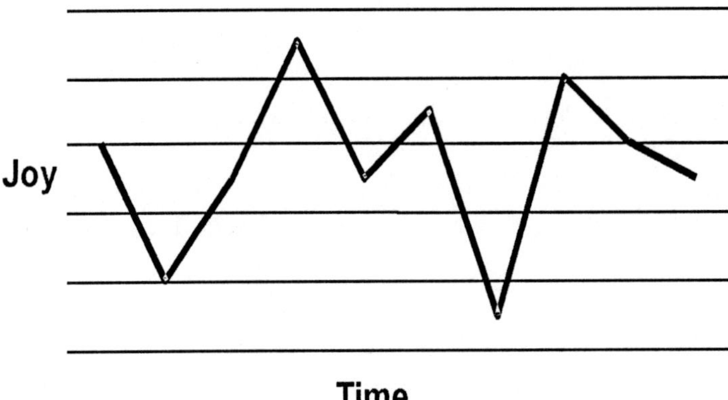

Joy and Happiness

People often associate joy with happiness, believing that both words carry the same meaning, or that a joyful person is a happy person by extension. But when correctly interpreted, there are major differences between happiness and joy. Happiness is circumstantial; joy is intrinsic. Happiness is an emotion; joy is inner peace. Happiness is temporary; joy is eternal.

When I was a child, Christmas was a magical time, full of happiness and euphoria. Presents were opened with delight, and shiny new toys played with all day. I was *always* happy on Christmas day! But within a short time—usually just a few days—euphoria would once again give way to normality.

Happiness relies on circumstances that are to our liking, while joy comes independent of circumstances. And though happiness is a wonderful gift that we should delight in, by itself it's not lasting. Life is not about *just* being happy—it's also about despair, uncertainty, and sadness. During difficult times, happiness is often elusive, but when we have real, genuine joy, we are equipped to deal with anything and everything life throws at us.

People who experience a deep sense of joy are those who take solace in and give praise to its Source: the Lord Jesus Christ:

> *Rejoice in the Lord always. I will say it again: Rejoice! Let your gentleness be evident to all. The Lord is near. Do not be anxious about anything, but in everything, by prayer and petition, with thanksgiving, present your requests to God. And the peace of God, which transcends all understanding, will guard your hearts and your minds in Christ Jesus.*
>
> *(Philippians 4:4–7)*

God's Word says to rejoice in the Lord always, not just when things are going our way. We discover deep, lasting joy when we turn our full attention to the Lord. Our hearts are filled with wonder and awe, and we are able to navigate through difficult times because of the joy derived through faith in Christ.

Experiencing Joy during Difficult Times

Harriet Ross became a slave when she was five years old. Although she was a hard worker, Ross was openly defiant and therefore routinely beat by her masters. At fifteen years old, she tried to help a runaway slave, and was punished by being hit on the head with a lead weight, which put her into a coma. She recovered but for the rest of her life suffered from blackouts. In 1844 Ross married John Tubman, a free black man, although she herself was still a slave. In 1849 she received word that she was to be sold, most likely to a southern plantation. Knowing that her husband would expose her if she told him, Harriet Tubman informed only her sister of her plans to escape. She then hiked 90 miles through swamps and heavy woods to the Mason-Dixon Line. After settling in Philadelphia, she went back to rescue her sister's family, then later her brothers, and still later her husband, who by that time had remarried and decided to stay. A few years later she rescued her parents. With each daring rescue, Harriet Tubman was considered to be increasingly threatening to the plantation owners, who offered a $40,000 reward for her capture. She was never captured. During her nineteen trips through the Underground Railroad, Harriet Tubman freed over 300 slaves. Later, she was a spy for the Union in the Civil War, and eventually worked for women's rights and improved care for the elderly.

Harriet Tubman led a difficult, turbulent life filled with abuse, life-long poverty, and the very real threat of imprisonment or death. She was constantly on the run, chronically fatigued, and not able to settle down until late in life (she didn't remarry until she was fifty years old). Harriet Tubman didn't have much to be happy about, but in spite of dire circumstances, she had a never-ending reservoir of joy in her life.

Although Harriet Tubman was forced at an early age to be a slave to men, she refused to be a slave to circumstance. She had purpose, passion, and above all, unwavering conviction. Her absolute faith in the Lord Jesus Christ transcended her struggles with mankind, and provided comfort and joy. In July 1863, *The Commonwealth* published a biographical article on Harriet Tubman. The excerpt below gives a glimpse of the depth of her faith:

> *"When going on these journeys she often lay alone in the forests all night. Her whole soul was filled with awe of the mysterious Unseen Presence, which thrilled her with such depths of emotion, that all other care and fear vanished. Then she seemed to speak with her Maker 'as a man talketh with his friend'; her child-like petitions had direct answers, and beautiful visions lifted her up above all doubt and anxiety into serene trust and faith."*

My guess is that Harriet Tubman's "Joy Graph" would look a lot different than the graph shown at the beginning of this chapter. For starters, happiness and joy would be separated, not mistaken for one another. The happiness line would likely show significant variation, while the joy line would have limited variation. The chasm between happiness and joy would be filled through strength found in the Lord, emanating from her strong faith. I believe that Harriet Tubman's Joy Graph would look something like this:

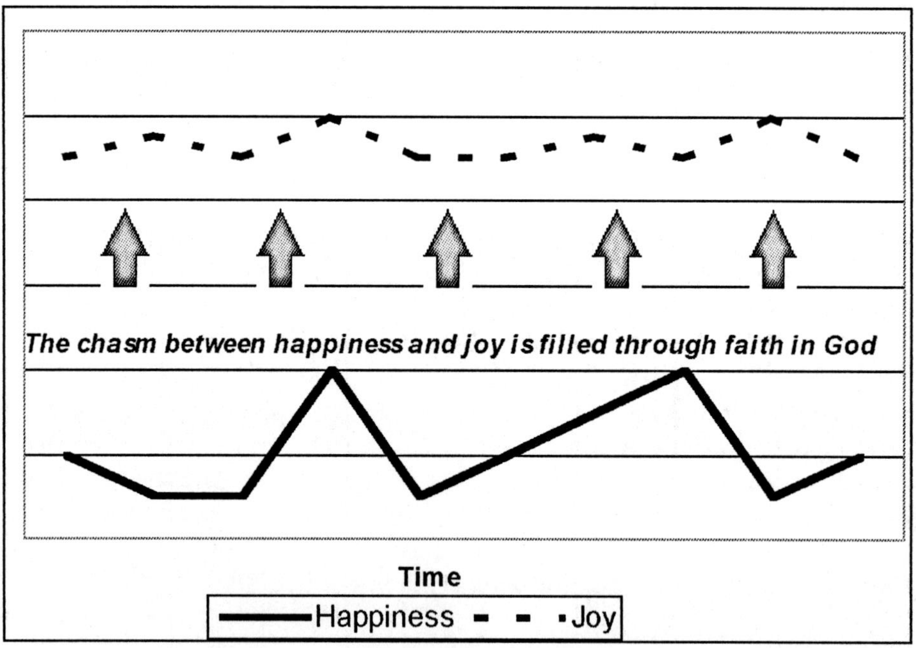

Fortunately, most of us will never come close to experiencing the pain and anguish that Harriet Tubman went through, since happiness is likely to be in much higher supply for us. But the incredible joy that Harriet Tubman had in her life is elusive to most people. We are often consumed with finding happiness, usually at the expense of missing out on joy.

Our Relentless Pursuit of Happiness keeps us from Joy

Thomas Jefferson captured the American dream when writing the first paragraph of the Declaration of Independence: *"We hold these truths to be self-evident: that all men are created equal, that they are endowed by their Creator with certain inalienable rights, among these are life, liberty, and the pursuit of happiness."*

Jefferson's words provided clarity and assurance in 1776, just as they do today. But happiness is subjective and can only be ascertained on an individual basis. By placing *"pursuit"* in front of *"happiness,"* Jefferson recognized that *enabling* people to seek happiness—whatever that meant to each individual—was critical to democracy. This stands in contrast to life and liberty, which were deemed "inalienable rights" that needed no such qualifiers. While the government could guarantee life and liberty, happiness is categorically different. It can only be *pursued*, which implies that we are to chase after something elusive, hoping we can somehow find, catch, and keep it. But isn't happiness a moving target?

I live in a 3-bedroom, 1.5 bathroom ranch house. I have "basic" cable television that allows me to access 68 different channels on any of my three televisions. If I choose to exercise available credit, I can travel to virtually any place in the world at any time. There are over 100 restaurants for me to choose from in the community I live. I am not lacking in food, clothing, or shelter, and I have many non-essential possessions that would be considered luxurious by most people in the world.

Amazingly, by United States standards, I fall into the "middle class." But by global standards—the only true barometer for comparison—I have riches that most people can only dream about. I seemingly have everything a person would require in order to live happily. I own a home, have a college education, am secure in my job, and am happily married with two wonderful children. I am free to worship God without fear of persecution, own three televisions and two VCR's, and live five minutes away from Lake Michigan. Isn't that enough to be happy?

Yes. No. Maybe? It appears that I have everything necessary in order to be happy. And I readily acknowledge that I have been blessed abundantly. But there is a part of us—all of us—that will *never* be completely satisfied with our circumstances, and therefore clamors for alternatives to increase happiness.

Take communications for example: In 1829 the typewriter was invented and people were amazed. In 1837 came the telegraph and people were amazed. In 1876 Alexander Graham Bell gave us the telephone and people were amazed. 1877 brought the first phonograph and more amazement. Cameras, television, motion pictures, and home videos followed, and while most people were impressed with those developments, few were actually amazed. More recently, satellite television, personal computers, the Internet, and palm pilots have been introduced, and our ability to be amazed has subsided dramatically. We have replaced our sense of amazement with a sense of entitlement, and are finding that the chasm between happiness and joy is wider than ever. The world we live in is ever changing, and happiness felt through material possessions is fleeting, to say the least.

How we pursue happiness is similar to how we deal with hunger. Satiety (fullness) comes from eating and gives necessary relief. If a person is disciplined and eats only what is necessary, they experience a greater sense of satiety and therefore less hunger. But if a person eats excessively in order to ward off hunger, he actually has *less* satiety and more hunger, and may even become gluttonous, which brings about numbness of the mind and greed of the soul. God's Word clearly warns us of the danger of gluttony:

> *Do not join those who drink too much wine or gorge themselves on meat, for drunkards and gluttons become poor, and drowsiness clothes them in rags.*
>
> *(Proverbs 23:20–21)*

Joy is the Great Equalizer

While discipline is essential for temporarily satisfying our hunger for happiness, the long-term solution is joy that comes through acceptance of Jesus Christ as Lord and Savior. When God gave us His only begotten Son, He provided the means for lasting fulfillment. Jesus' arrival was signaled by the promise of joy available to all through Him:

An angel of the Lord appeared to them, and the glory of the Lord shone around them, and they were terrified. But the angel said to them, "Do not be afraid. I bring you good news of great joy that will be for all the people. Today in the town of David a Savior has been born to you; he is Christ the Lord."

(*Luke 2:9–11*)

Joy is a precious gift from the Lord, and available to everyone. Whereas happiness is determined by individuals and relies on desirable circumstances, joy is available *universally* to those who trade earthly desires for eternal promises.

We are sustained by joy under any and all circumstances. In good times it provides a balanced perspective, helping us to acknowledge and give thanks to God as the source of our blessings. In bad times, we persevere and are further strengthened by looking beyond circumstances and focusing on God's eternal promise.

Jesus' words assure us that joy through Him is real and lasting, even during our most difficult times:

"I tell you the truth, you will weep and mourn while the world rejoices. You will grieve, but your grief will turn to joy. A woman giving birth to a child has pain because her time has come; but when her baby is born she forgets the anguish because of her joy that a child is born into the world. So with you: Now is your time of grief, but I will see you again and you will rejoice, and no one will take away your joy."

(*John 16:20–22*)

If You're Joyful and You Know It, Clap Your Hands!

Perhaps you are familiar with the popular children's song, "If you're happy and you know it, clap your hands (clap) (clap)." On and on the song goes as hands clap, feet stomp, voices shout "hooray," and the tempo becomes faster and faster. When you see children singing this song you cannot help but be happy!

Although we are usually quick to demonstrate happiness, we frequently fail to demonstrate joy. Even after coming to an understanding that joy through Christ is a gift to be treasured, we tend to keep it in our back pocket. Scripture instructs us to do otherwise:

"You are the light of the world—like a city on a mountain, glowing in the night for all to see. Don't hide your light under a basket! Instead, put it on a stand and let it shine for all. In the same way, let your good deeds shine out for all to see, so that everyone will praise your heavenly Father."
(Matthew 5:14–16)

Understand that there is a fine line between demonstration and flamboyancy. A demonstrative person allows their *true* feelings to be displayed openly, while a flamboyant person seeks recognition while exhibiting *contrived* behavior. God does not desire Christians to be flamboyant, but rather to demonstrate faith accordingly (and humbly) through words and deeds.

I love music, even though my taste is somewhat limited and I have never played an instrument. In my mind, a great song is one that elicits some type of emotional response. It can tug at my heart or cause me to move faster, but the common denominator is that I react in a manner that I wouldn't have without hearing the song. And I find that the most powerful songs are those that are written and performed with artistic integrity, minus *excessive* vocals and instrumentation. A great song does not require much embellishment.

The same is true when we demonstrate joy. When our intentions are pure, there is no mistaking that we bask in God's presence. We let our light shine for all to see, just as God desires. But when we manipulate joy—that is, when we dress joy up as something that it's not—we detract from God's kingdom. People can only see the purity of our joy when it is demonstrated in its natural state. Just as a great song doesn't need much embellishment, neither does the joy we have in Jesus Christ.

Emotions Change But Joy is Constant

I believe that the underlying reason for Christians not consistently demonstrating joy is the mistaken belief that joy is an emotion. People tend to erect barriers that prevent emotion from surfacing. Displaying emotion produces a feeling of vulnerability, which most people choose to avoid.

But as I stated earlier, joy is not an emotion, it is intrinsic. We can be joyous no matter what emotional state we are in. Whether we are remorseful, desperate, happy, sad, or full of love, joy is a constant if we choose to let Jesus' dwell within us. And on those occasions when we feel angry, bitter or jealous, joy through Jesus Christ helps us to overcome sinful emotions.

The key is to disassociate joy from emotion. Emotions come and go like the wind, provoking corresponding words and actions. But joy anchors us even as the winds of emotion threaten to carry us away. When we allow Jesus to dwell within us, joy isn't a variable, it's a constant. But because we tend to think of joy as just another emotion derived from circumstances, we often deny ourselves the constancy and fullness of joy through Jesus Christ.

Jesus' prayed for his disciples to have the full measure of joy available to them through His presence in their hearts. He knew that only joy could carry them through the difficult days that lay ahead:

> *"While I was with them, I protected them and kept them safe by that name you gave me. None has been lost except the one doomed to destruction so that Scripture would be fulfilled. I am coming to you now, but I say these things while I am still in the world, so that they may have the full measure of my joy within them."*
>
> *(John 17:12–13)*

If someone offered you a gift that would provide peace-of-mind during every minute of every day, and would *last forever,* wouldn't you take it? God gives joy to those who are open to receiving it.

Rejoice.

Soccer 101

My sons started playing soccer a few weeks ago in a Kindergarten co-ed league. Beyond learning the basics of the sport, the primary objective of the league and its coaches is to enable the kids to have fun. To this point, after four practices and one game, they have been overwhelmingly successful in reaching their objective.

Now here's the kicker (no pun intended): nobody keeps score in this league! With the objective being to learn fundamentals and have fun, keeping score is considered to be an unnecessary deterrent. The kids don't seem to mind at all. They celebrate when someone scores a goal, and they clearly understand that outscoring the other team is desirable, but mostly they simply enjoy playing the game.

Can you imagine going to a professional sporting event where nobody kept score? No one would show up! We feverishly root for "our" team to win the game, and are happy when they do. But when they lose, we're not nearly as happy with the outcome.

In sports and in life, our obsession with winning prevents us from experiencing joy. Just think what would happen if the simple, pure joy displayed by these Kindergarten soccer players carried over into their adult lives. They would appreciate what they have instead of worrying about what they don't have. They would treat others respectfully instead of manipulating them to get their own way. And they would embody the old adage, "It's not whether you win or lose, it's how you play the game."

Unfortunately, within a few years most of these Kindergartners will replace the natural joy of playing with an intense desire for winning. And while healthy competition is necessary for people to reach their full potential, too often self-value becomes tied to desirable outcomes.

We can learn from these Kindergarten soccer players. Don't stop trying to score goals in life, but remember that winning and losing are not nearly as important as how we live. With the Lord as our coach and the Bible as our playbook, we can't help but be joyful in life.

Kindness

A few years ago a movie called *"Pay It Forward"* was showing at theaters nationwide. Though only moderately successful at the box office while receiving mixed reviews from critics, the movie was unique in its simple premise that kindness begets kindness. The story centered on a young boy named Trevor who comes up with a novel idea for a class project in which he helps three people do something they could not have accomplished on their own. Those three people in turn help three other people, and so on and so on, until the cycle is repeated enough so that ultimately the world ends up being a better place to live. There are other plot twists, but essentially that was the idea behind *"Pay It Forward."*

"Pay It Forward" is a fictitious story, but its basic message that kindness begets kindness is not at all fictitious. Kindness does in fact beget kindness, though certainly not on the scale depicted in the movie. It is unrealistic to expect, in a world dominated by selfishness and greed, that the kindness we show toward others will be further perpetuated by them in all cases, or for that matter, in most cases. As we are incapable of controlling how other people think and act, we can only *influence* people to show kindness toward others. It is worth remembering that *deeply rooted* changes do not generally come about quickly and dramatically, but rather slowly and methodically. When we are kind to others, we *do* make the world a better place to live. Indeed, kindness begets kindness, but it happens slowly and on an individual basis, not quickly and en masse.

Of even greater significance is that kindness is requisite for godliness. As we are all sinful beings, to pursue godliness is to always come up short. But regardless, the Lord calls us to *strive* to be godly:

> *Have nothing to do with godless myths and old wives' tales; rather, train yourself to be godly. For physical training is of some value, but godliness has value for all things, holding promise for both the present life and the life to come.*
>
> (1Timothy 4:7–8)

God's Word provides additional clarification regarding the importance of pursuing godliness and the connection between kindness and godliness:

> *His divine power has given us everything we need for life and godliness through our knowledge of him who called us by his own glory and goodness. Through these he has given us his very great and precious promises, so that through them you may participate in the divine nature and escape the corruption in the world caused by evil desires. For this very reason, make every effort to add to your faith goodness; and to goodness, knowledge; and to knowledge, self-control; and to self-control, perseverance; and to perseverance, godliness; and to godliness, brotherly kindness; and to brotherly kindness, love. For if you possess these qualities in increasing measure, they will keep you from being ineffective and unproductive in your knowledge of our Lord Jesus Christ.*
>
> (2 Peter 1:3–8)

Of Kindness and Sternness

> *Consider therefore the kindness and sternness of God: sternness to those who fell, but kindness to you, provided that you continue in his kindness. Otherwise, you also will be cut off.*
>
> (Romans 11:22)

The message is clear in that kindness from God is assured provided that we reciprocate toward Him and toward our fellow man. God's kindness emanates from His love, and as God *is* love, His kindness is inherent. On the other hand, sternness from God is not inherent; it's reactionary. *We* determine whether God will be kind or stern toward us. God's commands are fixed and infinite, so when it comes to His kindness or sternness toward us, we are the only variable in the equation. We *must* be kind to others to find favor with God. And while it seems that kindness to other people should come naturally, a quick peek at the morning newspaper presents a different argument. Thus the question: "What state are we *naturally* inclined toward: kindness or sternness?"

Merriam-Webster's on-line dictionary defines sternness as *"having a definite hardness or severity of nature or manner."* When Adam and Eve succumbed to temptation, selfishness became us, with our inheritance marked by sinful desire. Indeed, while the thought of humankind being naturally disposed to sternness seems extreme, an objective view of our history suggests that we have earned that dubious distinction. Still, when we examine the paradoxical relationship between our sinful desires and our desire for fulfillment—both of which are inherent—determining whether we are naturally inclined toward kindness or toward sternness requires further investigation.

Regardless of whether or not we have accepted Jesus as Lord and Savior, we are *all* guilty of giving into sinful desires. The only variables are the nature of the sins we commit, the frequency with which we sin, and whether we repent for our sins in order to have restoration. Our sinful desire can to some extent be controlled, but it never completely leaves us.

In competition with our sinful nature is a desire for fulfillment. The Source of fulfillment is frequently mistaken, and many people erroneously equate fulfillment with happiness (which is temporary as well as circumstantial). *Genuine* fulfillment is found only through the pursuance of godliness (ref.1 Timothy 4:7–8). Furthermore, to become godly requires acceptance of Jesus Christ as Lord and Savior, along with a desire to live according to God's Word.

During the struggle between acting on sinful desires and searching for lasting fulfillment, elements of godliness hold natural appeal for many people, regardless of whether or not they have accepted Jesus Christ as Lord and Savior.

As indicated earlier (ref. 2 Peter 1:3–8), we have been given assurance that *"His divine power has given us everything we need for life and godliness through our knowledge of him who called us by his own glory and goodness."* Peter goes on to list several characteristics (faith, goodness, knowledge, self-control, perseverance, godliness, kindness, love) that we are to evolve in order to become more like Christ. He further states that ". . . *if you possess these qualities in increasing measure, they will keep you from being ineffective and unproductive in your knowledge of our Lord Jesus Christ."*

Taken individually, these characteristics hold natural appeal to believers as well as most non-believers. In particular, goodness, knowledge, self-control, perseverance, and kindness are almost universal in terms of greater societal *(but not necessarily individual)* acceptance. Going back to the question of whether we are naturally inclined toward kindness or sternness, a reasonable case can be made that the answer for most people is kindness. However, the validity of such a claim is severely lessened when considering that any "natural" inclination we have toward kindness is done on *our* terms only—not God's terms.

If we truly live according to God's Word, the kindness we show others will naturally reflect our love for them.

Do you love people—*all people*—so much that kindness becomes you? Speaking for myself, while many people may consider me to be loving and compassionate, the truth is that too often I *selectively* choose who I will love. And even though we are told to "love your neighbor as yourself" nine different times in the Bible, it still goes against our nature to love one another unconditionally. Given that kindness is a subset of love, how can we possibly believe that we are *naturally* inclined toward kindness?

If you're thinking that love and kindness can be separate and distinct, I agree but only in human terms. We must be kind to others, including people we don't know and people we don't see eye-to-eye with, but kindness without love is incomplete. Just as a dog will obey a stranger if he believes there is something to be gained by it, we will be kind to others if it helps us to feel better about ourselves.

Ask yourself this question: When you are kind to people whom you don't know, are you kind out of obligation, out of habit, or out of love?

If the answer is obligation or habit, then any kindness you show toward others brings about a temporary, false sense of self-satisfaction. But kindness out of love produces a much deeper state of satisfaction, one that focuses not on how we feel but rather on the welfare of another person. Kindness borne of love equates to godliness. And while I am not suggesting that we give up on kindness when it doesn't directly emanate from love, I am suggesting that we should always be kind to others *while working on removing barriers to unconditional love.* Eventually our kindness *will* reflect our love, and we will move one step closer to spiritual fulfillment.

Our sinful nature requires us to openly receive God's grace in order to be restored, yet even people who have not yet accepted Jesus into their lives gain satisfaction by showing kindness and compassion to others. And as we naturally seek fulfillment, the satisfaction derived from kindness—incomplete as it is without love—is enough for some people to halt their quest for lasting fulfillment. In doing so they not only deny themselves genuine fulfillment, they also relegate love to a secondary position.

Again, the bottom line is that God expects us be kind out of love, not obligation or self-satisfaction. The answer to the question posed initially can only be that we most assuredly *do not* naturally gravitate toward kindness, but rather toward sternness. We can fool one another by cloaking kindness as love, but we can't fool God. He knows that our inability to love one another unconditionally is rooted in sternness, which can only be alleviated through submission of our will to His:

> *For the sinful nature desires what is contrary to the Spirit, and the Spirit what is contrary to the sinful nature. They are in conflict with each other, so that you do not do what you want. But if you are led by the Spirit, you are not under law. Those who belong to Christ Jesus have crucified the sinful nature with its passions and desires. Since we live by the Spirit, let us keep in step with the Spirit.*
>
> (Galatians 5:17–18, 24–25)

Faith without Deeds Doesn't Amount to Much

According to research compiled by *Barna Research Online* (www.barna.org), as of January 2000, 40% of American adults were attending church during a typical weekend. The research also indicates that 71% of Americans adults had a period of time during their childhood when they regularly attended a Christian church.

I find these statistics to be frightening! Only 2 out of 5 American adults are attending church, *and* 3 out of 10 children who attend church will drop out as adults. Why are we losing the battle?

While the issue in its entirety is complex, we can certainly make some valid assumptions based on the "*Top Ten Reasons to Attend a Church Service,*" as reported via the research from Barna:

1. The theological beliefs and doctrine of the church.
2. How much the people seem to care about each other.
3. The quality of the sermons that are preached.
4. How friendly the people in the church are to visitors.
5. How involved the church is in helping the poor and disadvantaged.
6. The quality of the programs and classes for children.
7. How much you like the pastor.
8. The denomination the church is affiliated with.
9. The quality of the adult Sunday school classes.
10. The convenience of the times of their weekend services

Note that three of the top ten reasons for people attending church relate *directly* to kindness (numbers 2, 4, and 5 above).

When seeking to understand why people *don't* come to church, including those who once attended church, we can ascertain from the Barna research that a significant contributing factor is a lack of kindness from church members and, in some cases, church leaders.

It is not acceptable in God's eyes to attend church yet not demonstrate kindness to others. As churchgoers, it is imperative to understand that we *directly represent Christ.* Many people, in particular those who are not yet firm in their faith, see us as the embodiment of God's kingdom. Talk about a heavy responsibility! We *must* reflect our beliefs and make kindness a priority. When we aren't kind toward others, we dishonor ourselves as well as the church.

God's Word tells us rather succinctly that faith without deeds is not good enough:

> *In the same way, faith by itself, if it is not accompanied by action, is dead. But someone will say, 'You have faith; I have deeds.' Show me your faith without deeds, and I will show you my faith by what I do. You believe that there is one God. Good! Even the demons believe that—and shudder. You*

foolish man, do you want evidence that faith without deeds is useless? Was not our ancestor Abraham considered righteous for what he did when he offered his son Isaac on the altar? You see that his faith and his actions were working together, and his faith was made complete by what he did. And the scripture was fulfilled that says, 'Abraham believed God, and it was credited to him as righteousness,' and he was called God's friend. You see that a person is justified by what he does and not by faith alone. In the same way, was not even Rahab the prostitute considered righteous for what she did when she gave lodging to the spies and sent them off in a different direction? As the body without the spirit is dead, so faith without deeds is dead.

(*James 2:17–26*)

Beware of False Kindness

It must be mentioned that there are many people who blatantly use *false* kindness as a means of personal gain. This is a vastly different scenario than kindness out of obligation or habit, during which if we work toward removing barriers that hold us back from unconditional love we inevitably progress toward godliness. But people who *purposefully* use kindness as a means of getting something are not progressing toward godliness—they are digressing toward *godlessness*.

Most of us appreciate when people do nice things for us. We tend to place a lot of trust in people who seem interested in helping us. But beware of people who will exploit our trust for their own purposes.

If you think back to your high school days, you will invariably recall the bully who was known to be "kind" to the kid who did his homework for him. Or the boy who used "kindness" to persuade his girlfriend to have sex with him. Or the pretty girl who feigned kindness to the shy boy so that he would give her a ride to school every day. The list goes on and on!

Sadly, false kindness is not limited to just High Schools; it is predominant everywhere. In workplaces, families, governments, churches, etc., false kindness abounds. We must be alert and on guard against people whose supposed kindness serves only to benefit themselves:

I urge you, brothers, to watch out for those who cause divisions and put obstacles in your way that are contrary to the teaching you have learned.

Keep away from them. For such people are not serving our Lord Christ, but their own appetites. By smooth talk and flattery they deceive the minds of naive people.

(*Romans 16:17–18*)

Kindness is not always a 2-way Street

One of the barriers that many people have to kindness is an expectation to be treated in the same manner that they treat others. I wish it was that simple, but the fact is that regardless of the kindness we show people, some will not reciprocate in kind. We all *desire* to be treated with respect, dignity, and kindness, but often we are not. In acknowledging that fact, the question is whether we let other people dictate how kind we will be toward them.

Make no mistake about it—being kind to people who aren't kind to us is not an easy thing to do! How difficult it is to not give into pettiness and negativity. Yet *we* alone determine whether to be kind toward people. And the actions of others aren't sufficient reason to abandon God's instruction. Indeed, we are to be kind toward others even when they aren't toward us.

Perhaps you are thinking that this approach is in conflict with the "eye for an eye" passage sprinkled throughout the Old Testament (Exodus 21:24, Leviticus 24:20, Deuteronomy 19:21). But that passage is frequently misinterpreted. Its context is not one of disproportionate sternness but rather appropriate retribution. During the time in which the passage was written, the prevailing approach in Palestine was to react to injustice upon oneself by inflicting a much more severe punishment on the perpetrator. Violence borne out of a false sense of honor was the rule of the day and threatened to destroy society. Thus the "eye for an eye" passage essentially placed a ceiling on uncontrolled, escalating violence. There are many passages in the Bible that call for appropriate (and proportionate) earthly punishment in response to criminal acts. But in terms of kindness, regardless of whether or not people reciprocate, Christians are to be kind *no matter what.*

Bear in mind that God expects our kindness to be done out of love, which takes many forms. Just as the Bible calls for appropriate punishment for criminal acts, it also calls for appropriate discipline in order for a person to become godly. Even when administering punishment or discipline—*especially when administering punishment or discipline*—we must be kind to others out of love.

God sets the expectation for displaying kindness to others at all times:

Share with God's people who are in need. Practice hospitality. Bless those who persecute you; bless and do not curse. Rejoice with those who rejoice; mourn with those who mourn. Live in harmony with one another. Do not be proud, but be willing to associate with people of low position. Do not be conceited. Do not repay anyone evil for evil. Be careful to do what is right in the eyes of everybody.

(Romans 12:13–17)

Romans 12:13–17 sounds a lot like *"Pay It Forward."* The world is a better place when we live according to God's Word.

Kindness Makes a Difference!

After becoming engaged, Pam and I quickly realized that we would have to find a church to get married in! Though we had both been inactive in our respective churches for several years, we were in agreement that not only would we find a church to marry us, we would find one that would help bring about spiritual nourishment. Without having much familiarity with churches in the area, we were uncertain as to whether one church would meet both of our needs.

A few months later, after visiting several churches in the area, we decided to get married at St. Paul's United Church of Christ. The church was willing to conduct our wedding service prior to any commitment on our part to join the church.

As we spent more time in church and with its Pastor (Reverend Wallace Zink), we felt increasingly drawn to it. We were especially enamored with the sincerity and kindness shown to us from Reverend Zink, and quickly determined that he cared a lot more about our spiritual condition than whether or not we became members of St. Paul's.

Reverend Zink challenged Pam and I to be true disciples of the Lord Jesus Christ. He actively counseled us on our forthcoming marriage, making sure to remind us that God's place in a marriage was at the forefront. Not once did he make us feel less than worthy to be married in the church, despite the fact that we were not yet officially part of it.

Reverend Zink never pressured us into making a rash, regrettable decision, and because of that we were able to attend church for several months before *comfortably* deciding to become members of St. Paul's. His unfailing politeness and patience were exactly what we needed at the time. We also felt a strong sense of kindness and acceptance from other church members.

We will always have a special place in our hearts for Reverend Zink and for St. Paul's United Church of Christ. We were married in the church, made a lot of friends in the church, and found the spiritual nourishment we were seeking from the church. It was home. And in our hearts, it's *still* home.

Love

Love is patient, love is kind. It does not envy, it does not boast, it is not proud. It is not rude, it is not self-seeking, it is not easily angered, it keeps no record of wrongs.

(1 Corinthians 13:4)

This simple, eloquent definition of love offers strong appeal to our basic human desire for acceptance and value. A true love is one where selflessness, patience, and kindness are ever present. Seemingly the only place where this kind of love exists is in fairy tales, but even in fairy tales true love is absent as the good characters and bad characters are contrived to be diametrically opposed, allowing for selectivity when it comes to love. And since fairy tales are human creations with human biases, they tend to overlook the hardest part of love, which contrary to popular belief isn't remaining in love, it's having a *desire* to love. Not just a desire to love those who we're closest with—a desire to love all people.

For most of us, any attempts at adhering to what 1 Corinthians 13:4 teaches us are contingent on being allowed to determine *who* and *when* we will love in this manner. And even then, how many of us are willing to love even one person unconditionally, all of the time? How can we possibly even think about loving all people unconditionally, all of the time, when we can't even do that with the people we are closest to? The sad truth is that despite having an agreement in principle with 1 Corinthians 13:4, very few people are successful in *living* according to its precepts.

As was noted in the "*Kindness*" chapter, without love everything we do is incomplete. If a professed belief in Jesus Christ as Lord and Savior is the basis of Christianity, then love is the *manifestation* of Christianity. Our love from, and our love for, Jesus Christ should govern our every thought and action. All of our solemn prayers, all of our good deeds, all of our accomplishments don't amount to anything when love is absent. This becomes especially acute when considering the verse directly *preceding* 1 Corinthians 13:4:

> *If I give all I possess to the poor and surrender my body to the flames, but have not love, I gain nothing.*
>
> *(1 Corinthians 13:3)*

The Source of True Love

Any "love" that we show toward others is flawed. As we are all sinful beings, even on those rare occasions when we make legitimate attempts to completely focus on another person, we never quite succeed. Our personal agendas never completely disappear, even when we desire that they would. It is rather sobering to think that I will never be able to demonstrate *pure* love. And it is an *especially* sobering thought coming on the heels of the last paragraph, in which it is acknowledged that anything we do in life is rendered meaningless without love.

But the cure for what ails us is God's love. While we are incapable of demonstrating true love, God most assuredly is not. God is *the* source of love, a love so pure that we can hardly even begin to comprehend it.

For many Christians, a favorite Bible verse is John 3:16: "*For God so loved the world that he gave his one and only Son, that whoever believes in him shall not perish but have eternal life.*"

We take comfort in knowing that God's love for us runs so deep that He willingly gave us His only begotten Son. We mocked, tortured and crucified the Lord. *We did this to God's Son.* How can God possibly love us? It just doesn't add up—according to our math.

Nevertheless, for reasons known only to God, we are gifted with eternal life in heaven when we believe in Jesus and strive to follow Him. What greater love could there possibly be?

Jesus spoke to His disciples about what true love entails:

"My command is this: Love each other as I have loved you. Greater love has no one than this, that he lay down his life for his friends."
(John 15:12–13)

At first glance, Jesus' command doesn't seem all that difficult to follow. I can say with absolute certainty that I would willingly lay down my life for my wife, kids, and other loved ones. I am sure you would do the same for the people you love. But would you sacrifice yourself for people you've never met? How about for people who despise you? Would you *allow* people who hate you to kill you, just so you could give them something precious?

Honest answers to these questions prompt us to revisit John 15:12–13 with significantly more appreciation for God's sacrifice. The Lord essentially tells His disciples that He *is* love, knowing full well that He was to sacrifice Himself in order to save His friends—every man, woman, and child who ever was or ever will be.

My willingness to begrudgingly lay down my life as a last resort to save a few *select* people comes up well short compared with Jesus' command to "Love each other as I have loved you." If I truly loved other people as the Lord loves me, I would commit myself to helping others every minute of every day, even to the point of giving my life for *anyone* who would benefit from my death. And everything I do for others would be done out of love and desire, not obligation or self-satisfaction.

Recognizing that love is essential for Christian living, and that demonstrating *true* love is impossible, how can we possibly find favor with God?

By ourselves, we *can't*. But through acceptance of Jesus Christ as Lord and Savior we are extended grace that allows us to live in favor with God:

> *For the law was given through Moses; grace and truth came through Jesus Christ. No one has ever seen God, but the only Begotten Son, who is at the Father's side, has made him known.*
>
> *(John 1:17–18)*

We are further assured of God's eternal love for us when remembering that of the 41,473 verses found in the Bible, its last two speak volumes about Jesus' promise to His followers:

> *He who testifies to these things says, "Yes, I am coming soon." Amen. Come, Lord Jesus. The grace of the Lord Jesus be with God's people. Amen.*
>
> *(Revelation 22:20–21)*

Love Is Difficult But Rewarding

The nourishment, comfort, and security we provide for our children during their first few years of life is done out of unwavering love that flows easily and continuously in our understanding that *we* are the sole providers for nearly all of their needs. In spite of considerable fatigue, stress, and personal sacrifice, commitment to our children is rarely in question.

But then something changes along the way. Our children become increasingly independent. They take care of their own needs, develop distinct personalities and (gasp!) talk back to us.

As we lose control over our children, it becomes a much greater challenge to love them unconditionally. And while we can easily forgive them for spilling milk when they're three years old, how about when they spill milk a few years later during a temper tantrum? We *know* in our minds that loving our children isn't supposed to be circumstantial, yet realistically it is much harder to love them when they are behaving badly than it is when they are not.

Indeed, when people behave in a manner that we approve of, love comes easy. But unconditional love requires us to love people regardless of how they behave. And while we are *not* to ignore behavior altogether, we *are* to relegate behavior to a secondary position when it comes to love, keeping in mind that as God loves all His children all of the time, so must we. By focusing first and foremost on loving the person—even when we don't love what the person does—we find favor with the Lord:

Above all, love each other deeply because love covers over a multitude of sins.

(1 Peter 4:8)

True Love isn't Easy

In striving to love others unconditionally, it becomes vitally important to know what love is and is not. Love takes many forms, some obvious and some not so obvious. *True* love is often painful, yet always rewarding in the long run. And as we are sinful beings by nature, our human tendency is to avoid the pain that accompanies true love. We want to love others in a manner that feels good, so that both the people we love as well as ourselves do not suffer pain or agony. But often the easy road leads not to love but to decay.

Genuine love requires that we do not accept or condone behavior that is of a significantly sinful nature. This may appear to be in conflict with unconditional love, but in fact it not only doesn't conflict with unconditional love, it's essential for it. How can we love a person—truly love a person—if we are unwilling to help them overcome destructive behavior? Love is all about sacrifice. To have genuine love for a person is to *never* stop loving them no matter what they do, while at the same time helping to steer them toward the path of righteousness. Realizing that what is at stake is eternal life, we need to lovingly rebuke one another as required:

Do not hate your brother in your heart. Rebuke your neighbor frankly so you will not share in his guilt.

(Leviticus 19:17)

Unfortunately, many people mistake unconditional acceptance for unconditional love, which in truth are at odds with one another.

Unconditional acceptance is a form of cowardice. It is far too convenient to ignore sinful behavior under the guise of *"that's not my issue to worry about, let God take care of it."* How can we possibly feel comfortable while watching people we claim to love live in sin? Are we afraid of confronting others with the truth? Have we deluded ourselves into believing that God's grace precludes us from calling people into account for their actions?

The answer to these questions lies in one word: deception. Satan gains great satisfaction watching Christians take a lackadaisical approach to bringing others toward the saving truth of Jesus Christ. The "I'm okay, you're okay" world we live in suits the devil just fine. He knows that when we fail to call others into account for their actions, *we* contribute to the likelihood of them missing out on eternal life in heaven.

Scripture gives us the weapons for fighting against deception:

Put on the full armor of God so that you can take your stand against the devil's schemes.

(Ephesians 6:11).

The "armor" Paul refers to includes truth, righteousness, readiness, faith, salvation, and God's Word (ref. Ephesians 6:13–17). This armor is vital to godly living, especially when considering that even the most faithful, ardent believers are guilty on occasion of mistaking unconditional acceptance for unconditional love; it's an easy trap to fall into. Unconditional acceptance *feels* good, but unconditional love *is* good. Be assured that we embody Christian love when we compassionately call people into account for their actions *while* redirecting them toward the Lord Jesus Christ:

Love must be sincere. Hate what is evil; cling to what is good. Do not be overcome by evil, but overcome evil with good.

(Romans 12: 9, 21)

While acknowledging that true love requires us to occasionally rebuke others for significant transgressions, we must always examine our own hearts prior to doing so. It is far too easy (and tempting) to judge others while overlooking our own thoughts and actions. Rebuking others must be done with a clean heart, one that seeks to help people out of love, not judgement. *Do not* look past yourself when calling another into question:

"Why do you look at the speck of sawdust in your brother's eye and pay no attention to the plank in your own eye?"

(Matthew 7:3–5)

When calling others into account, we should steer clear of accusations and judgements, focusing instead on the importance of godly behavior. Unless done within the confines of established societal law, judgements rendered against others tend to be counter-productive and, more importantly, rarely done out of love. Much better results are derived from showing genuine care, concern, and compassion. Failure to do so is an indication that you are acting not out of love, but out of judgement.

I am *not* suggesting that we coddle others, but rather that everything we say and do be out of love. Suppose that a close friend is abusing alcohol. The loving thing to do is confront them with it, even though such a confrontation may well be met with defensiveness and/or resistance. You will likely be tempted to counter their anger with some of your own, but if you allow anger to supercede care, concern, and compassion, then any "love" you have for your friend will be buried beneath accusations and judgement. Instead of helping your friend, you'll alienate him. And regaining his trust will not be easy.

Beyond calling people into account for their actions, we are also called to *discipline* those we love in order to bring them closer to God. Discipline is uncomfortable for many and misunderstood by most, but to correctly discipline others is to simply mirror the discipline we receive from the Lord. God's discipline is *always* designed to redirect our focus to the eternal:

> *But God disciplines us for our good that we may share in his holiness. No discipline seems pleasant at the time, but painful. Later on, however, it produces a harvest of righteousness and peace for those who have been trained by it.*
>
> *(Hebrews 12:10–11)*

God's discipline is never spiteful, always loving:

> *My son, do not despise the Lord's discipline and do not resent his rebuke, because the Lord disciplines those he loves, and he punishes the son he delights in.*
>
> *(Proverbs 3:11–12)*

When we consider discipline in a *Biblical* context, we clearly see that it is a gift from God. God's discipline is often painful and takes forms such as hardship, suffering, loss, grief, persecution, etc. Even as we bemoan our circumstances, God knows that it is during trials and tribulations—times when we are most desperate—that we are much more likely to seek Him. God strongly desires that we accept His offer of salvation, using discipline as a means of shifting our focus from ourselves to His saving grace.

Although Scripture clearly shows that discipline is a form of love, there are those who mistakenly label *brutality* (particularly toward spouses and children) as a form of love. In doing so, they disregard the fact that everything done and/or taught to us by the Lord is out of love, intended to bring us closer to a saving knowledge of Him. It is deceitful, sinful behavior to inflict physical or mental punishment toward another person out of anything other than love. And any punishment we render must have reasonable boundaries, understanding that the goal of discipline is to simply correct wrongful behavior. People who feel compelled to mercilessly beat their wives and/or children are acting out of hatred, not love. Some may claim that what they do is out of love, but they're either delusional or lying. And those who seek to justify their brutality by quoting Scriptures like Proverbs 13:24 (*"He who spares the rod hates his son, but he who loves him is careful to discipline him"*) either purposefully overlook or are woefully ignorant of the context and *totality* of God's Word. Though convenient, it is also dangerous to seek specific Bible passages that, taken out of context, support one's personal agenda. We are to study Scripture incrementally and in totality, but above all we must set aside personal bias if we are to experience the Truth of God's Word. And just as it is dangerous to selectively seek passages in support of one's personal agenda, it is also dangerous to selectively *discard* passages that don't cater to one's agenda. Put simply, God's Word will speak to us in ways we can scarcely imagine *if* we are willing to set aside our prejudices.

To reinforce the importance of interpreting Scripture in its proper context, let's re-examine Proverbs 13:24 (*"He who spares the rod hates his son, but he who loves him is careful to discipline him."*). For starters, we must consider what the writer of Proverbs says a bit later (*Proverbs 19:18: "Discipline your son, for in that there is hope; do not be a willing party to his death."*). Clearly this is a warning to discipline our children early so as to prevent problems later. Have you ever tried to get a six-year old to clean up their room on a regular basis, after not enforcing such a requirement earlier? Speaking from experience, it's not easy! We are further told, *"Do not withhold discipline from a child; if you punish him with the rod, he will not die. Punish him with the rod and save his soul from death." (Proverbs 23:13–14)*. In considering all three verses (Proverbs 13:24, 19:18, and 23:13–14), we understand that we are to discipline children early in life, out of love, and within reasonable limitations, so that we help them to live eternally with God. In its overall context, Proverbs 13:24 does not give us a license to cruelly and mercilessly beat our children, it simply legitimizes disciplining our children *when necessary, under controlled conditions, and out of love.*

Don't Keep Score

Think back to when you were a child. Can you remember how it felt when a parent consoled you shortly after scolding you? Or took you out somewhere special shortly after punishing you? Or perhaps, for no apparent reason, surprised you in some way? Chances are you felt loved. Children cherish attention, praise, and recognition, *without* keeping track of when they feel mistreated. That's an important aspect of love that children seem to understand while many adults don't. 1 Corinthians 13:4 tells us that love *"keeps no record of wrongs."*

I admire how kids bounce back quickly when things don't go their way. Even when disciplined in some manner, kids are usually quick to forgive and forget. But for some reason that tendency diminishes over time. It seems that we ought to become wiser as we become older, but in many ways we do not. When criticized, children pout and carry on for a bit before moving on, but most adults who feel criticized or in some way slighted take considerably longer before letting go of their anger. Some *never* let go of the grudges they keep.

Instead of loving others unconditionally as God loves us, we tend to keep score against one another. Sometimes we even go so far as to frame our rejection of others as though *they* were the ones rejecting us!

> *"Well, normally I wouldn't think twice about watching Mary's kids while she's at the hospital. But you see there's just this one little problem: I heard through the grapevine that she didn't like my idea for the church play. It's obvious to me that she just doesn't like me and probably wouldn't want me around her kids anyway."*

The example above might sound extreme, but don't be too quick to discount it. Whether it's not saying "hello" to someone at work because they've never said it to you first, or not bothering to call a relative because it's "their turn," or ignoring the guy sitting next to you on the bus because he "looks weird," chances are that you have kept score.

There is no panacea that gets us out of the scorekeeping mode, but we are wise to remember how we willingly received and expressed love as children. Life is too short to hold petty grudges.

Love's Many Splendors

While recognizing that love's ultimate rewards are of an eternal nature, it is certainly worth noting that there are significant earthly benefits to be gained from love as well. Our inherent human condition is one of intense desire for love and affirmation. We need to feel loved, and we need to express love.

As we are made in God's image, and our God is one of love, we live for love. It is incredibly gratifying to look into another's eyes and sincerely, honestly tell that person how much you love them—not out of obligation or with a hidden agenda, but out of love. And when we are on the receiving end of such a conversation, the feeling is just as good!

The love we have for other people doesn't always have to be verbalized, but it sure helps. Too many people have felt the sting of rejection that comes from never hearing the three words we all long to hear: *"I love you."* Many families have been shattered by one or more people being unable (unwilling?) to express love. When we don't express our innermost feelings to those who mean the most to us, we shouldn't be surprised later when they feel unloved. "Implied" love is not good enough. It's a bit like a used car salesman telling you that he wouldn't be at all surprised if the car he just sold you ran for another 100,000 miles. Wouldn't you prefer that he gave you a *guarantee* that it will run for another 100,000 miles? Granted, while there are no such guarantees when it comes to love between two people, we still prefer express assurances to implied assumptions.

And let us never forget that when it comes to God's love, the Bible is the ultimate repair manual. It has the answers for anything and everything that hold us back from living in His love. What's more, the Bible is not just a repair manual, it is also God's *express guarantee* that regardless of our sinful past, we are assured eternal life when we accept Christ as our Lord and Savior and seek to follow Him for the rest of our days.

> *If anyone acknowledges that Jesus is the Son of God, God lives in him and he in God. And so we know and rely on the love God has for us. God is love. Whoever lives in love lives in God, and God in him. In this way, love is made complete among us so that we will have confidence on the day of judgement, because in this world we are like him.*
>
> *(1 John 4:15–17)*

Love is precious. Love is timeless. Love is God. God is Love.

From The Mouths of Babes

As of this writing my wife and I haven't faced many days where our children misbehaved for extended periods of time. But having just turned six, they obviously have had occasional bouts—increasingly as of late—of bad behavior. Nevertheless, we have been blessed with two very good boys.

But then there was the evening last February. It started innocently enough, with me losing myself in the local newspaper after coming home from work. Even after Pam told me that the boys had been wild all day, I didn't think much of it. After all, the sports section beckoned.

After dinner I walked downstairs and could not find the carpet—it was covered with toys. Hot wheels were everywhere, play dough plastered on walls and—shriek!—my tabletop hockey game covered with monster trucks.

Needless to say I was not happy. It had already been a long day, and it was about to get longer! Though I rarely raise my voice to our kids, I did then and with ample authority. Spencer and Trevor started to pick up their toys after they quickly realized they had no room to negotiate.

Shortly thereafter, the basement floor was cleaned up (well, almost) and tempers calmed. Before going to bed, Spencer hugged me, saying that he was sorry for making a mess and hoped we could play together tomorrow. After telling Spencer that I loved him, I gave him another hug, tucked him in bed, and assured him that we would play together tomorrow. In the meantime, Trevor had fallen asleep so I tucked him into bed.

The next morning, after waking up a bit after 5:00 a.m., I heard footsteps and realized it was Trevor. We talked for a bit and I told him that I looked forward to playing with him and Spencer after work. After showering, I walked back to the living room and saw that Trevor had fallen asleep on the sofa. Just as I kissed Pam goodbye and grabbed my coat, Trevor's eyes opened and his exact words were "You know, dad, I really treasure you, mom, and Spencer. I love you, see you later."

The love of children is precious: no scorecards, no grudges. Just a whole lot of honesty!

Marriage

Allow me to preface this chapter by telling you how abundantly blessed I am to have married my best friend. My wife is my rock and inspiration, my heart and soul. And though I will fall short in any attempt to document the depth of my feelings for Pam, it is with love, gratitude, and devotion that I dedicate this chapter to her.

Warning: Be Careful What You Commit To

Perhaps you are feeling a bit bewildered as to why I would issue a warning about marriage immediately after lovingly paying tribute to my wife. Is a cautionary warning a necessary component of a chapter on marriage? Absolutely! There is a definite correlation between a measured, serious commitment, and the fullness of joy that such a commitment can bring about.

Marriage is not for the faint of heart, nor is it to be taken lightly. Making a lifetime commitment to another person is serious business, as indicated by Jesus' words:

> *"I tell you that anyone who divorces his wife, except for marital unfaithfulness, and marries another woman commits adultery." The disciples said to him, "If this is the situation between a husband and wife, it is better not to marry." Jesus replied, "Not everyone can accept this word, but only those to whom it has been given. For some are eunuchs because they were*

> *born that way; others were made that way by men; and others have renounced marriage because of the kingdom of heaven. The one who can accept this should accept it."*
>
> (Matthew 19:9–12)

Even as the fruits of marriage are abundant, its most precious, lasting rewards come less from passion than from commitment. Starting a fire is easy, but fanning the flames to keep a fire burning requires persistence and dedication.

Before entering into marriage, we must thoroughly examine our heart, mind, and soul. To put it another way, we must carefully and prayerfully reach positive conclusions in each of the following areas:

1) *Emotional.* How deep is my love for my partner? How deep is my partner's love for me? Is our mutual desire for oneness strong enough to bring about a willingness to make necessary individual sacrifices?

2) *Logical.* Setting aside matters of the heart, will I be marrying this person for the "right" reasons? Do I honestly and objectively believe that the marriage will be one of *mutual* lifelong commitment?

3) *Eternal.* Will the marriage be Christ-centered? Will my spouse join me in walking as a disciple of the Lord Jesus Christ?

Although the next three sections are written for people *considering* marriage, the thoughts and ideas contained within also offer application for those who are already married.

Examining Our Hearts Prior to Marriage

On the surface, examining one's heart prior to marriage appears to be a foregone conclusion. The logical assumption is that anyone considering marriage must feel love for his or her partner. Yet the fundamental consideration isn't whether love exists, it's whether a strong mutual desire for *oneness* exists, such that both people are willing to make significant individual sacrifices.

There is a strong association between *desire* and *willingness*, and both are critical for a strong marriage.

Marriage

Desire governs willingness. When we desire something, the question that always follows is "How bad do you want it?" When it comes to marriage, both people must have a strong desire for a loving, healthy, lasting relationship. Merely having a *willingness* to commit to such a relationship is insufficient.

To illustrate the point, a desire for healthy teeth and gums *produces* a willingness to occasionally endure some degree of pain from a Dentist. Nobody desires to undergo dental work, but if that's what it takes to support a desire for health, most will.

A willingness to make personal sacrifices *based on* a willingness to commit to a strong, healthy marriage will nearly always result in an unsuccessful marriage. Willingness without desire leads to disillusionment and frustration.

To further reinforce the point, a comparison can be made between being in a marriage and working in a job. Abraham Maslow developed a general theory on motivation called the "*Hierarchy of Needs*," in which he suggested that beyond food, shelter, social needs, and self-esteem, people are driven by an intrinsic desire for self-fulfillment, of which recognition, growth, and creativity are elements. In the workplace, when we don't feel valued, aren't sufficiently challenged, or lack development opportunities, we either search for a different place of employment or simply go through the motions from one day to the next. Neither scenario brings about self-fulfillment. When people move from one company to the next, more often than not they repeat the same scenario over and over. Each change brings more disillusionment, and any desire to seek fulfillment through work is eventually replaced with mere willingness. As for those who simply show up and go through the motions, they have essentially abandoned hope of finding self-fulfillment through work. In accepting their situation, they bypass their higher needs.

In marriage the vows we make to one another are *binding*. While acknowledging that divorce is inevitable in certain scenarios, the fact remains that God *intended* marriage to last a lifetime. Unlike the job market where we are free to explore other opportunities, marriage affords no such options. And unlike the workplace where a person can go through the motions every day and not have a significant adverse effect on others, in marriage everything we do and say effects at least one other person. One person's disillusionment or discontentment can have a devastating effect on his or her spouse.

Our answers to the *"How bad do you want it"* question reveal the extent of our desire. If a man and woman mutually desire a loving, healthy, lasting marriage such that they are willing to make personal sacrifices for the sake of oneness, then they have successfully answered the essential questions of the heart. But be sure to examine your heart—and your partner's heart—carefully and objectively. It is a mistake to believe that you can easily transform willingness into desire, as more often than not willingness stems *from* desire. Desire either exists or it doesn't, and attempts to manufacture it are generally misguided.

Examining one's heart really is a delicate matter. So often one person fervently wishes for the other to share in their dreams and desires, making it difficult to separate fact from fiction. What we *want* can overcome us and result in bad—and permanent—decisions. Exercising caution beforehand prevents considerable heartache and pain later on.

Examining Our Minds Prior to Marriage

Since examining one's heart is indeed a delicate matter, it is necessary to balance the heart with the *mind*. Examining the mind in preparation for marriage is tantamount to *intellectual* ascertainment of the viability of sustaining a loving, happy, healthy marriage with a particular person.

Whereas the heart represents our emotional state, with key elements being love and desire, the mind represents our logical state, with a primary focus on assessing the viability of a prospective marriage *from the outside looking in*.

When examining our minds before marriage, it is necessary to isolate matters of the heart to whatever extent possible. We cannot assess anything logically and objectively if there are significant natural biases interfering.

From there, as with any logical assessment, a desirable result(s) needs to be defined. This may sound easy, but in fact it is rather difficult. My criteria for a successful marriage may very well conflict with yours. Of much more importance, your criteria for a successful marriage may conflict with your partner's. If you believe that maintaining an active social life is essential for a healthy marriage, but your partner believes that *scaling back* on social activities makes for a healthy marriage, then your disagreement in this area will likely be a source of discontentment and resentment—unless you agree in advance on mutually acceptable middle ground.

When defining criteria for a successful marriage, do so independently of your partner. If you do this exercise together, the heart will get in the way and one or both of you will compromise its validity.

After both of you have compiled separate lists, go through them together point-by-point. Do not be surprised or frustrated with disagreements—they are to be expected. Talk about how you might handle certain situations, with an emphasis on determining how flexible you and your partner are about different criteria. Seek to understand the things that each person is most territorial about and least territorial about, and look for major stumbling blocks.

At this point, you will both have defined criteria for a successful marriage and had several honest discussions about what each person seeks from the marriage. You will likely have discovered some criteria in which you or your partner are willing to give ground, as well as other criteria in which one or both of you are not. Keep in mind that there are no "wrong" answers during this time. You are simply assessing the viability of marrying this individual. And when you're on opposite ends, focus not on who's right or wrong but rather on how you will address the disagreement to the satisfaction of both people. If one person strongly desires to have children early in the marriage, while the other would prefer to wait until later, then the logical approach is to find a middle ground. And don't just focus on your partner—focus on yourself too. Are *you* willing to give ground and still be happy with the outcome? These are important discussions to have before entering into marriage.

If both people can logically conclude that theirs will be a marriage not only of love, but also of self-sacrifice *and* give-and-take, chances are good that the marriage will last throughout their lifetime.

But the additional element that increases the odds of a loving, healthy marriage from good to great, is God.

Examining Our Souls Prior to Marriage

"Do you promise before God to love her, comfort her, honor and keep her in sickness and in health, forsaking all others so long as you both shall live? What God has joined together let no one put asunder."

Webster's on-line dictionary defines a vow as *"a solemn promise or assertion . . ."* While not legally binding, a vow represents major commitment. As it relates to marriage, that commitment is magnified considerably based on the belief that God Himself has decreed the marriage.

Traditional wedding vows take into account that an abundantly rewarding, lifelong marriage not only requires requisite love and commitment for one another, but also for the Lord Jesus Christ. In reciting the vows, we agree to love, comfort, honor, keep, and be faithful to each other through good times and bad, *as God is our witness*. Furthermore, the commitment to one another is made not only before God, it is made *to* God. And while traditional wedding vows may seem dated in our present age, in truth they simply reflect Jesus' teaching:

> *"But at the beginning of creation God made them male and female. For this reason a man will leave his father and mother and be united to his wife, and the two will become one flesh. So they are no longer two, but one. Therefore what God has joined together, let man not separate."*
> *(Mark 10:6–9)*

As God created us to be in communion with one another and with Him, a major consideration prior to marriage is whether both you and your partner will put Christ at the center of your relationship. If you both choose to do so, God will abundantly bless your union. But if either partner lacks the desire to make Jesus foundational, the marriage will inevitably be based on worldly considerations rather than God's will. The difference is that compromise and self-satisfaction govern a worldly marriage, while living according to God's Word (with an eternal sense of purpose) governs a Christ-centered marriage. To put it more succinctly, Jesus is the compass every marriage needs to find its true north.

A final question to consider prior to marriage is, "Do I feel the need for a prenuptial agreement?"

If your answer is "yes," then my opinion is that the commitment to your spouse (and in some cases to marriage as an institution) is lacking. A prenuptial agreement is tantamount to marriage insurance, and the only reason to ever take out insurance is to protect against risk. If you believe—if you *really* believe—that you have carefully and objectively concluded that the heart, mind, and soul of both you and your partner are prepared for marriage, then your vows to one another and to your Creator are all the insurance you need.

Appreciating Your Spouse

The Lord God said, "It is not good for the man to be alone. I will make a helper suitable for him."

(Genesis 2:18)

I do not pause nearly enough to ponder how truly blessed I am. My love for Pam runs deep and my commitment to her is unquestionable, yet too often I take her for granted. It's easy to do, what with non-stop appointments and events, work demands, children's activities, etc. It has been said that the best things in life are those which are right in front of us, yet are often unrecognized. When standing two feet away from an exquisite painting we don't quite fathom its beauty, but when stepping back the picture crystallizes, and its depth and beauty are breathtaking.

That's what marriage is like sometimes. From one day to the next, it is easy to overlook how blessed we are to have somebody to love and cherish us. It is incredibly humbling when I consider that Pam loves me unconditionally, choosing to overlook my many shortcomings. She may not like my occasional moodiness or selfishness, but the fact that she tolerates it out of love means more to me than she can know, and gives me impetus to be a better husband.

As we are all selfish by nature, we need to occasionally step back and take stock of our love for our spouse, and their love for us. This is especially true when we feel like we're just going through the motions. It is essential to keep the proper perspective (appreciation) in order to maintain a vibrant, healthy marriage.

Understand that while "stepping back" helps to *reinforce* love and appreciation for our spouse, it is not a replacement for an active relationship. A healthy marriage is one where a husband and wife are actively engaged *while* regularly taking time to reflect on their love for one another. The old saying, "absence makes the heart grow fond," is true mostly because we fail to fully appreciate those we love on a daily basis. It is during the "normality" of life—when one day *seems* indistinguishable from the next—that we should love our spouse the *most*. Too often we mistakenly associate anniversary dates and holidays as designated times when we're to demonstrate love and appreciation for our spouse; on the contrary, *every day* is an opportunity to appreciate and demonstrate love. If you don't believe me, ask anyone whose husband or wife has passed away about the importance of cherishing your spouse every minute of every day.

God in his infinite wisdom addressed man's emptiness with companionship. Beyond salvation through Jesus Christ, there is no better earthly gift than one in which a man and a woman share their innermost desire, passion, and love for a lifetime. As my wife is a gift from God, and as I love the Lord, so do I love, honor, and cherish Pam as she so richly deserves.

Of God and Marriage

How much value does God place on marriage? Enough that He instructs newlyweds early in their marriage to focus solely on what brings happiness to one another. In this way, a husband and wife will grow in appreciation and understanding for each other:

> *If a man has recently married, he must not be sent to war or have any other duty laid on him. For one year he is to be free to stay at home and bring happiness to the wife he has married.*
>
> *(Deuteronomy 24:5)*

Without a doubt, God desires for men and women to marry; in fact, not only does He desire that we marry, He *entices* us to marry:

> *He who finds a wife finds what is good and receives favor from the Lord.*
>
> *(Proverbs 18:22)*

Think about what that verse tells us: our spouse is a gift from God, and acceptance of God's gift allows us to find favor in Him. That's like having your cake and eating it too!

Lest we get too carried away with ourselves, it is necessary to understand *why* God places such a value on marriage. While gifting us with human companionship (ref. Deuteronomy 24:5), He also calls us into a deep relationship with our Lord and Savior, Jesus Christ. Indeed, marriage represents commitment to another person *and* to Jesus. When the Lord is the foundation for a marriage, fulfillment and joy are sure to follow.

Marriage

Taking into account that we are to love the Lord our God above all else, and acknowledging that we have real physiological and psychological human desires, it becomes essential to understand and harness unhealthy desire. And make no mistake, the question is not whether we have unhealthy desires (we all do), but how we *control* those desires.

To illustrate, regardless of whether or not you are married, it is perfectly natural to be attracted to more than one person of the opposite sex. Thus it is vitally important to recognize and acknowledge our condition of human weakness, as failure to do so is to deny Truth and increase the likelihood of rationalizing sinful behavior. We must recognize that we are all *capable* of acting on desires of the flesh, which makes it essential to *control* desire. And any attempts to "control" desire by ignoring its existence are futile. Lying to oneself is not nearly as effective as seeking the Lord's protection and guidance—proactively for determining non—negotiable foundational beliefs, and reactively when facing temptations likely to weaken resolve. It is also important to remember that as desire governs willingness, a fundamental question is "which desire overrides all others?" In other words, which of your desires is so powerful that it can stop all others in their tracks?

The answer can only be a desire to live according to God's Word. The Holy Spirit will envelop and protect those who *genuinely* strive for godliness.

For most of us, it is an ongoing challenge to place our desire to live for God ahead of all other desires. For that reason, God gifts us with marriage. The Lord knows that as we have a strong desire for love, companionship, and physical gratification, we are able to *better* serve Him by being in a healthy marriage. Still, there are those who are so focused on bringing forth the kingdom of God that seeking a mate would be detrimental to their unique purpose on earth. The Apostle Paul was one of these, though he taught that for most people, marriage is a path to godliness:

> *But since there is so much immorality, each man should have his own wife, and each woman her own husband. The husband should fulfill his marital duty to his wife, and likewise the wife to her husband. The wife's body does not belong to her alone but also to her husband. In the same way, the husband's body does not belong to him alone but also to his wife.*
> *(1Corinthians 7:2–4)*

Sacrifice Has Its Rewards

I mentioned previously the need to relegate personal interests to a secondary position in a marriage, recognizing that the marriage as a whole is of much greater significance than either individual. But while sacrifice is a necessary component for marriage, there is a common misconception that when the "two become one," individuality goes out the window.

On the contrary, in a nurturing, healthy marriage, individuality is *enhanced.* Pam and I *are* one, but as God made us unique individuals, we are *also* two. Through honesty, love, and solidarity, we draw out each other's best qualities while helping to dispense with the worst. Neither of us desires that the other forego individuality in order to fit some pre-determined standard, but rather that we help one another become the people God calls us to be:

> *"For this reason a man will leave his father and mother and be united to his wife, and the two will become one flesh." This is a profound mystery—but I am talking about Christ and the church. However, each one of you also must love his wife as he loves himself, and the wife must respect her husband.*
>
> (Ephesians 5 :31–33)

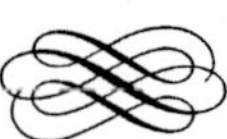

When You Least Expect It

I wasn't looking for Pam Scott, nor was she looking for me. But God had a plan to bring us together, and regardless of my efforts to undermine His plan, His will prevailed.

Before I met Pam during my junior year of college, I had officially sworn off women for the rest of my days! The previous year consisted of getting unceremoniously dumped by my then girlfriend, followed by a series of unsuccessful attempts to convince a close female friend to enter into full-fledged romance. I was through with women . . . or so I thought.

A funny thing happened on my way to the monastery! It was a cold February evening, and even though at that time I went out nearly every Friday, I had no desire to do so that night. Dan and Tom, the roommates I was closest with, had already left for the evening, leaving me with Dale, whom I wasn't especially close with.

For some reason, Dale decided that he really wanted to go to a Valentine's Day dance that night on campus, and insisted that I go with him. After intense lobbying, he finally talked me into it, mostly because I was tired of hearing him tell me I should go!

Attendance at the dance was sparse and I comfortably receded into my chair thinking it would be a short night. The dance floor was empty save for two girls who were energetically dancing the night away. Dale had a funny look on his face and I knew I was in trouble.

Sure enough, he dragged me out to dance with the two girls. I immediately gravitated toward the prettiest girl and struck up a conversation. She said her name was Pam. My evening began to get a lot better as I got to know this pretty, soft-spoken girl from Northern Michigan. I decided that maybe I would stay at the dance a little longer, maybe even a lot longer.

And so it was that on Valentine's Day 1984 I met the love of my life. I had heard it said that when you least expect something to happen, expect it to happen. But never in my wildest dreams did I imagine that the best day of my life would come on an otherwise uneventful February night.

Nourishment

"Give a man a fish, and he'll eat for a day. Teach him how to fish and he'll eat forever."

(*Ancient Chinese Proverb*)

Many people think of nourishment as strictly a physical requirement, overlooking its deeper implications. The ancient Chinese proverb effectively captures the true essence of *nourishment*. To nourish—or nurture—is not merely to satisfy a temporary need, it is to *sustain wellness*. To illustrate, if every meal consisted of an unlimited supply of chocolate chip cookies, our basic appetite would be satisfied even as we remained bereft of nutrition necessary to sustain us.

To remain in a state of wellness is *impossible* without proper nourishment, which extends beyond our physical needs and into the intellectual, social, and spiritual areas of our lives.

Intellectual Nourishment

If lacking in stimulating learning opportunities, we will never realize our true potential. I wonder how many people in third world countries fail to realize their potential because they lack educational opportunities. Closer to home, I wonder how many people in impoverished areas of the United States fail to realize their potential for the same reason. My guess is that there are a lot of doctors, teachers, artists, and scientists trapped beneath the underbelly of poverty.

Everyone—regardless of natural limitations—needs intellectual nourishment. God gifts us with the ability to learn new things every day, and without using and expanding our intellect we not only shortchange ourselves, we shortchange others. And while I am not suggesting that we all become doctors and lawyers, I am suggesting that we cannot afford to stand pat with what we know. It is of much greater significance to grow in knowledge than to attain a position of status, and it's even more significant to use our knowledge for the betterment of others and to advance God's kingdom. Where would we be today if the Apostle Paul didn't share what he learned about Christ and how to apply it accordingly?

Indeed, the primary reason to nurture our minds is to contribute to society. And personal growth *positions* us to be a resource to others. What a privilege!

Unfortunately, many people base their pursuit of knowledge on personal *gain* rather than personal growth. It is easy to ignore or forget that everything we have, including our minds, comes from God. We are effective ambassadors for the kingdom when bearing in mind that how we *act* on knowledge is of much greater significance than whether or not we acquire it:

> *If we deliberately keep on sinning after we have received the knowledge of the truth, no sacrifice for sins is left, but only a fearful expectation of judgment and of raging fire that will consume the enemies of God.*
> *(Hebrews 10:26–27)*

Sometimes good intentions lead to negative consequences, which nevertheless do not excuse us from further contributing to the welfare of others. If a student who is naturally gifted in Math while naturally deficient in English studies diligently for an English exam but still receives a "C," should she put her academic aspirations on hold? Logically, the answer is "no," but out of frustration or simply a lack of confidence, she may well resign herself to being less than what God created her for. We should take solace in knowing that, even when we fail, when we *try* to do God's will we find favor in Him. I cannot think of a more convincing argument for not allowing frustration to impede good intentions.

Alfred Nobel is a shining example of someone who overcame a significant setback to positively contribute to mankind. Born in Stockholm, Sweden in 1833, Nobel developed into a brilliant Chemist despite never having attended college. In 1867, Nobel obtained a patent on a new type of nitroglycerine, which he called "dynamite." Nobel's invention quickly became a staple for building and construction. Nobel considered the betterment of mankind to be his life's mission, and thus was understandably distraught to learn that dynamite was being used by some as an instrument of evil.

Nobel's frustration did not deter him from filling his life's mission. In 1895, he placed the bulk of his estate in a fund that would annually recognize and reward people who provided the greatest benefit to humanity. Nobel's legacy lives on, and his passion for contributing to mankind is evident in this excerpt from his last will and testament:

> *"The whole of my remaining realizable estate shall be dealt with in the following way. The capital shall be invested by my executors in safe securities and shall constitute a fund, the interest on which shall be annually distributed in the form of prizes to those who during the preceding year shall have conferred the greatest benefit on mankind . . ."*

Social Nourishment

Nurturing one another through encouragement, prayer, and counsel fills a basic human need. Whether we acknowledge it or not, we all require social nourishment.

To understand the importance of social nourishment, contrast those who receive it abundantly with those who do not. Economic success, righteousness, and a solid education often result from strong, regular nourishment from others, while poverty, substance abuse, and illiteracy often result when nourishment is lacking. Regardless of race, gender, or religion, anybody lacking a sufficient network of friends, family, clergy, etc. faces a difficult challenge. Even people who are *naturally* independent or strong willed need nourishment, and no one should be exempt from receiving it.

I live in Holland, Michigan, where we are blessed with one of the finest homeless shelters in the country. A major factor in the Holland Rescue Mission's success comes from nurturing residents in all areas: physically, intellectually, socially, and spiritually. Based on their unique situation, residents are *temporarily* provided shelter, meals, life skills, counseling and, most importantly, exposure to the saving Truth of Jesus Christ. In exchange, residents are required to attend daily chapel services, find steady work, follow all rules, and in general contribute to the community in which they live. The Holland Rescue Mission recognizes and rewards its residents based on demonstrated commitment to God and community. The Mission truly embodies what the Bible teaches us about nourishment—people who come there don't simply receive a square meal and a place to sleep, they receive life changing nourishment.

A friend of mine recently began working at the Mission after several years of being a supervisor for a public company. One of his immediate challenges was to *not* allow residents to have something without first working for it, as decreed by the Mission. He recently told me of a man whose shoes were in such bad shape that the soles were literally worn through. In order to get a new pair of shoes, the man would need to work at the Mission for a portion of that day, which the man did willingly and earnestly, and without complaint. My friend recounted to me that in all his years of supervision, rarely did he see people work as hard as this man did. The man *earned* his shoes and can wear them with pride and dignity.

When we help others, particularly those less fortunate, we should do so out of love, humility, and kindness. "Helping" is not always the same as "giving"; indeed, reciprocity of some form is usually a necessary element for proper social nourishment. The simple fact is that we help others best by helping them help themselves. Handouts are temporary but true nourishment sustains. We can give people a fish or we can teach them how to fish; which will help them the most?

People who have been blessed through nourishment must give back. In fact, the surest way to maintain healthy social nourishment is to provide it to others whenever possible. Whether it's volunteering at a charity or school, mentoring a student, or simply being a good friend, nourishing others helps you more than it does them. And best of all, it draws you closer to God:

> *And we urge you, brothers, warn those who are idle, encourage the timid, help the weak, be patient with everyone. Make sure that nobody pays back wrong for wrong, but always try to be kind to each other and to everyone else. Be joyful always; pray continually; give thanks in all circumstances, for this is God's will for you in Christ Jesus.*
>
> *(1 Thessalonians 5:14–18)*

How does providing social nourishment to other people nourish us? Put simply, when you're a child, it is more rewarding to receive a gift than to give one, but when you're an adult, it is more rewarding to give than to receive. We reach a point when giving brings about a deep sense of social nourishment.

People who receive abundant social nourishment will still lack fulfillment if they fail to nourish others. Many successful managers experience an epiphany during their careers when they start focusing less on themselves and more on others. In essence, they replace taking with giving and find it to be much more rewarding.

Jesus was hungry and tired during a stop in Samaria as part of a long journey from Judea to Galilee (ref. John 4:1–6). But after bringing a Samaritan woman he met at Jacob's well to a saving knowledge of His Truth, Jesus' hunger and fatigue were replaced with vitality and purpose:

> *Meanwhile his disciples urged him, "Rabbi, eat something." But he said to them, "I have food to eat that you know nothing about." Then his disciples said to each other, "Could someone have brought him food?" "My food," said Jesus, "is to do the will of him who sent me and to finish his work. Do you not say, 'Four months more and then the harvest'? I tell you, open your eyes and look at the fields! They are ripe for harvest. Even now the reaper draws his wages, even now he harvests the crop for eternal life, so that the sower and the reaper may be glad together. Thus the saying 'One sows and another reaps' is true. I sent you to reap what you have not worked for. Others have done the hard work, and you have reaped the benefits of their labor."*
>
> (John 4:31–38)

Spiritual Nourishment

Physiological, intellectual, and social nourishment are vital, but without spiritual nourishment they are rendered meaningless. Spiritual nourishment is of absolute importance for godly living, and it is a colossal mistake to believe otherwise. To be fulfilled, we must regularly and vigilantly seek spiritual nourishment.

Scripture is the primary component of spiritual nourishment. Everything we need to know about how to live is found in God's Word:

Man does not live on bread alone but on every word that comes from the mouth of the Lord.

(Deuteronomy 8:3)

Never underestimate the nutritional value derived from reading and studying Scripture. The effect of twenty or thirty minutes each day spent in God's Holy Word is amazing. Even when I miss a few days during the week, I have benefited enormously over the past three years from taking time in the morning to dwell in God's Word. I often gravitate to specific books and/or verses that address my unique needs on a given day, and more importantly, I *anchor* myself in His Word to start the day. As we are all "wired" to seek truth, when reading Scripture I feel personally validated knowing that God loves me so much that He has given me the answers I need to live a godly life.

Conversely, when going through periods when I don't often dwell in the Word, I feel unfulfilled. Speaking from firsthand experience, I do not recommend a spiritual hunger strike, especially when the source of nourishment is so readily available. The Lord's Prayer does not refer to His nourishment as "occasional bread," but as "daily bread." (ref. Matthew 6:11) Jesus extends an open invitation to join Him at His table, but we frequently decline:

Jesus replied: "A certain man was preparing a great banquet and invited many guests. At the time of the banquet he sent his servant to tell those who had been invited, 'Come, for everything is now ready.'" But they all alike began to make excuses. The first said, 'I have just bought a field, and I must go and see it. Please excuse me.' "Another said, 'I have just bought five yoke of oxen, and I'm on my way to try them out. Please excuse me.'" Still another said, 'I just got married, so I can't come.' "The servant came back and reported this to his master. Then the owner of the house became angry and ordered his servant, 'Go out quickly into the streets and alleys of the town and bring in the poor, the crippled, the blind and the lame.'" 'Sir,' the servant said, 'what you ordered has been done, but there is still room.' "Then the master told his servant, 'Go out to the roads and country lanes and make them come in, so that my house will be full. I tell you, not one of those men who were invited will get a taste of my banquet.'"

(Luke 14:16–23)

I believe that many people get frustrated when not experiencing a spiritual breakthrough shortly after beginning to study Scripture. Frustration of this sort is natural and to be expected. In everyday life, most of us are impatient and seek *quick* gratification, so why should the study of Scripture be any different? We *expect* something dramatic and are disappointed when we don't get it, yet in reality even when we think we're not being nourished, we are.

I'll use an analogy for dealing with frustration over not experiencing spiritual breakthrough. Think back to when you started Kindergarten. If you're like me, you probably don't remember much, but it is certain that you learned *basic* elements of English, Math, Art, Music, etc. As the years went by, you learned and applied more and more, to the point where you undoubtedly became proficient in certain subjects. Upon successfully completing 13 years of school, you were rewarded with a diploma. Looking back, do you attribute your accomplishment to a few watershed moments, or to the cumulative effect of 13 years of learning, study, and application? Even while recognizing that some people do indeed have watershed moments of extreme clarity, *nobody* accomplishes anything of significance and lasting value without investing time and effort. Spiritual fulfillment through study and application of Scriptures is no different; a solid spiritual foundation *opens the door to* spiritual breakthrough:

> *Brothers, I could not address you as spiritual but as worldly—mere infants in Christ. I gave you milk, not solid food, for you were not yet ready for it. Indeed, you are still not ready.*
>
> *(1 Corinthians 3:1–2)*

Just as the Scriptures teach us, try to maintain a healthy sense of perspective when seeking spiritual nourishment. Rest assured that your efforts are not in vane, and that God *is* at work in you. But also recognize that as you begin to grow spiritually, if you fail to deepen your quest for spiritual nourishment, you will inevitably feel undernourished in short order. Just as eating baby food won't properly nourish a 10-year old, an inadequate spiritual "diet" won't properly nourish a growing disciple of Jesus Christ.

Thankfully, God's Word is relatively easily deciphered, yet never fails to inspire and amaze. Regardless of whether we started reading Scripture yesterday or fifty years ago, the Bible always provides nourishment. And in the United States, we are abundantly blessed with Christian Book Stores, churches, Internet sites, etc., offering a wealth of options for Bible study. Never before has God's Word been so accessible! For developed nations like ours, we have absolutely *no excuses* for not dwelling in the Word.

Spiritual Nourishment is not Spiritual Enlightenment

One of the truly distressing aspects of recent history is the ever increasing belief that spiritual health can be found independent of God. But this is not a new development; our sinful nature is such that we have always been susceptible to deceit. Paul knew that even as he prepared Timothy for Missionary work:

> *Timothy, guard what has been entrusted to your care. Turn away from godless chatter and the opposing ideas of what is falsely called knowledge, which some have professed and in so doing have wandered from the faith. Grace be with you.*
>
> *(1Timothy 6:20–21)*

In America, "popular culture" places a premium on so-called spiritual *enlightenment* while ignoring lasting spiritual *nourishment*. People who subscribe to non-traditional beliefs are looked upon as open-minded, independent thinkers, while Christians are considered closed-minded, dependent thinkers. Yet published demographics suggest that the majority of people in America *are not* active Christians, which begs the question, "Are Christians *more* open-minded than non-Christians?"

If we logically consider the question, the answer can only be "yes." It is *easy* to go along with whatever is accepted en masse, but not so easy to go against the grain. Our country was founded on (and still largely governed by) Christian principles, but culturally speaking we have moved away from God as our anchor. In many regions of our nation, it is simply not fashionable to be a Christian. On the other hand, alternately exploring various approaches to finding "enlightenment," or cycling through miscellaneous "alternate" beliefs, will doubtless be seen by most as progressive and independent. But how progressive is it to *purposefully* deny oneself the opportunity to learn about Christianity? Not opening one's mind to the *possibility* that Christianity might represent truth amounts to sticking one's head in the sand. Indeed, a desire to seek spiritual enlightenment from virtually any source *except* that which is viewed as "traditional" is hardly open-minded. And contrary to being the least bit spiritually progressive, such an approach equates to spiritual paralysis. If you really want to try something radical, try Christianity.

I will, however, agree with those who consider Christians to be dependent in nature, though our dependence is not based on affirmation or acceptance by worldly sources, but on knowledge of the saving Truth of Jesus Christ. We *need* Jesus, and we acknowledge Him as *the* provider of spiritual nourishment:

> *Jesus answered, "I tell you the truth, you are looking for me, not because you saw miraculous signs but because you ate the loaves and had your fill. Do not work for food that spoils, but for food that endures to eternal life, which the Son of Man will give you. On him God the Father has placed his seal of approval." Then they asked him, "What must we do to do the works God requires?" Jesus answered, "The work of God is this: to believe in the one he has sent." So they asked him, "What miraculous sign then will you give that we may see it and believe you? What will you do? Our forefathers ate the manna in the desert; as it is written: 'He gave them bread from heaven to eat.'" Jesus said to them, "I tell you the truth, it is not Moses who has given you the bread from heaven, but it is my Father who gives you the true bread from heaven. For the bread of God is he who comes down from heaven and gives life to the world." "Sir," they said, "from now on give us this bread."*
>
> (John 6:26–34)

The Importance of Church

A major effect of our societal movement from God is erosion in the church, as evidenced by a significant decline in attendance over the past several years. There was a time in our nation's history when Christians would likely have been more concerned about such a trend than we appear to be now. But as with a lot of things, acceptance becomes us. And frankly, the Christian church has in many ways been its own worst enemy. Too frequently, we have allowed petty disagreements, divisiveness, exclusiveness, and on rare occasions, criminal acts to bring shame to the church. God's people are called to bring forth His kingdom, yet we often do our best to tear it down. We *must* do better at becoming a united Body of Christ, for that is exactly what God calls us to be:

> *For by the grace given me I say to every one of you: Do not think of yourself more highly than you ought, but rather think of yourself with sober judgment, in accordance with the measure of faith God has given you. Just as each of us has one body with many members, and these members do not all have the same function, so in Christ we who are many form one body, and each member belongs to all the others. We have different gifts, according to the grace given us. If a man's gift is prophesying, let*

him use it in proportion to his faith. If it is serving, let him serve; if it is teaching, let him teach; if it is encouraging, let him encourage; if it is contributing to the needs of others, let him give generously; if it is leadership, let him govern diligently; if it is showing mercy, let him do it cheerfully.

(*Romans 12:3–8*)

This passage speaks volumes about why the church is so vital to spiritual nourishment. When we are a united Body of Christ such that *"each member belongs to all the others,"* we cannot help but nurture one another! Indeed, the church in its intended form is such a perfect provider of spiritual nourishment that we are to ensure its sanctity by replacing personal bias with God's will. To put it differently, if we recognize Jesus as the Head of the church, then the Christian church will once again thrive. There is no doubt that a committed, Spirit led church community is capable of bringing nourishment in abundance to its members and its greater community. And if you're thinking that the church is incapable of such an undertaking, you're absolutely correct—*if* we omit Jesus from the equation. But when we allow the Lord to take His rightful place at the head of our table, we can't fail.

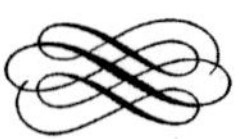

Men Working

A couple years ago my father-in-law invited my two brother-in-laws and myself to attend a Promise Keepers event. Having never attended Promise Keepers, I enthusiastically accepted his invitation.

The event was spiritually invigorating, with passion, energy, and fellowship clearly on display. The Holy Spirit was definitely at work!

After the event I felt an increased need for spiritual nourishment. I had previously started doing daily devotions and felt significant spiritual nourishment from doing so, but the Promise Keepers event awakened me to a need for even more nourishment.

In the meantime, just prior to the event, a group called "Men Working" formed at our church. The group met weekly and was open to Christian men from within the church as well as outside the church. I didn't attend right away, preferring instead to rationalize my morning devotions and weekly church attendance as "good enough."

Finally, on a crisp autumn morning, I decided to attend Men Working. Almost immediately I felt the Holy Spirit's presence much as I did while at Promise Keepers, except there weren't 10,000 men at our church that morning, there were more like 12. Apparently the Holy Spirit does not need a big crowd to make its presence felt. I could hardly wait to come back the next week, and beyond learning more about what being a man of God entails, I was rather impressed with how much coffee a small group of Christian men could slurp down in an hour!

As I have become increasingly active in Men Working, leading several discussions and coordinating and scheduling our group, I have realized just how vital it is to be in communion with fellow believers. This is especially true for men; we *need* fellowship in order to offset our independent nature and bring us closer to God and to one another. The men in our group share successes, failures, and everything in between. I believe the bond we have is similar *on some level* to the bond the early Christians had. Granted, we don't have to deal with widespread persecution or legal issues, but just as the Lord was present with the early saints, so is He with our group on Tuesday mornings.

Optimism

Genuine optimism requires genuine realism. It makes no sense to artificially manufacture optimism in order to feel better or to avoid becoming a pessimist. In fact, the only times we should be optimistic are when we have *good reason* to be optimistic. Being *realistic* allows foundational beliefs and specific life circumstances to be incorporated into our outlook, and is markedly different from the prevailing philosophy that we ought to "choose" our outlook independent of specific inputs. Said differently, the "choose our outlook" philosophy suggests that we should be optimistic simply because it's conducive to health, happiness, and fulfillment; but if truth is absent from such an outlook, doesn't "optimism" equate to delusion?

Indeed, we *can* choose our outlook, but doing so without incorporating beliefs and circumstances requires us to forego truth in favor of falsehood. This approach requires one to believe that artificially manufactured optimism leads to a sort of self-fulfilled prophecy, in which even when lacking a basis for optimism, good things inevitably happen. It's similar to the "If you build it they will come" theme from the movie *"Field of Dreams."*

The fundamental question is this: If I choose to be optimistic without having a *basis* for optimism, am I not deluding myself?

There can be no answer other than "yes." And given that, I would propose that rather than simply *choosing* our outlook, we should *formulate* our outlook—based on foundational beliefs and specific life circumstances.

If you agree that realism is indeed requisite for optimism, then the logical question that comes next is "what is there to be optimistic about?"

Our answers to this question define the basis of our outlook. Any mention of one's glass being "half full" or "half empty" should invariably be countered with the question, "why?"

What is there to be Optimistic about?

The basis for my optimism is faith in the Lord Jesus Christ. I believe with all my heart, soul, and mind in the authenticity of God's Word, which promises eternal life to those who accept Jesus as Lord and Savior and strive to live accordingly. There is no greater basis for optimism than the promise of eternal life, a promise so powerful that it can sustain us even during dire circumstances:

> *Praise be to the God and Father of our Lord Jesus Christ! In his great mercy he has given us new birth into a living hope through the resurrection of Jesus Christ from the dead, and into an inheritance that can never perish, spoil or fade—kept in heaven for you, who through faith are shielded by God's power until the coming of the salvation that is ready to be revealed in the last time. In this you greatly rejoice, though now for a little while you may have had to suffer grief in all kinds of trials.*
>
> *(1 Peter 1:3–6)*

While God's promise is sufficient for us to remain unendingly optimistic, many Christians overlook that faith requires corresponding deeds in order to be of value (ref. James 2:19–20). As the basis for my optimism is faith in the Lord Jesus Christ, if my actions aren't in accordance with my faith, then my optimistic outlook is *selectively* inclusive of what I believe to be reality (God's Word), and has therefore been manufactured under false pretenses. To believe in restoration through Jesus Christ entails that we subscribe in *totality* to God's

Word, without selectively ignoring the parts with which we are not comfortable. Indeed, to conveniently ignore specific Bible verses' is to convert God's Word into *our* word, contorting our professed definition of reality so that it conforms to what we *want* reality to be. If we're not careful, rather than living according to God's will, we will simply bend His Word to be in accordance with our will. That is a dangerous trap, and the most effective way to avoid falling into it is through ongoing study of Scripture, prayer, fellowship, and discernment. When encountering Scripture that doesn't reconcile with your own beliefs, do not merely discard it, but *study* it through leveraging available resources so that you can accurately interpret the passage: Is the passage to be taken literally or figuratively? Do I understand the context in which it was written? How does it effect me? To find the answers, you must first ask the questions.

Other Eternal Considerations

While having strong faith and acting accordingly are essential for optimism stemming from God's promise of eternal life, there are other "eternal" considerations that give us even more reason to be optimistic.

One such consideration is that acceptance of Jesus as Lord and Savior allows for *increased* realism to permeate our every thought. Put another way, without discovering and accepting the Truth of Jesus' Holy and living sacrifice, much of our time is spent in search of temporary happiness rather than lasting fulfillment. Our human desire is to feel good, and bypassing or ignoring truth (joy and fulfillment through Jesus Christ) allows deception (worldly "happiness") to become an increasingly attractive alternative.

It has often been noted that many comedians suffer from depression. The irony of such an allegation is obvious, given that the underlying goal of a comic is to make people laugh. A common approach comedians take for inducing laughter is to make light of our human condition. Jokes about bodily functions, individual mannerisms, and gender and ethnic stereotypes are almost always guaranteed to generate laughs, mainly because people connect on some level with what the comedian says and/or acts out.

But how would we react if the comedian's "routine" consisted of saying and acting according to how he felt that day? Would we laugh at a comedian who tells us that he is depressed and looking for a reason—any reason—to be optimistic? (I am not talking about a comedian whose *act* is based on self-depreciation, but one who speaks honestly and openly of his current outlook on life). After taking a few minutes to realize that the comedian is no longer performing, I suspect that people would react in one of two ways: either listening intently to what the comedian had to say, or walking out and demanding a refund. I would further suspect that the very large majority of people would exercise the latter option. Why?

Because we have an inherent desire to be happy. People do not attend comedy shows to hear someone talk about their depressing life in *genuinely* truthful terms; in fact, a primary reason people attend comedy shows is to momentarily *escape* reality. (And using comedy to escape reality isn't limited to the audience; it's also true of many comedians. Rodney Dangerfield, on the PBS show *"Healthweek,"* told interviewer Sharyl Attkisson, *"I was writing jokes at 15. Not out of happiness, you write it to escape from reality perhaps."*)

We are comfortable when the comedian's "truth" encapsulates humorous aspects of our human condition, but most people would be rather uncomfortable if the comedian's "truth" included honest commentary on his current mental and spiritual state.

Can you see how deception becomes increasingly attractive when truth is absent from our outlook? Just as we have no desire to hear *real* truth and meaning from a comedian, we shy away from acknowledging real truth in everyday life. And as we move further and further away from the eternal Truth of Jesus Christ, we increasingly gravitate toward the pursuit of worldly happiness, which provides little incentive to *appreciate* reality. On the other hand, when we submerge ourselves in the absolute Truth of God's Word, reality is our ally and we have reason to be *legitimately* optimistic about our eternal future.

Absolute acceptance of Jesus as Lord and Savior allows us to minimize the tangible effects of our inherent sinful desires. Knowing that eternity waits should give us all the impetus we need to be content with our earthly blessings:

> *I know what it is to be in need, and I know what it is to have plenty. I have learned the secret of being content in any and every situation, whether well fed or hungry, whether living in plenty or in want. I can do everything through him who gives me strength.*
>
> *(Philippians 4:12–13)*

Situational Optimism

While believing and living according to God's Word allows us to maintain a perpetually optimistic eternal outlook, we must also recognize that each day brings about unique scenarios during which our immediate (short-term) outlook is heavily influenced by circumstantial reality.

For example, I have played golf for many years but have never been very good at it. Although I only play around nine or ten times a year, I've played enough to clearly understand my limitations. I have changed stances, grips and clubs, and recently took lessons, and I have *rare* moments when I make a good shot, but I have yet to sustain my good shots. And given that I usually shoot around 115 for 18 holes—and have only shot below 100 once—should I be optimistic that the next time I play I'll shoot an 89?

As a professed optimist, the answer I am *supposed* to give is "yes;" but as an optimist whose optimism is predicated on reality, the only answer I can truthfully give is "no."

In contrast with an eternal outlook of optimism where there is little or no variation, our short-term outlook can vary widely depending on circumstances. Yet despite occasional disconnects between our short-term outlook and our eternal outlook, the common denominator is that both require reality to be the *basis* thereof. I am not optimistic that I will shoot an 89 the next time I play golf, but I am optimistic that at some point in my life I will.

Note that while I am being realistic about my golf skills, I am not being self-limiting. Presently, I have no good reason to believe that I will suddenly cut 25 strokes from my golf game, yet I do believe that over the course of time, through determination, practice and skill, I can justifiably expect to shoot under 90.

It is essential to avoid labeling self-limiting behavior as "reality." As previously noted, when determining our outlook, the question that must be asked is, "why?" Or, to ask the question in a slightly different manner, "why not?" The question is essentially the same, but how we go about answering it may well be different. In my case, the *only* basis for believing that I will never shoot an 89 would be limitations that I have placed upon myself. And given that many golfers struggle for years before realizing a sustainable level of performance, and that shooting an 89 is hardly a lofty goal for many golfers, should I limit myself by believing that I just don't have what it takes? Of course not!

The caveat to the "why not?" approach to optimism is that there still must be good reason to be optimistic. I had stated earlier that my optimism about breaking 90 on the golf course is predicated on "determination, practice and skill." If I lose my determination, I will likely quit practicing, which in turn will prevent sustained improvement in skill. Self-limitation is the enemy of determination—do not let doubt and insecurity reduce you to being less than what you are capable of being.

Balance Results with Process

We in western society are consumed with results. Think about our mindset when it comes to sports, school, work, etc. Our tendency is to initially focus on what results we're after, then to ascertain how to attain those results. We feel a need to *explicitly* understand desirable outcomes (results) prior to determining how to go about attaining them. In sports, we assess success or failure based on a final score; in school, we assess success or failure based on grades; and at work, *others* assess our success or failure based in large part on whether we've met pre-determined goals and objectives.

For example, by making a specific result (shooting less than 90) the criterion by which I will ultimately gauge success or failure on the golf course, I have essentially discounted the satisfaction derived through merely playing better, regardless of what my score might be. Would I be better off by allowing "determination, practice and skill" to be my primary focus, with success or failure determined by whether I've acted in accordance? Doing so would seemingly bring about positive results at some point in the future, though one could argue that not having a specific, measurable goal identified beforehand prevents an objective assessment of success or failure, and may well produce a degree of complacency and acceptance of mediocrity.

My "results governs process" approach is representative of western society as a whole, though the opposite is true in ancient eastern cultures, where the primary focus is not on the explicit but on the implicit. Jesus' exemplified eastern thought through frequent use of parables, with their meanings ascertained rather than explicitly stated. The Lord's approach is indicative of the long-standing eastern philosophy of implicit teaching and learning, wherein the journey is placed ahead of results.

Is one approach better than the other? Discounting partiality from both east and west, the answer can only be "no," since both have proven to be effective when properly aligned within a given culture. We cannot ignore the significance of cultural traditions and paradigms. It has been shown time and time again that sustaining an *imposed* cultural change is next to impossible; in essence, cultures become a sort of life form unto themselves, with a natural resistance to imposed change and a natural gravitation toward standing traditions. The bottom-line is that trying to compare the effectiveness of a results-driven culture with a process-driven culture is a losing proposition, as both approaches are effective when properly utilized in a given environment.

But one thing that we can all do better—regardless of where we are from or whether we are governed by results or process—is learn how to optimally *combine* the best of both approaches.

In 1962, at Rice University, President John F. Kennedy addressed students, faculty members, politicians, and scientists regarding the nation's space effort. He boldly declared that we would put a man on the moon within the next seven years, drawing wild applause from his audience even as many of them wondered how Kennedy could possibly make such an assertion. But while Kennedy took a considerable risk, it was not necessarily uncalculated; in fact, earlier in his speech he laid out *how* his administration would support this lofty goal:

> *"Houston . . . will become the heart of a large scientific and engineering community. During the next 5 years the National Aeronautics and Space Administration expects to double the number of scientists and engineers in this area, to increase its outlays for salaries and expenses to $60 million a year; to invest some $200 million in plant and laboratory facilities; and to direct or contract for new space efforts over $1 billion from this Center in this City."*

Kennedy didn't have all the answers, but after meeting with Vice-President Lyndon Johnson and a host of scientific advisors, he felt confident that the United States would realize his stated objective. Kennedy successfully combined focusing on a specific, desired result with an aggressive yet feasible approach to successfully achieving the result. He pledged to provide necessary financial and scientific resources, knowing that doing otherwise would bring about failure.

We know the rest of the story: the United States space program has been enormously successful ever since aligning itself with Kennedy's vision some forty years ago. Kennedy demonstrated the power that comes when *combining* a "results first" approach with a "process first" approach. Had he articulated the same objective without having received prior assurances from experts—and a preliminary commitment for funding and resources—our space program (and nation as a whole) would likely have been set back many years while scientific advances went unrealized due to bureaucratic gridlock. And had he provided funding and resources *without* articulating what needed to be accomplished and when it needed to happen, we would likely have had unproductive debate and indecision leading to inaction, with the end result being a failed initiative or worse.

A healthy situational outlook is based on a combination of reality and self-empowerment. We can't ignore reality, yet we must also guard against imposing limitations on ourselves. Be bold and think positive, never losing sight that your constant ally is none other than the Lord Jesus Christ.

The Relationship between our Eternal Outlook and Short-term Outlook

In the "*Joy*" chapter, I pointed out that happiness is often mistaken for joy, but that while happiness relies on circumstance, joy does not. Just as happiness isn't a factor in determining joy, neither is it a factor in determining *eternal* optimism. The reasons are the same: joy and eternal optimism are exclusive of emotion and circumstance, relying instead on the promise of God's Word.

Without exception, our eternal outlook must always govern our immediate (short-term) outlook. Too often we allow the opposite scenario to occur, in which our outlook pertaining to a worldly situation interferes with our ability to live according to God's will. The reality of living for Christ is enough to overcome *any* earthly situation we encounter, and to allow eternal optimism to be overcome by circumstantial emotion is to ignore God's Word:

> *I have set the Lord always before me. Because he is at my right hand, I will not be shaken.*
>
> *(Psalm 16:8)*

Said simply and succinctly, do not cheat yourself of eternal joy and optimism that comes through faith in Jesus Christ. Being a slave to worldly pursuits is a losing proposition.

Nonetheless, we should not completely remove emotion from our *short-term* outlook. Although it may appear that this contradicts separating emotion from joy and eternal optimism, it doesn't. Emotion *is* a factor in how we assess situations. It is to be expected that our short-term outlook may be one of disappointment or frustration *while* we remain eternally joyful and optimistic. The key is to recognize our feelings while not completely surrendering to them. There is too much at stake to allow emotion to overcome us. Anchoring ourselves in God's saving Truth allows for an eternal outlook of optimism to consistently prevail over situational emotion, so that even when we are down, we are never out:

> *Therefore we do not lose heart. Though outwardly we are wasting away, yet inwardly we are being renewed day by day. For our light and momentary troubles are achieving for us an eternal glory that far outweighs them all. So we fix our eyes not on what is seen, but on what is unseen. For what is seen is temporary, but what is unseen is eternal.*
>
> *(2 Corinthians 4:16–18)*

Optimism and Pessimism Aren't All That Different

Optimism and pessimism are not nearly as different as they might appear. The optimist whose optimism excludes reality is no better off than the pessimist whose pessimism excludes reality. As it regards the basis of their outlook, both have failed to ask the question "why?" and have therefore bought into a delusional outlook. But in western society, optimism for the sake of optimism is considered by most to be a virtue, while pessimism for the sake of pessimism is not.

When viewed objectively, one can only conclude that there is little difference between unfounded optimism and unfounded pessimism. Unless there is a real, genuine basis for leaning one way or the other, both are flawed, although the pessimist is likely to have a *better* grasp on reality than the optimist. Why?

Because without having discovered and/or given in to the source of Truth and eternal life, the pessimist actually has reason to feel the way he does. His outlook may be *intentionally* pessimistic, but without assurance of eternal life, what is there for him to be optimistic about anyway? The challenge for the pessimist is to move away from what the world values and toward the saving

Truth of Jesus Christ. If his heart is willing, he will discover the source of legitimate optimism and have a completely new outlook to show for it.

As for the optimist, the challenge is no different: Stop being *intentionally* optimistic and start discovering reasons to be optimistic. You will develop a real—and fulfilling—optimistic outlook when you seek the Lord as never before.

Don't hide. Seek.

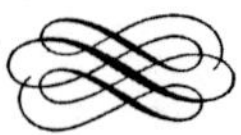

Spelling Be

When I was in sixth grade, I was decidedly pessimistic. Short and scrawny with thick glasses and psoriasis of the scalp, I was the poster child for adolescent insecurity. But that winter I learned a valuable lesson about optimism.

It was announced that the school Spelling Bee would begin in three weeks. Each student was informed of the rules and given a study guide. At first I didn't think much of it: what chance would I—an average student at best—have at winning our school Spelling Bee?

I set the study guide aside, determining that I would look at it when sufficiently motivated, whatever that meant. Fortunately, my mother sensed that my outlook during that time wasn't exactly overflowing with optimism, and she was bound and determined to help me gain some much-needed self-confidence.

Thinking that I would never have to look at the study guide again, I was surprised a few days later when, upon coming home from school, it was sitting atop our dinner table. My mother offered to work with me in preparation for "the Bee," and for some strange reason I accepted her invitation. Still, I didn't even think about actually winning.

Over the next few weeks leading up to the Bee, my mom and I studied together every evening. During that time my spelling improved dramatically, culminating in justifiable optimism on the day of the Bee.

Finally that day came, and I watched as slowly but surely nearly all the other students were eliminated from contention. As the number of students became fewer and fewer, a group of my friends began cheering for me. I was delighted by their gesture, and was more determined than ever to win.

Finally, there were only two students left: a girl named Daria and myself. The tension mounted as we went back-and-forth, until I was asked to spell toboggan. "T-O-B-B-O-G-A-N" I replied confidently. But alas, my confidence quickly dissipated as the error of my spelling was pointed out, and Daria proceeded to spell the word correctly.

Despite having missed my objective, I felt proud to finish in second place. I am forever grateful to my mother for teaching me that hard work, faith, and self-empowerment produce legitimate optimism.

As a side-note, I also finished in second place in our school Spelling Bee the next year. Who did I lose to? Daria, of course! Oh well, at least I still enjoy going tobboganing . . . I mean, tobogganing!

Prayer

Calling on the Lord is a bit like calling a trusted friend. Then again, we never have to worry about God not answering us—He invites us to call on Him during good times and bad, when flourishing and when floundering, and at every point in between. And God *always* responds to our prayers, sometimes in a manner exactly as we hope for, other times in a manner opposite of what we hope for. Through it all, regardless of whether we're complacent, bitter, ungrateful or thankful, God never shuns us and always welcomes our call.

Make the Call

Perhaps you remember the catchy 70's song from the Spinners titled "*I'll Be Around:*"

> *"Whenever you call me I'll be there . . . Whenever you want me I'll be there . . . Whenever you need me I'll be there . . . I'll be around."*

While the Spinners sang about true love for one person and the commitment that such a love entails, God's love runs much deeper and applies to *all* people. The Lord's love is boundless and limitless; in fact, the only boundaries or limitations of His love are those that we place upon ourselves.

But realistically (and contrary to the Spinners' song), just as we shouldn't expect a distant lover to *intuitively* know when to be there for us, neither should we expect Jesus to make His presence fully known to us without being invited first. In order to *abide* in Jesus' healing presence, we must reach out to Him. Indeed, while Jesus is not some distant lover (He's ever present), *we* decide whether to *invite* Him to dwell within us. God gives us free will, and with it comes free choice.

When failing to call on the Lord, we essentially cheat ourselves of an intimate and fulfilling relationship with Him. We might think that independence, intelligence and sheer determination are sufficient to bring about lasting fulfillment, but without an ongoing, active relationship with our Redeemer, that is simply not the case. Just as no one in his right mind would build a dream house on an unstable foundation, neither should we risk the promise of eternal life on an unstable foundation:

> *As it is written: "See, I lay in Zion a stone that causes men to stumble and a rock that makes them fall, and the one who trusts in him will never be put to shame.*
>
> *(Romans 9:33)*

Jesus is our rock-our foundation. Insecurity, unworthiness, and emptiness are replaced with a deep sense of purpose, self-worth, and fulfillment when we live according to Jesus' saving Truth. And unlike our relationships with other people (even those we love the most), our relationship with Christ is not based on "give-and-take"—it's based on "take." Since everything we have is from God, anything we "give" Him was merely on loan to us anyway. Our tithes and offerings, the time we spend helping others, the prayers we offer in praise and thanksgiving—all please the Lord, yet in reality all are gifts *from* Him. God does not need our tithes and offerings—they're His to begin with, and we are merely His stewards—but *we* need to give them in order to be strengthened in faith and perpetually joyful. God does not need us to help others—our actions have no effect on His kingdom—but *we* need to help others in order to gain the full measure of His blessings. And God certainly does not need our prayers of thanks and praise—He requires no validation—but *we* need to offer thanks and praise to fully receive grace and assurance. Indeed, while we are to "give" to the Lord with humility and contrite hearts, let us never lose sight that our relationship with God is forever destined to be one-sided. When Jesus suffered, died and ascended into heaven, the ledger tipped squarely in *our* favor. Jesus purchased our eternal life in heaven, and all we have to do is acknowledge that fact and seek to live as He teaches us. And the more we "give" to God, the more we get back. Sometimes it may feel like all we're doing is giving, but those are often the times when God is blessing us the most. How? When our earthly circumstances are not to our liking, out of necessity we tend to turn to God, and any time we can move closer to God, we are blessed!

And how does Jesus respond when we call on Him? Unlike the responses we sometimes get from people, the Lord *never* rejects those who approach Him with contrition and humility. We may reject *ourselves* as unworthy, but He doesn't. How can we possibly consider ourselves unworthy when considering that God allowed His only begotten Son to die at our hands, so that *our* sins could be forgiven? Although I am a sinner, if God considers me to be worthy of salvation, that's good enough for me.

That being the case, why wouldn't we call out to the Lord? He's waiting, ready to gift us with the full measure of His grace and love if only we will let Him. All it takes is one "call" to begin releasing the bonds that keep us from joy.

Make the call—He's anxious to hear from you!

Of Goodness and Godliness

There are those who believe that goodness and godliness are essentially the same. But even when we are empathetic and helpful to others, raise our children morally and ethically, and contribute to the betterment of society, if we fail to *purposefully* live according to God's Word we assume a neutral position in the battle between heaven and the world. Neutrality does nothing to further God's kingdom and everything to further Satan's agenda. The devil's ultimate goal is to bring about evil, and his weapons are lies and deception. Satan knows that the surest way—the *only* way—to bring about evil is to separate people from the Truth of Jesus Christ. When people discover Jesus' Truth and seek to live accordingly, Satan's task becomes significantly more difficult, though not impossible since lulling God's people into complacency is a tactic he employs frequently, often with great success. But Satan also knows that the large majority of people aren't going to *knowingly* turn from God, which necessitates that he employ a strategy of subtle lies and deception in order to further his agenda. He is successful when people mistake goodness for godliness, because without discovering the Truth of Jesus Christ and living according to that Truth, there is absolutely no possibility for people to advance God's kingdom. And if we are not helping to advance God's kingdom, we are helping to suppress it:

> *"No one can serve two masters. Either he will hate the one and love the other, or he will be devoted to the one and despise the other."*
>
> *(Matthew 6:24a)*

Spiritual fulfillment is often directly proportional to the effort we put into our walk with Christ. We shouldn't be surprised or disappointed when feeling less than fulfilled while passively seeking the Lord. *Any* relationship approached with passivity will be less than optimal. It takes time, effort, and dedication to forge a deep, lasting relationship, and that's what's required in order to abide in Jesus.

Make Prayer a Vital Part of Your Life

Given that goodness is no substitute for godliness, and that Satan actively seeks to separate us from God, it is absolutely essential that prayer be an active component of our lives. There is little doubt that nearly all Christians would travel great distances if they were somehow guaranteed that doing so would allow them to spend five minutes with Jesus. But Scripture tells us that we don't need to travel great distances to talk with Jesus; if we simply reach out to Him, Jesus will live within us!

> *Let your gentleness be evident to all. The Lord is near. Do not be anxious about anything, but in everything, by prayer and petition, with thanksgiving, present your requests to God.*
>
> *(Philippians 4:5–6)*

As first mentioned in the *Christianity* chapter, most Christians—knowingly or unknowingly—follow this path en route to abiding in Jesus Christ:

1. *Inheritance of beliefs*
2. *Compliance to inherited beliefs*
3. *Search for truth and meaning*
4. *Acceptance of Jesus Christ as Lord and Savior*
5. *Obedience to God*

6. *Search for meaning*
7. *Abiding in God's love*

While many people reach the fourth step (acceptance of Jesus as Lord and Savior), significantly less reach the fifth, sixth, and seventh steps. I believe that prayer is a major determinant for how far we progress in our spiritual journey.

Imagine that you have just won the lottery. Everything has changed! Yesterday you faced an uncertain future, but today you look forward to collecting riches beyond your imagination. Still, you are faced with a decision: you can elect to receive your winnings in one lump sum, or you can amortize your winnings such that you receive a healthy annual check every year for the rest of your life. This is a major decision, so think carefully before choosing: if you take your winnings in one lump sum, will you be disciplined enough to not fritter it away? If you elect to amortize your winnings, will increased *security* compensate for not being as instantly rich as you could be?

That's a tough choice! Many lottery winners who elect to receive a lump sum quickly squander it away; after all, most people who become millionaires overnight have no idea how to manage their riches, and without trustworthy consultation and guidance, their lives can quickly become *worse* than they were before. On the other hand, many lottery winners who elect to amortize winnings later regret their decision, finding that the increased security from receiving annual dividends doesn't necessarily bring about significant wealth.

When we first confess Jesus as Lord and Savior, we essentially win a *spiritual* lottery. Just as being an instant millionaire brings about immediate joy that borders on the indescribable, so does "winning" salvation through new life in Jesus Christ.

But what happens next? Are we to simply "cash in" by receiving a lump sum distribution of Jesus' saving grace? That may work for a while, but it certainly won't sustain joy.

Should we instead amortize His grace, taking a little at a time but never too much? That may help us feel *secure*, but will likely prevent us from experiencing *deep* joy that comes through an intimate, perpetual relationship with Jesus.

The answer to the "what happens next" question is given to us through Scripture:

Devote yourselves to prayer, being watchful and thankful.
(Colossians 4:2)

Prayer is a vital component for spiritual fulfillment. It is *impossible* to make it to the fifth, sixth, and seventh steps of the spiritual journey (obedience to God, search for meaning, and abiding in God's love, respectively) without earnest, ongoing prayer. And prayer is vital not only for fulfillment, but for gaining spiritual maturity and preventing backsliding into old habits and beliefs. We must fight with everything we have against complacency, and prayer is a potent weapon for doing so.

Although we may think that discovering Jesus as Lord and Savior is the culmination of our spiritual journey, in reality it's just the beginning. Inherited beliefs, compliance to inherited beliefs, and the search for truth and meaning are *pre-requisites* for discovering Jesus' saving Truth; but accepting Christ as Lord and Savior assures us of eternal life in heaven only if we renew our commitment to Christ on an ongoing basis. It becomes imperative to continuously grow in faith and knowledge, so that we can increase our sense of fulfillment, advance God's kingdom, and protect our interests. When inheriting something of great value, we are wise to do whatever it takes to safeguard it; if you win a million dollars, will you announce your good fortune to a known thief? Our salvation is the most precious gift we will ever receive, and Satan would enjoy nothing more than robbing us of our inheritance. Prior to accepting Christ, our neutral position posed no threat to Satan. But upon discovering the Truth of Jesus Christ and vowing to live accordingly, we have not only foiled the devil's intent to separate us from God, but we now pose a much greater threat to him since we may well bring others to a saving knowledge of Truth.

When it comes to dealing with Satan, to borrow an often used sports cliché, our best defense is a great offense. Furthermore, the best way to generate a potent offense is through commitment, obedience, vigilance, and . . . weakness—at least from a human perspective. Fighting against Satan's weapons (temptation, deception, complacency, rationalization, etc.) requires an unending reservoir of strength, one only found when *humbly* seeking and relying on Jesus. Simply put, our human weakness is converted to godly strength when we place absolute faith and confidence in the Lord. On our own we lack the strength to defeat Satan, but with Jesus as our source of strength we are able to withstand the devil's arsenal.

Pray to Jesus. Seek Him. Call out to Him. Jesus will protect and enlighten, bless and redeem you, if only you ask Him.

Troubleshooting

Before abiding in Jesus, we must first become obedient, not out of compliance but out of love and desire. But if after confessing Jesus as Lord and Savior we don't *consistently* feel strong love and desire for Him, what are we to do? Should we attempt to somehow *generate* love and desire?

These are difficult yet common questions. I am convinced that most Christians experience some frustration *after* accepting Jesus as Lord and Savior. This frustration often stems from unrealistically expecting chronic euphoria to follow our initial confession of Jesus as Lord and Savior, while in reality, without prayer, Bible study and fellowship, initial exuberance at finding the key to eternal life will quickly give way to doubt and uncertainty.

To draw an analogy, think of a time when you were offered a job you really wanted. Initially, you probably felt excitement, pride, and anticipation as you prepared to start in your new position. But within a few days, your excitement, pride, and anticipation were likely tempered to a degree by better understanding what you needed to do in order to be successful in your new position. Perhaps you felt overwhelmed at how much you had to learn prior to making significant contributions. And it's likely that you relied on other people to help gain necessary knowledge and skill. Shouldn't we use a similar approach when seeking to advance God's kingdom?

Being gifted with grace does not excuse us from growing in faith and understanding. In fact, we *must* grow in faith and understanding, because doing otherwise prohibits us from doing God's will and stops our spiritual journey in its tracks. How tragic it is when the *culmination* of one's spiritual journey occurs upon discovering and accepting the saving Truth of Jesus Christ. Discovery and acceptance of the Lord ought to fuel our desire to know and serve Jesus with all of our heart, mind, and soul. We relegate ourselves to a state of spiritual paralysis when failing to actively seek Christ. Joy and fulfillment come and go like the wind when we're spiritually stagnant, but are ever present when perpetually seeking the Lord.

Attaining anything of real and lasting value—including fulfillment through Jesus Christ—requires effort. Obedience to Christ serves as an essential gateway to abiding in Him, and as such requires that we actively seek Him. Indeed, when deep love and desire for the Lord are absent or faint, we ought to work that much harder at generating them, remembering that love and desire for Christ will grow in direct proportion to growth in knowledge, wisdom, and faith. It's Economics 101: Supply and Demand—God will supply us with grace, fulfillment, and eternal life *if* there is a demand for it. *We* determine levels of demand for what God supplies us, generating that demand through studying and living according to God's Word, being active in the church, helping others, and remaining prayerful.

B2B

Even while growing in knowledge, wisdom and faith, we will inevitably struggle on occasion during our life of prayer. Human weakness frequently interferes with our ability to give our entire focus to God, and nearly everyone goes through dry spells from time to time, feeling spiritually undernourished.

Thankfully, Jesus knows our weaknesses much better than we do ourselves. He taught us how to pray and what to pray for. The *"Our Father"* is a special gift from the Lord. It is important that we think of the Lord's Prayer *as* a prayer—too often we *recite* the "Our Father" without actually *praying* it. We should honor such a gift by not only learning His words, but by cherishing and *praying* them:

> *He said to them, "When you pray, say:" "Father, hallowed be your name, your kingdom come. Give us each day our daily bread. Forgive us our sins, for we also forgive everyone who sins against us. And lead us not into temptation."*
>
> *(Luke 11:2–4)*

With all due respect to the *"Prayer of Jabez"* (a wonderful, powerful prayer), the one prayer that should absolutely be prayed every day is the "*Our Father.*" It is a prayer that gives thanks and praise to God, recognizes His power, glory and dominion, asks for spiritual nourishment, grace and protection, and serves as a pledge to forgive others of their sins against us.

I am not suggesting that our prayers be *limited* to the Lord's Prayer, but that we should consider it as foundational. By no means should we ignore what's in our hearts and minds when praying to the Lord, yet we should also be careful to not stray far from how Jesus taught us to pray.

The title of this section—B2B—is an acronym for "Back to Basics." In a world where creativity and independence are almost universally admired, it is essential that we purposefully approach our walk of faith with a "B2B" mindset. While God gives us free will and discerning minds, we should never lose sight that Scripture—His Word—anchors us. Indeed, pour your heart out to the Lord when praying—offer thanksgiving, ask for grace and discernment, request Him to intervene on behalf of specific people and situations, ask to be blessed—do all those things and more, but do not lose sight of what's most important. The Lord's Prayer never goes out of style, and always serves to redirect us toward Him.

Two Traps to Avoid

There are those who convince themselves that God is not interested in their prayer requests, mistakenly believing that, unless they have something "significant" to bring to the Lord, they are not worthy of His time. This belief is not supported by God's Word, and comes from buying into Satan's lies and deception. God welcomes and takes our prayer requests seriously, regardless of how insignificant they may seem to us. Think of it this way: if a toddler asks you to help write, "I love you" on a card she plans on giving to her mother, would you turn her down? Probably not! Yet objectively speaking, it's not important that the words be spelled correctly on the card; after all, it's the thought that counts, and the child's mother will be thrilled regardless of whether the card says "I love you" or "Ei Louv Uwe." Nonetheless, you would likely recognize that while correct spelling may not be important to you or to the card's recipient, it *is* important to the little girl. And that's why you decide to help her.

Now, turning our attention to God, when we ponder whether to pray for help and/or intervention during specific situations, how can we possibly believe that our problems don't merit His attention? Given our limited capacity to love others, if *we* can acknowledge and act on a seemingly insignificant request from a small child, who are we to assume that God, with an *unlimited* capacity to love, won't consider our requests worthy of His attention?

Don't listen to Satan's whispers; instead, follow the Word of God:

"Ask and it will be given to you; seek and you will find; knock and the door will be opened to you. For everyone who asks receives; he who seeks finds; and to him who knocks, the door will be opened. "Which of you, if his son asks for bread, will give him a stone? Or if he asks for a fish, will give him a snake? If you, then, though you are evil, know how to give good gifts to your children, how much more will your Father in heaven give good gifts to those who ask him!"

(Matthew 7:7–11)

Finally, avoid keeping track of how often you *think* God has answered your prayer requests. When we approach God with contrition and humility, He always answers our prayers. When God grants you exactly what you've asked for, praise Him and proclaim His goodness. And when God doesn't grant you what you've asked for, praise Him and proclaim His goodness even louder! Too often, our preoccupation with present circumstances prevents us from understanding *why* God allows certain things to happen. But God focuses first and foremost on our eternal future. In spite of whatever circumstances we encounter in life, when we pray in earnest to the Lord, we are blessed. Things may get a bit crazy at times in our world, but rest assured that in heaven the saints and angels are forever singing God's praises.

Why not bring a little bit of heaven to earth? Ask and you shall receive.

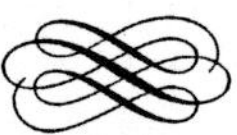

A Lesson about Prayer

I knew Jack from the Leadership Development Program that we were both part of, but I didn't really *know* him. Since we had never said much beyond "hello" and "how are you?" to one another, I naturally approached our lunch meeting with some uncertainty.

Nonetheless, I wasn't meeting him to make a friend; my intention was to simply find out as much as possible about the new position I was starting the next week—a position he held at that time.

We sat down and exchanged some light banter. I mentioned how anxious I was to start, and that I appreciated his willingness to meet me so that we could talk about the position. Within a few minutes, I felt very much at ease with Jack, as it became apparent that he and I had much in common. He quickly exhibited the same kind of offbeat sense of humor that I have, yet also provided insightful information about what I could expect in my new role.

As our food was being served, I readied myself to dig in. Across the table, Jack politely excused himself, closing his eyes as he silently prayed. I was genuinely surprised! I had never dined with anyone who prayed prior to eating in a public restaurant. For whatever reason, I immediately closed my eyes and prayed too. What was absolutely natural to Jack felt rather unnatural to me; I *usually* prayed before meals, but never in a restaurant and definitely never in front of someone I barely knew.

After our lunch I thought about Jack's actions: Here was someone who had no reservations about demonstrating his faith in God; I, on the other hand, was strong in faith but often slow to demonstrate it. I felt that perhaps God had led me to Jack so that I could learn how to act according to my beliefs.

In the slightly more than two years since we first met for lunch, Jack and I have become the strongest of friends. Yet Jack is much more than a friend—he's a mentor. He has taught me much about what it means to be a disciple of Jesus Christ and how to go about living for Him. We talk nearly every day, laugh a lot, and confide a great deal in one another. And every time we go out for a meal, we pray first. In fact, the last time that I didn't pray before a meal—anywhere, anytime, with anyone—was the day before my first lunch with Jack.

Quest

My Quest:
Help bring forth God's kingdom

We are all on a journey through life. Some of us think about our journey often, while others hardly think of it at all. But regardless of how often or to what extent we contemplate it, suffice to say that we are all, without a doubt, on a unique journey through life. And given that fact, a key question is "*what is it that guides you through life?*"

If we were to carry an imaginary "spiritual compass" throughout the course of our lives, after discovering and accepting the saving Truth of Jesus Christ we would see that God's will is located true north. Yet to advance toward *abiding* in Him, we must first progress from discovery and acceptance of Truth to seeking additional meaning behind God's Truth. Yes, discovering Truth is essential for abiding in Jesus but so too is learning how to best handle such an important discovery.

An integral part of our progression toward abiding in Jesus is to discern God's will for us *as individuals*. God gifts us with a unique purpose in life, and it's up to us to seek it. If we patiently, prayerfully, and carefully seek to understand our unique purpose, we will inevitably discover that our quest is located true north, *directly in line* with God's will. Indeed, it is our quest—*our unique purpose that supports God's will*—that guides us through life.

When I successfully *"Help bring forth God's kingdom,"* my life is filled with significance and purpose, and I know for certain that I am headed north. But when I fail to live according to my quest, my spiritual compass points everywhere *except* north.

To ensure that I don't remain lost for long, I regularly compare my current spiritual position against that of true north on my spiritual compass. Even though I inevitably (and frequently) find myself journeying in different directions, my quest never fails to point true north, and serves to redirect me toward God.

I start each week by writing my quest in my planner and thinking about how to best live it out during the coming days. And I start most days by looking at my quest, then vowing to live accordingly. When lapsing into a temporary crisis of faith and/or fortitude, by restating my quest every week and recommitting to it nearly every day, I am constantly reminded of what I have been called to do.

My quest consists of five small words, but in combination their significance is immeasurable. The words are sacred to me, and in large part define me.

The Difference between a Journey and a Quest

Having already devoted portions of two chapters to the spiritual journey that many Christians take, and recognizing that *journey* and *quest* are frequently mistaken as one and the same, I feel it necessary to draw a distinction between the two words.

Merriam-Webster's on-line dictionary defines a *Journey* as *"something suggesting travel or passage from one place to another."*

Webster's defines a *Quest* as *"an act or instance of seeking."*

Upon successfully discerning our quest—our unique purpose—our *journey* through life changes dramatically. Far from seeking truth, we seek to *live* according to Truth. And rather than groping our way through life, we know *exactly* which direction to take. Put simply, without discerning our quest, our spiritual compass will never be perfectly calibrated; we may think that we are heading north, but without a specific, fixed quest in support of God's will, our compass is inevitably out of calibration.

To further illustrate the fundamental difference between a quest and a journey, think of a quest as the *direction* we are to travel, and a journey as the *process* of actually getting there. Clearly, if our quest does not align with God's will—if it's not fixed true north—our journey will lack direction and ultimately bring about failure.

Jesus made sure that His quest aligned perfectly with His Father's will:

> *"For I have come down from heaven not to do my will but to do the will of him who sent me. And this is the will of him who sent me, that I shall lose none of all that he has given me, but raise them up at the last day. For my Father's will is that everyone who looks to the Son and believes in him shall have eternal life, and I will raise him up at the last day."*
> *(John 6:38–40)*

My quest is to help bring forth God's kingdom. I believe that is God's will for me, and that my quest is located directly north on my spiritual compass, overlapping God's will. And as I journey accordingly, I will encounter many twists, turns and forks in the road, but keeping my quest in front of me will help ensure that I never stray too far off course.

Obedience to God + Searching for Meaning = Clarity of Quest

You may recall that the fifth step of the spiritual journey toward abiding in Christ is "Obedience to God," and that the "Search for Meaning" step directly follows it. This may appear to conflict with what I have advocated so far in this chapter—that upon discovering and accepting the Truth of Jesus Christ, we must patiently, carefully and prayerfully discern our life's quest prior to earnestly proceeding toward abiding in Jesus—but in fact it does not.

To clarify, to "patiently, carefully and prayerfully" discern our life's quest *is* to be obedient to God. Furthermore, it is impossible to find genuine, deep meaning behind the Truth of Jesus Christ without also being obedient to the Lord.

Indeed, obedience to the Lord is absolutely requisite for uncovering purpose and meaning. To ignore obedience as a vital element of the search for meaning is to fall prey to either spiritual malnutrition over having accepted Jesus as Lord and Savior but not understanding what that really means, or declaring (usually abruptly) a quest that does not necessarily align with God's will *for you*. Under the first scenario, without properly understanding what the Truth of Jesus Christ entails, over the course of time we will likely begin thinking of God's "Truth" as little more than theory without significant application thereof. In the latter scenario, even though a self-declared quest may well support God's Word, it is not likely to align with God's *will* for you as an individual, effectively diminishing spiritual fulfillment.

We must live godly lives, but without a quest, or with a quest that does not take into account God's will, we fail to fully accept all that God offers, essentially rendering us spiritually undernourished. Just as a student who is naturally gifted in Physics shouldn't be content with receiving a "B" on a Physics exam, neither should a Christian be content with living in a manner less than what God has made him for.

Obedience to God is essential for bringing us ever closer to comprehending the breadth of His Truth.

To illustrate, suppose you learn in a History class that there were 620,000 soldiers killed during America's civil war, nearly equaling the *total* number of American soldiers killed in action ever since. Let's further suppose that the *only* thing taught in your History class about the civil war was how many soldiers died. Your teacher then informs you that there will be no material on the next exam that isn't first covered in a lecture.

Your initial thought may be that you have learned everything you need to know about the civil war. Your "success" hinges on answering test questions correctly, and you now possess all the necessary knowledge to answer exam questions pertaining to the civil war. But would merely knowing how many soldiers died in the war satisfy your intellectual curiosity as to *why* they died?

For some people, the answer would be "yes," but for many it would be a resounding "no." Yet even of those people who would seek additional information, how many would actually seek additional *meaning*? Most would simply gravitate toward finding additional facts and figures, effectively limiting their ability to develop a deeper understanding of the war's significance. But for those who are not content to merely skim facts and figures, and who long for *real* understanding, there would doubtless be a slow, methodical, and introspective search for meaning. Such a search would require patience and perseverance, but would return abundant intellectual and, perhaps, spiritual nourishment.

When it comes to faith, which group do you belong to? Are you content to learn just enough about the saving Truth of Jesus Christ, without understanding its deeper implications? Are you a collector of facts and information, perhaps even committing Scriptures to memory, but haven't developed the obedience necessary to discern God's will for you? Or are you the rare individual who thirsts for meaning and purpose, spending time with God, studying the Word, being in prayer, and actively participating and contributing to the church?

To discern our life's quest, we must be *questful*. Being questful is not genetic; we choose to seek an understanding of meaning behind truth; we choose to be obedient to the Lord (knowing that obedience draws us ever closer to Him); and we choose to ask God to reveal His plan for us.

The Psalmist's questful approach to life helped bring him ever closer to God:

> *Show me your ways, O Lord, teach me your paths; guide me in your truth and teach me, for you are God my Savior, and my hope is in you all day long.*
>
> *(Psalm 25:4–5)*

The process of discerning one's quest tends to be arduous and often frustrating. But if we model the approach the Psalmist used—praying regularly and passionately, dwelling in God's Word, and asking God to reveal our purpose—we will undoubtedly find it. Nothing worthwhile in life comes easy, and our quest is no exception.

The Crossword Puzzle Approach to discerning our Quest

If you are seeking to *initially* discern your quest, I highly recommend taking an approach similar to how one would go about solving a complex, challenging crossword puzzle.

Just as we aren't likely to complete a crossword puzzle by randomly and aimlessly trying to solve every word, neither should we attempt to discern our quest without employing a basic, methodical approach for doing so.

Most people begin a crossword puzzle by filling in words that are relatively easy to identify. Discerning our quest entails the same initial approach, only instead of quickly identifying words, we identify *essential* elements for godliness. Those elements—grace, love, humility, redemption, salvation, etc.—must become ingrained in us before we are able to solve the rest of the "puzzle." To illustrate the point, it goes without saying that if a person has a quest to "embody and promote authentic Christian living," it would be impossible to live accordingly without a proper understanding of the *basis* for Christianity.

When working on a crossword puzzle, after initially filling in words that can be identified quickly and with relative ease, we would then build from what we've completed; knowing the answer to one-across gives us a much better chance of determining the answer to one-down. This approach should also apply to determining our quest; after increasing our knowledge and understanding of the essential elements of God's Word, we can move ahead toward further application and personalization of what His Word means for us. We may not be ready to solve the puzzle in totality, but by building off what we have learned (and what we will continue to learn), we can complete more and more of it over time.

But as is often the case when trying to complete a difficult crossword puzzle, when discerning our quest we are likely to reach a point when we have got most of the answers but cannot quite figure out the last few in order to complete the puzzle. This is the critical point where we have to decide whether to give up or continue on. Hopefully our decision is to forge ahead, which entails that we leverage our resources, including (but not be limited to) our family, pastors, church members and close friends, and so on. At this point we ought to have our spiritual antenna fully raised, for God will answer our prayers for discernment, but *how* He answers them is unknown to us. He may speak to us through any of the "resources" you tap into, through a song or book, through Scriptures, or through simply placing a thought in your mind from which you can't escape. Whatever the case, *be ready and be open to receiving an answer to your prayers!*

An Important Disclaimer

It is vitally important to understand that discerning a unique, specific quest in no way excludes other key elements for godly living. First and foremost, we are to abide by Scripture—God's Word. Even as God gifts us with a unique, individual purpose that represents His will, we are never to exclude or overlook the *totality* of His will. Think of your quest as being one element (albeit a rather important one) included on a list of many significant elements for godliness. While the other elements may be shown in "normal" font on your list, your quest would be shown in bold italic. But all the elements on your list are important, and excluding any one of them does not support God's will.

Upon discerning your quest, make sure that you don't become so consumed with it that you inadvertently ignore other key elements for godly living.

For example, many Christians consider bringing others to a saving knowledge of the Truth of Jesus Christ to be their personal quest. I have no doubt that in nearly every case, they have discerned their quest patiently, prayerfully and carefully, and are absolutely correct about what they have been called to do. Indeed, bringing others to a knowledge of the Truth of Jesus Christ is not only Biblical, it is essential. But there are those who, in their zealousness to fulfill their quest, ignore or disregard other essential elements of God's Word, such as love, humility, and forgiveness. In those cases, even as their quest in itself is aligned perfectly with God's will, in disregarding critical aspects of God's Word they fail to bring their quest to fruition. Attempting to bring others to Christ in a manner that is threatening (not loving), self-righteous (not humble), and condemning (not forgiving), is to act in a manner not at all like Jesus.

Without taking into account the totality of God's Word, we risk compromising the very thing that we have been called to do.

The Significance of our Quest

I mentioned earlier that although I often fail to live according to my quest, I make a habit of regularly writing and renewing my commitment to it. Yet in spite of my good intentions and disciplined approach, I still routinely proceed in directions other than north.

Have you ever thought you were driving in a particular direction only to find later that you weren't? More to the point, have you ever thought you were driving in a particular direction only to find out that you weren't, *even as a map or compass was readily available to you?*

We do that a lot during our journey through life! Even though we desire that our journey be continuously aligned with our quest, we often fail to properly ascertain where true north lies. I write my quest out weekly and commit to it nearly every day, but doing so does not guarantee success. While healthy habits are indeed essential for healthy living, if we simply act out of habit while failing to recognize the *purpose* behind our habits, then we effectively follow in the footsteps of the Pharisees, losing sight of *why* we should live according to our quest.

It is vitally important to not lose sight of the significance of our quest, especially considering that we have patiently, carefully, and prayerfully discerned it in the first place. We need to regularly ask ourselves *why* our quest is as important today as when we first discerned it. Our answer to that question will serve to reinforce our passion and commitment to our quest, and motivate us to live according to it. On the other hand, if we act merely out of habit, we will never fully understand what our quest entails. Indeed, just as we are called to continually renew our commitment to the Lord, so are we to continually renew our commitment to our quest, for if we have discerned our quest correctly, our commitment to it and our commitment to the Lord are essentially one and the same. Furthermore, just as renewing our commitment to the Lord—and I mean *really* renewing it—entails that we discern why He alone is worthy of our thanks and praise, so should we discern why our quest is worthy of absolute commitment.

I often stray off course while attempting to live for Jesus, which restricts me from perpetually abiding in Him. Yet I take solace in knowing that *attempting* to maintain my focus on Jesus ensures that my quest glorifies the Lord and will eventually lead me to naturally and perpetually abide in Him:

It is better to take refuge in the Lord than to trust in man.
(Psalm 118:8)

The Importance of Forward Progress

I became interested in football when I was around seven years old. Growing up in the Detroit area, my favorite team was (and still is) the Detroit Lions

(I'm a glutton for punishment!). I knew next to nothing about football when I first started watching it, but my dad was always willing and able to answer my questions. One thing that confused me was why a referee would mark the ball at the furthest point a ball carrier got to, as opposed to the place where he was actually tackled. I couldn't understand how a player could run to the twenty-yard line, get pushed back and tackled at the fifteen-yard line, and have the next play start not at the fifteen, but at the twenty-yard line. "Why does the referee mark the ball farther up field than where the player was tackled?" I asked. My dad proceeded to explain the rule of *forward progress:* that because the player was able to advance as far as he did, the next play starts at his furthest point up the field.

Forward progress throughout our life journey is essential for remaining questful. It is inevitable that we will experience many setbacks during our journey through life: financial difficulties, marital problems, the loss of loved ones—all these and much more will come our way during life. But while our journey is absolutely impacted by difficult circumstances, we must maintain an attitude of forward progress when it comes to living according to our quest.

Whether it's exercising, reading, praying, or, for that matter, just about anything else, sustaining motion is essential for sustaining positive results. Spiritually speaking, it is much easier to travel north if we are already heading that way to begin with. But when we find ourselves traveling south—when our life circumstances distract us from living according to our quest—then we are to start anew, not where we've been "tackled," but where our forward progress took us prior to being pushed back and tackled.

To illustrate further, "Linda" has a quest of helping others who are less fortunate than her. One of the ways that Linda lives out her quest is to spend three hours each week visiting hospitalized children. But a situation at work has occupied her time and focus, pushing her quest to the background. After a few weeks of missing her weekly hospital visits, Linda realizes that she has inadvertently lost sight of her quest. In football terms, Linda *feels* as if she has lost some "field position." But in reality, what counts is her forward progress, not where she was tackled. By renewing her commitment to God and to her quest, Linda doesn't lose any ground whatsoever. In fact, the only way she can lose ground is if she allows guilt to consume her, which is what Satan wants. Linda's *forward progress* approach allows God to mark the ball for the next play—not Satan. And God's rules are that when we earnestly, contritely seek grace, and renew our commitment, our field position is not only restored, but we may even gain a few yards. First down!

Selecting Which Mountains to Scale

Living questfully requires that we *regularly* assess the validity and scope of our quest.

I wrote earlier of the need to regularly ask *why* our quest is so vitally important to us, and *why* its alignment with God's will is so important. I further mentioned that the answers we uncover to those questions do not weaken our resolve, but strengthen it through reinforcement of our Creator's goodness and our own life's purpose. But while a correctly discerned quest remains fixed on true north, what about its *scope?*

The short answer is that the scope of our quest should change frequently. My quest—to *help bring forth God's kingdom*—is rather broad, to say the least! If I asked a million people what those five words meant to them, I am certain that I would get a million different answers. Many would be similar, but none would be absolutely identical. In fact, *my* interpretation of my quest changes all the time! Some days I feel that to live my quest is to simply conduct myself in a manner not blatantly sinful, while other days I feel that living my quest requires that I boldly declare the gospel Truth of Jesus Christ. The message here is that even though how I live my quest varies, the *nature* of it is unchanging.

On the other hand, although how we interpret and live our quest can change daily, we should *always* hold ourselves accountable to a well-defined minimum standard. Each and every day of my life I am responsible for living according to my faith in Christ. I may not be as bold or zealous in faith today as I was yesterday, and that's to be expected, but I must at a minimum behave in a manner consistent with my faith. There can be no tolerance for conduct unbecoming a professed follower of Christ.

Beyond the daily variation that comes naturally with living according to our quest, we cannot completely ignore larger scale opportunities that God gifts us with. For example, *the* reason I am writing this book at this time is that I feel called to do so. And the essence of this book, at least as I see it, clearly supports my quest—to *help bring forth God's kingdom*. Along the way, even as my commitment to finishing the book has remained strong, there have been moments of doubt and uncertainty. I have *never* in my life undertaken an endeavor this challenging, but with God's hand upon me, and in knowing that my quest is in line with His will, I proceed north.

From Questions to a Quest

In Search of Truth
I am an ocean, forever drifting away
My mind's in motion but I will always be
In isolation from mainstream society
For I am different—I know my identity
Fiction gets mixed with fact (opposites attract)
Is harmony a story from the past?
Cold stares from angry eyes help me to realize
That man's weakness is his willingness to fight . . .
The Truth
(I'm in search of Truth)

From early childhood, I believed in the saving Truth of Jesus Christ. Yet for most of my life, while rarely exhibiting blatantly *unchristian* behavior, I didn't consistently exhibit unmistakable *Christian* behavior either.

But even while spiritually neutral on the outside, God was working on me on the inside. Allow me to explain further.

Written eighteen years ago while I was in college, "*In Search of Truth*" reveals an incomplete commitment to the Lord. The lyrics are confounding; while disavowing worldliness and asserting that through knowledge of Jesus Christ I knew my "identity," and after lamenting persecution of Christians, I declare that "I'm in search of Truth." Why would I need to search for Truth if I had already found it?

The answer lies within the words: my so-called "isolation from mainstream society" was not physical, it was spiritual. I didn't *literally* isolate myself from people, but by outwardly suppressing my faith I isolated the essence of my being from other people; I didn't let them see the "real" me, the Christian me. And in declaring a search for Truth immediately after declaring that man's weakness is in *turning from* Truth, I basically indict myself. Deep inside I knew I wasn't *living* for Jesus, and these lyrics represented a sort of confession of faith.

Although it has taken many years to discern my quest, writing these confusing (yet honest and confessional) words in 1984 helped point me north. God speaks to us in many ways, including, on occasion, our own words. I understood later that I wasn't really searching for Truth as much as acknowledging a failure to live *according* to Truth. I know now that faith is at its strongest when living according to a quest that perfectly aligns with God's Word and will.

Relationships

Jesus is far and away the most influential person to have ever walked the earth. Though His public ministry only lasted around three years, the words, teachings, and grace Jesus gave us are timeless. Our Lord lived without sin—something that nobody else had ever done or ever will do—and brought passion, conviction, and purpose to everything He did. And the depth of our Lord's love for us can scarcely be imagined, given that He willingly died at our hands so that *we* could be forgiven of sin. Can there be any doubt whatsoever that the historical significance of Jesus Christ dwarfs that of all others?

For those who subscribe to the absolute saving Truth of Jesus Christ, there is no hesitation when answering with a resounding "no." But while nearly all Christians—and many non-Christians—are more than willing to acknowledge Jesus' historical significance, relatively few are willing to consistently place Jesus at the forefront of their lives. What's more, even after reaching some level of understanding and appreciation, many nevertheless frequently fail to *seek* Jesus, essentially (and often unintentionally) viewing Him as a distant, inaccessible icon, rather than the living Redeemer that He is.

We should not be surprised that many Christians inadvertently develop a passive approach to seeking Jesus. We live in a world that values and rewards behavior contrary to Christian teachings and principles. As our secular society increasingly embraces cart blanche acceptance of almost everything, we invariably push God further and further away from our everyday life. In fact, just a few days ago a ruling was handed down by the U.S. Court of Appeals that decreed the Pledge of Allegiance to be unconstitutional, with the phrase "under God" interpreted to be forbidden under the establishment clause in the First Amendment.

It is a daunting challenge to live according to God's Word in a world overrun by the wickedness of men. Yet it is even more daunting when we relegate Christ to being a distant or absent historical figure instead of our ever present, *living* Messiah. We must purposefully and vigilantly seek Jesus, as failure to do so will inevitably bring about erosion of faith accompanied by increased adherence to worldly values and pursuits. It is only through actively and earnestly seeking Christ that we develop a dynamic, sustained *relationship* with Him that serves as an unending source of strength, empowering us to consistently place godliness over worldliness. Contrary to being uninterested and distant, Jesus is a loving and trusted Counselor, Father, and Friend. Our risen Lord is ready and eager to be in constant communion with us, but for that to happen we must first seek Him. And rest assured that while Jesus isn't *directly* visible to us, He is most definitely tangible.

Do you talk with Jesus? He is always eager to listen and respond—just call on Him.

Have you submitted your will to His? Do this, and your life will never be the same. The unquenchable pursuit of earthly happiness and the unending pursuit of truth and meaning will quickly yield to sustained joy and fulfillment through Jesus Christ.

Do you *desire* to have an active, joyful relationship with your Redeemer? You certainly ought to! Doing otherwise prevents knowing Jesus as the present, loving, *living* Friend and Savior that He is.

It is only fitting that a chapter on *Relationships* should focus on our relationship with Christ prior to our relationships with others, for it is only through an evolving, living relationship with the Lord that we can relate to others in *optimal* Christian fashion. To maintain proper Christian communion with other people, we must first be in regular communion with Jesus. The Lord awaits our call, but if we choose to procrastinate or avoid seeking Him, then in essence we reject Him. We are given new life when confessing Jesus as Lord and

Savior, and when striving to live according to God's Word, but if we don't regularly seek His presence, then we cannot fully appreciate what He offers us. What a shame it is when we place Jesus' priceless gift of joy, fulfillment, grace and salvation on a shelf, all but forgetting about it except on rare occasions.

Through discipline, prayer, fellowship, Bible study, etc., as we increasingly seek Christ, the perceived distance between Jesus and ourselves becomes less and less, such that we eventually invite Him to live within us on a perpetual basis. And in surrendering our will to His, our relationship with Jesus prospers, serving as an essential gateway to spiritual fulfillment. Inevitably, our relationship with Jesus is *outwardly* reflected by our relationships with other people. Indeed, a vibrant relationship with our Savior is requisite for making sure that others see us as a new creation in Christ:

> *Therefore, if anyone is in Christ, he is a new creation; the old has gone, the new has come!*
>
> *(2 Corinthians 5:17)*

A Key to Healthy Relationships: Try To See People Through God's Eyes

> *There is neither Jew nor Greek, slave nor free, male nor female, for you are all one in Christ Jesus.*
>
> *(Galatians 3:28)*

It is absolutely essential that we try our best to see others through God's eyes. God loves and cherishes *all* of His children, and commands us to do the same. Yet because of our sinful nature, we regularly and routinely levy unfair judgements on others. And while many people manage to convince themselves that they are free from prejudice, none really are.

Most of us instinctively think of prejudice as a brand of unmistakable, hostile behavior from one person or group toward another person or group. And indeed-and most unfortunately—blatant, hostile prejudice is alive and well, permeating every corner of our world and constantly pitting people against one another. This type of prejudice is *relatively* easy to detect, borne out primarily through inappropriate words and actions. Even in our democratic society, there is a long and tragic legacy of societal toleration and, at times, mass acceptance of various brands of institutionalized prejudice. And while recognizing that blatant prejudice is still embraced in many corners of the world, and that genuine equality is non-existent *everywhere* in the world, it's probably fair to state that in our present age the vast majority of people in civilized nations consider blatant prejudice to be unacceptable. If indeed that is the case, then it follows that those who engage in such behavior are themselves considered to be outside the boundaries of acceptable society, thereby significantly discounting their credibility and scope of influence. To illustrate, whereas at one point in our nation's history many white people were overly accepting of others who swore allegiance to racist groups like the Ku Klux Clan, today such acceptance is rare. In fact, people who align themselves with overtly prejudiced groups or causes almost always face widespread scorn and disdain from people of *all* races.

Nevertheless, the fact remains that blatant prejudice is still relatively common, bringing about considerable danger and devastation.

Beyond blatant prejudice lies subtle prejudice. This brand of prejudice isn't normally visible, dramatic or bold, and its effects are rarely devastating, but it is highly prevalent and impacts each one of us every day. Unlike blatant prejudice, subtle prejudice often goes undetected and/or unacknowledged—*what you don't know can't hurt you*. But it can hurt, and it does hurt.

Think for a moment about the labels we place on people very day. Democrat (left-wing liberal); Republican (right-wing conservative); Laborer (uneducated, low income); Manager (educated, high income); Widow (lonely, despondent); Bachelor (loner, independent); etc. The list could go on and on, but the point has been sufficiently made. We all label people in some fashion, then categorize them according to *our* belief system. It is pointless to deny this basic truth. The simple fact is that although we should always strive to see people as God does, we can never actually do so. We are all prejudiced whether we admit it or not; only God is capable of seeing people as they truly are, and only God can accurately judge a person's heart.

So what are we to do about this dilemma? Quite simply, *strive* to be godly while recognizing that you will fall short. Purposefully look beyond the obvious when you interact with people, for that is the only way you will ever come close to discovering what lies in their heart. Always bear in mind that an active, healthy relationship with Jesus is a necessary gateway for godly relationships with other people. And last but not least, follow the Word of God, in which we are taught to avoid judging other people:

> *Do not judge, and you will not be judged. Do not condemn, and you will not be condemned. Forgive, and you will be forgiven.*
> (*Luke 6:37*)

A Key to Healthy Relationships: Hospitality

> *Offer hospitality to one another without grumbling.*
> (*1 Peter 4:9*)

There is nothing quite so noble as placing the needs of others ahead of the needs of self. Jesus' paid the ultimate price for us, and if we are to be His followers then we must serve others in a similar manner. And make no mistake, hospitality toward others entails personal sacrifice, something most people aren't exactly enthusiastic about! Nonetheless, a surprisingly strong case can be made that when we are *purposefully and regularly* hospitable toward others—regardless of any immediate resistance or inconvenience we feel—we quickly develop a natural affinity for it.

God created us to commune with one another. Eve was given to Adam because *"It is not good for the man to be alone." (ref. Genesis 2:18)*. Indeed, despite our sinful, selfish nature, we experience immense satisfaction when being hospitable to others because it's at the very heart of what we were made for. Conversely, it's sad when we let selfishness inhibit a vital source of fulfillment, which hospitality toward others most assuredly is. Imagine how much better the world would be if even half the people in it consistently strove to live according to God's Word.

A few weeks ago, my father-in-law and stepmother-in-law, along with my neighbor (and friend) Chuck, came over on a Saturday to help cut and clear eight dead pine trees from our yard. Each of the trees exceeded fifty feet in height, and because of their proximity to our house and to the busy street we live on, taking them down was no small chore. And lest I forget to mention it, the temperature that day was close to ninety degrees Fahrenheit!

About the only thing we could afford to compensate the "help" with was lunch, dinner, and plenty of cold beverages throughout the day. Yet not only were there no complaints, there was a noticeable spirit of camaraderie and fellowship.

To say that my home repair skills are limited would be a vast understatement. My father-in-law is well aware of that fact, and though his home repair skills are opposite of mine (he's a recently retired custom homebuilder), he has never made any derogatory remarks about it. On the contrary, as long as I am willing to work with him (which I always am), he will help me with just about anything. Roofing, carpentry, whatever—he has helped me out—and has yet to complain, instead expressing satisfaction from being able to help.

As for Chuck, he wasn't content to stop at cutting, chipping, and stacking my trees! The day after we cut down the trees, Pam and I took the boys to Lake Ann for a scheduled five-day vacation at my father-in-law's house. Unfortunately, because we weren't able to disposition all the wood from the trees the day before, we left somewhere between three and four tons of wood stacked in our yard. As we left on vacation, I dreaded the thought of coming back to a major cleanup.

When we arrived home after our vacation, we found that all of the wood was gone save for a few stumps! Knowing that we were planning on scrapping the wood (it's not a wood that burns well), Chuck had taken it upon himself to load and dispose of nearly all the wood. I thanked Chuck, expressing my appreciation and indebtedness, to which he quickly corrected me, saying that in fact I owed him no such debt. If I can be half as hospitable to others as Chuck is, I'll be on the right track. I am truly blessed to have him as a neighbor and friend.

Although hospitality comes from a desire to help others, it is those who give graciously of themselves who derive the most benefit. This bears consideration, considering that from a logical, worldly viewpoint (assuming that one subjugates any hidden agendas, including the possibility of reciprocity), there is seemingly little to be gained by serving others and much to be gained by others serving us. But for devoted followers of Christ, "logic" takes a backseat to godliness. It certainly doesn't *seem* logical for God's Son to have washed the feet of His disciples, but it is in fact perfectly logical when taking into account our Lord's words immediately following His selfless actions:

"I tell you the truth, no servant is greater than his master, nor is a messenger greater than the one who sent him."

(John 13:16)

A Key to Healthy Relationships: Settle Disagreements Quickly

"Therefore, if you are offering your gift at the altar and there remember that your brother has something against you, leave your gift there in front of the altar. First go and be reconciled to your brother; then come and offer your gift."

(Matthew 5:23–24)

Jealousy, stubbornness and pride are cancers to healthy relationships. How often have you witnessed a vibrant relationship between people-one built on trust, respect, kindness, and love—quickly disintegrate over petty disagreements? We have all seen it happen, and if we think long and hard enough about it, we will likely conclude that we ourselves have been involved in such a relationship at some point in our lives.

Forgiving others is absolutely essential for healthy relationships. And the sooner we forgive others, the better! Every time that we allow a disagreement or argument to hold us back from having a healthy relationship with someone we care about, we fail to live according to God's Word. And by cutting off a relationship with someone we care about, we severely restrict fulfillment through godly living. We simply cannot go about our business of praising God, being active in church, doing morning devotions, etc., while purposefully removing ourselves from people we are to love. Jesus taught us the importance of forgiving others, even under the most arduous circumstances:

When they kept on questioning him, he straightened up and said to them, "If any one of you is without sin, let him be the first to throw a stone at her." Again he stooped down and wrote on the ground. At this, those who heard began to go away one at a time, the older ones first, until only Jesus was left, with the woman still standing there. Jesus straightened up and asked her, "Woman, where are they? Has no one condemned you?" "No one, sir," she said. "Then neither do I condemn you," Jesus declared. "Go now and leave your life of sin."

(John 8:7B–11)

The Pharisees were hoping to trap Jesus by their question, knowing that Moses' law commanded them to stone openly adulterous women. But in reality, the Pharisees had absolutely no regard for the woman, or for the law itself. Evidence strongly suggests that the Pharisees failed to regularly carry out Moses law, instead selectively interpreting and executing this and other laws at their discretion. Indeed, their intention was clearly to stone this woman to death *without* a fair trial (which the law allowed for, including opportunity for the condemned to confess their wrongs) while conveniently overlooking that Moses' law also stipulated that the woman *and the man* found in adultery be stoned together; the man was nowhere to be found. Recognizing that the Pharisees cared little for the law and nothing for the woman, it is evident that their true underlying intent of this exchange was to induce Jesus to either uphold the law (essentially condoning the stoning) or to break the law (openly disregarding God's Word). But Jesus did neither, for beyond knowing the law (the Word) and what it actually entailed, Jesus *is God's Son,* sent by the Father to establish a new covenant:

For God did not send his Son into the world to condemn the world, but to save the world through him.

(John 3:17)

If you truly desire to honor Jesus, then pay Him the ultimate tribute by seeking to live as He did, not allowing jealousy, stubbornness, and pride to supercede kindness, forgiveness, and love.

And bear in mind that our universal human nature is such that we have a strong desire for validation. Our relationships, particularly those with whom we are closest to, are a major source thereof. As a regular supplier of validation to others, you will be nourished accordingly.

A Key to Healthy Relationships: Never Compromise Your Belief in God

A dear friend once told me that the most important advice he ever gave his children was to always remember that their every word and action is a direct reflection of their belief in God. He wanted his children to know that consistently speaking and acting in accordance with their faith would bring honor to themselves and to their Creator. What an awesome gift he gave his children, the fruits of which are easily evidenced through transparent godliness and genuine love for the Lord.

How important is it that we never compromise our faith in God? *Vitally important.*

Inevitably, we find ourselves in situations that threaten to compromise our character and beliefs. Many of these situations involve someone with whom we have an established relationship, perhaps someone whose beliefs (and possibly morals and ethics) may be in conflict with our own. Should we behave differently around those people? Should we somehow conceal our faith when talking to them?

Of course not—but we must also recognize that the dynamics of individual relationships vary widely, dictating in large part how we ought to *best* embody our faith in Jesus. It is perfectly natural to assume that a church member will be more receptive to listening and talking about religious beliefs than the neighbor down the street who doesn't attend church. But that does not imply that it is okay to ignore our neighbor, or for that matter, to conceal our faith when we do talk to him. Indeed, we must respect him (and his worldview) while assessing his receptivity to hearing about the saving Truth of Jesus Christ. Too many Christians are guilty of approaching *all* of their relationships with far too much preaching and not nearly enough listening. If we really desire to do God's will then we will seek to foster relationships based on mutual trust, respect, and kindness, none of which require us to simply condone beliefs and/or behavior contrary to our own. But nothing turns people away faster than being spoken to in a manner that is condescending or judgmental, except perhaps being spoken to in a manner that is deceitful. Be open and honest with people about your faith, but if they are not receptive to hearing about it, don't just walk away from the relationship. Instead, consistently approach that person with trust, respect, and kindness, while never *denying* your faith, and they will quickly come to understand that you are a person whose faith is strong—so strong in fact that your words and actions never fail to align with your beliefs. And that is a very powerful statement in itself!

It is not easy to consistently *verbally* embody our belief in Jesus Christ. And recognizing that our individual relationships are going to be naturally (and healthily) unique, we must, *in all cases*, never fail to make our beliefs clear to others. While verbal expression of faith is indeed essential, let us not forget that our actions speak louder. We can detract from the kingdom, or we can embody the kingdom. If we choose to do the latter, then how we live, what we say, and the joy we display through having accepted Christ will inevitably help bring others to a saving knowledge of Jesus:

Make every effort to live in peace with all men and to be holy; without holiness no one will see the Lord.

(Hebrews 12:14)

Treasure Family and Friends

Jesus forged relationships with fishermen, children, prostitutes, religious leaders and many others from all walks of life. He dined with sinners, tax collectors, and lepers—all were of value in His eyes. And in His final hours, Jesus made sure that His *earthly* mother would be properly cared for after His death:

Near the cross of Jesus stood his mother, his mother's sister, Mary the wife of Clopas, and Mary Magdalene. When Jesus saw his mother there, and the disciple whom he loved standing nearby, he said to his mother, "Dear woman, here is your son," and to the disciple, "Here is your mother." From that time on, this disciple took her into his home.

(John 19:25–27)

Do you *treasure* the people who mean the most to you? Are your relationships filled with passion, vitality, and commitment?

My answer to both questions is "yes," but only with a significant qualifier: I fail to *regularly* convey my feelings to the people who mean the most to me. I have no qualms about expressing love to close family members and a select group of friends, but I rarely express *why* I love them. For this shortcoming, all I can offer at this point is a sincere apology and a solemn vow to do better in the future.

And while recognizing that to properly document the love I hold for all of my family and friends would entail filling far too many pages of this book, I nevertheless feel compelled, at a minimum, to document my love for immediate family.

What follows is not meant to imply that extended family, in-laws, and close friends are unworthy of receiving documented expressions of love and gratitude on these pages. On the contrary, I have been enormously blessed with a wonderful extended family, in-laws and close friends, and they are all absolutely worthy of documented expressions of my love. But alas, there are limits to the number of pages in a book that can be reserved for such expressions, and so at this time I will limit my words to immediate family.

Relationships

To Pam—marrying you was the smartest thing I have ever done. You are loving and compassionate, caring deeply for your family and other people. You have taught me what it means to be a loving, responsible husband and father. You mean everything to me, and you are my rock. I love you.

To Spencer—I am so blessed to be your father. I love your adventuresome spirit and your infectious personality. Our time together is always filled with laughter and joy. Thanks for being you. I love you.

To Trevor—what a sweet disposition you have! I am consistently amazed at the strong love (and curiosity) you have for God, and for your family. You are a wonderful boy, and I am blessed to call you my son. I love you.

To my mother (Angie)—you have taught me more than you can know. Your outward love for the Lord and for our family is absolutely apparent. You are a terrific mom and an even better grandmother. How blessed I am to have you as a mother! I love you.

To my dad (Alex), who now dwells with the Lord in heaven—my children know you and will never forget you. Your legacy—unending love for God, family, and friends—is alive and well. You have impacted my life so much, and I am richly blessed to have had you as a father. I love you.

To my brother (Tom)—although we naturally drifted apart after our teen years, I have a wealth of wonderful memories about growing up, most of which involve you. And I have nothing but admiration for the way you have overcome difficult circumstances at various times. You are a loving husband and father, and I am blessed to be your little brother. I love you.

To my sister (Denise)—what wonderful times we had growing up! I have so many fond memories, yet while memories themselves tend to fade over time, the bonds that come from them do not. I am blessed to be your brother! And I continue to marvel at what an awesome wife and mother you are. I love you.

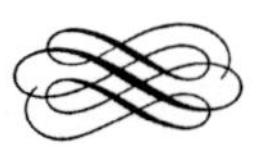

Shell Court

Between 1982 and 1993, NBC televised a popular sitcom called "*Cheers.*" *Cheers* premiered as the lowest rated show in America yet concluded its last few years as America's highest rated show. Based loosely on an actual bar in Boston, the setting for the show was inviting and engaging, a place "where everybody knows your name." And indeed, though the writing was crisp and the characters memorable, what really appealed to viewers was the bar's atmosphere.

While *Cheers* was set in a bar in Boston, the place where everyone knew my name was a neighborhood in Michigan. Like *Cheers*, Shell Court was inviting and engaging. I was three years old when my parents built a house at 26070 Shell Court, and I lived there until leaving for college.

Our neighborhood hearkened back to a simpler time. There were five houses directly located on our court, and each family knew the others well. There were cookouts in backyards, lunches on patios, and swimming on hot summer nights. There were sleepovers and get-togethers (usually impromptu), non-stop activities and plenty of laughter.

Amazingly, of the five houses on our little court, four contained young families. All told, there were five boys (all no more than three years apart) and seven girls (all no more than five years apart) on our court. And each family lived on Shell Court for many years. *We grew up together.*

I fondly remember playing pitch-and-catch; lawn jarts; tennis; street hockey; Evil Knievel bike jumps; roller-skating; kickball; tag; basketball; dodgeball; water fights; five-hundred; croquet; and, of course, chasing down the Ice Cream truck for grape popsicles.

Interspersed between all the fun things we did were occasional arguments and disagreements. But they never lasted long, usually dissipating within a day or two. There was an implicit feeling amongst the kids on Shell Court that even though we weren't blood relatives, we were connected in a manner that went beyond mere friendship.

I am not conclusive about many things in life, but one thing I can say with certainty is that the kids of Shell Court-Michelle, Lydia, Renee, Brian, Kim, Chris, Jeff, Suzanne, Cheryl, Denise, Tom, and myself—have fond memories of growing up in a place where life was undeniably simple, yet rich in texture.

Stewardship

What Is Stewardship?

Merriam-Webster's on-line dictionary defines *Stewardship* as: "*1: the office, duties, and obligations of a steward; 2: the conducting, supervising, or managing of something; especially: the careful and responsible management of something entrusted to one's care.*"

Biblically speaking, when it comes to stewardship we must initially seek to view the "bigger picture." It is far too easy (and instinctive) to limit our notions of stewardship to being rooted in ancient law and little more than a means of providing funding for our churches. And indeed, stewardship *is* rooted in the Old Testament and *is* vital to funding our churches, but it goes well beyond law and finance.

To properly ascertain the scope of stewardship, we need to go back to the origins of humankind. We were in perfect harmony with God until Adam and Eve sinned, which produced from that day forward *inherent* human sin and resultant separation between man and God:

> *But your iniquities have separated you from your God; your sins have hidden his face from you, so that he will not hear.*
>
> *(Isaiah 59:2)*

The chasm between God and humankind could only be reconciled through Jesus' sinless life, sacrificial death, and glorious ascension into heaven. Jesus' death and ascension atoned for our sins, and allowed us to be reconciled with our Creator. Even as we continue to sin, in our acceptance of Jesus Christ as Lord and Savior, we are forgiven:

> *Therefore, if anyone is in Christ, he is a new creation; the old has gone, the new has come!*
>
> *(2 Corinthians 5:17)*

So there you have it: Man was born in perfect harmony with God. Man destroyed that perfect harmony by sinning and separating himself from God. God's only begotten Son died and ascended into heaven so that man could once again be reconciled with God.

That pretty well describes the history of man's relationship with God. But what does it have to do with stewardship? Everything! At the risk of stating the obvious, the Truth of Jesus Christ *is* Christianity. Is that fact indelibly etched on our hearts and minds? It must be, because we are incapable of being good stewards if we fail to properly understand or appreciate *what* we are to steward. And as being a steward in any sense of the word requires one to supervise, manage, and be responsible for *"something entrusted to one's care,"* it goes without saying that Christian stewardship must always center on the gospel Truth of Jesus Christ—the *saving* Truth of Jesus Christ. Jesus is the *"what"* of Christian stewardship, and we are entrusted to carry the gospel forward.

It stands to reason that being properly equipped is essential for carrying forward something of great importance. Financial Institutions transport money and securities by specially armored Brink's trucks driven by armed guards—not by Couriers on Ten-speed bicycles. Christians cannot "transport" the Good News of Jesus Christ without being properly equipped. Active participation and leadership at church, participation in Bible Studies, reading and studying God's Word—all of these things and more are vital for equipping us to be good Christian stewards. We are simply incapable of bringing others to an understanding of Truth if we ourselves lack such understanding. Preparedness is paramount for Christian stewardship.

Jesus entrusts us to bring forth His message of Truth. When we submit our will to His, we bury our sins in the past and begin life anew:

> *And he died for all, that those who live should no longer live for themselves but for him who died for them and was raised again.*
>
> (2 Corinthians 5:15)

Jesus desires that *all* people be saved from their sins through knowing and accepting His Truth:

> *The Lord is not slow in keeping his promise, as some understand slowness. He is patient with you, not wanting anyone to perish, but everyone to come to repentance.*
>
> (2 Peter 3:9)

If you believe that Jesus *is* Truth, and that Truth is the essential thing that we are to be stewards for, then the question that follows is "*How* shall we bring forth the Truth of Jesus Christ?" To which I would answer, "Through optimal use of our resources."

Perhaps my answer seems incomplete or vague. But I would argue that, taken literally, it is absolutely complete. Optimal use of our resources, by and in itself, is enough to bring forth the gospel Truth of Jesus Christ.

And it would be just that simple, except for one little thing that continually holds us back: our selfish human nature. Selfishness blinds us to the basic, fundamental truth that *all* of our resources—our money, houses, cars, even our time and talents—belong to God. Everything we have is on loan to us; we are merely the beneficiaries of God's generosity. Yet this essential truth is often unacknowledged and only rarely embraced. Even those who have the best of intentions, and are in fact godly people, struggle with accepting and/or embracing that *everything* belongs to God. But grasp it we must, for failure to do so severely restricts our ability to be good Christian stewards. Scripture tells us that our earthly possessions are merely temporary:

> *For we brought nothing into the world, and we can take nothing out of it.*
>
> (1 Timothy 6:7)

God gifts us with time, money, possessions, and talents. And while all are temporary, what we do with them determines our eternal future. The resources we have been entrusted with are to be managed so that the Truth of Jesus Christ is shown to as many people as possible. That's the macro view of Christian stewardship—using *all* of our available resources, none of which belong to us and all of which are temporarily bestowed upon us, to bring forth Truth.

If we accept that as the macro view, then our micro view must focus on *how* we best put each of our basic resources (time, talent, and money) to work for the kingdom.

Being a Good Steward of Time

How frequently we fail to understand the precious nature of time! Most of us rarely appreciate how important time is, and on those rare occasions when we do, it's usually when time seems to either stand still or pass us by.

During our most difficult moments—the loss of a loved one, financial uncertainty, marital problems, unemployment, etc.—time doesn't seem to move. Our struggles so paralyze us with fear and uncertainty that we feverishly desire to push a sort of "fast-forward" button in order to get to whatever comes next. Time is our enemy during the down periods of life.

The old phrase "the devil finds work for idle hands" is not Biblical, but it does contain a certain degree of Biblical Truth. Not because idle people are somehow destined to commit vile acts, but because idle people are not as likely to spend ample time being good stewards for the Truth of Jesus Christ. And while the reality of everyday life in the twenty-first century necessitates that time be spent on many things not *directly* related to stewarding the Truth of Jesus Christ, it is equally realistic to state that every minute of every waking hour should, at a minimum, *indirectly* support such a cause. It is also fair to add that if we fail to adopt and apply this very mindset, then by *not* being an active steward for Christ we inadvertently help the enemy.

When life brings uncertainty and frustration, turn to God. Dwell in His Holy Word, seek Him out, and do something *constructively* with your time. Volunteer to work at a mission. Join a Bible Study group. Be a mentor to a child. Do *something* in stewardship for Jesus Christ. You will find that time is no longer your enemy but a trusted friend.

On the opposite end of the spectrum are those occasions when time seems to pass us by. Nearly all of us reach a point (and more commonly several points) in life when we feel suddenly awakened to the abrupt passage of time. "Milestone" birthdays—twenty, thirty, forty, and so on—tend to be such occasions. Those are times when we naturally reflect on what we have done in life, and perhaps what we hope to do in the future. Those are also times when priorities are examined and major decisions made. Indeed, not only is it healthy for us to take stock of our past, present and future, it's vital. Lasting change can only come about through strong motivation, and motivation generally comes about due to some degree of dissatisfaction with circumstances. It only makes sense that if we fail to adequately take stock of our lives—to ascertain satisfaction—then we will not change. And a failure to change is a failure to evolve, which as it relates to Christian stewardship is tantamount to not developing or utilizing the resources God gives us. So many "successful" people don't realize until too late that earthly success has little to do with eternal success, unless they *leverage* the former in order to further the latter.

Generally speaking, our culture is long on action but short on purpose. Yet Scripture teaches us that action without purpose is wasted energy, and that purpose must *govern* action. And since Scripture itself provides us with clarity of purpose (ushering forth the Truth of Jesus Christ), idleness of the mind, soul, or body is inexcusable for Christians:

> *We hear that some among you are idle. They are not busy; they are busybodies. Such people we command and urge in the Lord Jesus Christ to settle down and earn the bread they eat.*
>
> (*2 Thessalonians 3:11–12*)

When we reflect on what we have done with our time, let our reflections be in the form of celebration. Jesus entrusts us with time, and when we use it purposefully and wisely we help to steward in Truth. And make no mistake: our brief time on earth, when compared to eternity, barely registers; but *what* we do with our time is a major determinant for our eternal destination.

Being a Good Steward of Talent

> *We have different gifts, according to the grace given us. If a man's gift is prophesying, let him use it in proportion to his faith. If it is serving, let him serve; if it is teaching, let him teach; if it is encouraging, let him encourage; if it is contributing to the needs of others, let him give generously; if it is leadership, let him govern diligently; if it is showing mercy, let him do it cheerfully.*
>
> (*Romans 12:6–8*)

God has given all of us unique and special talents. Irrespective of where your talents lie, you are called to use them on behalf of our Lord. Indeed, putting our talents to good use—that is, leveraging our talents to usher forth the Truth of Jesus Christ—is necessary for spiritual fulfillment. It is not merely *recommended* for spiritual fulfillment—it is *necessary* for spiritual fulfillment.

In itself, the grace bestowed upon you through acceptance of Jesus Christ as Lord and Savior is sufficient to ensure eternal life, but if you are interested in attaining spiritual fulfillment in this world then you must utilize your talents in stewardship for the source of genuine fulfillment. And when you do apply your God-given talents on behalf of our Lord, you will be blessed *abundantly.* (But be careful to remember that the blessings we receive from above come in many different varieties; sometimes our blessings are pleasing to us, while at other times they are anything but pleasing. Although we may think of certain "blessings" as something closer to curses, in giving ourselves to the Lord we *are* blessed. Even in difficult times—especially in difficult times—we are able to draw ever nearer to Jesus).

Have you given ample consideration to what your talents are? Have you focused on what you *can* do rather than on what you can't?

As a child, I was always envious of my father and of my brother. Both were skilled mechanically, able to disassemble then reassemble anything from bicycles to cars. I, on the other hand, had difficulty reassembling ballpoint pens if they happened to pop open! For many years, I lamented my mechanical shortcomings, considering myself inferior on account of them.

As time went on, I increasingly came to grips with being mechanically challenged. It became less and less of an issue, though it never quite subsided until I began focusing on my talents rather than shortcomings. I eventually realized that God gifted me with much, including but not limited to leadership, writing, public speaking, sports (exempting golf), compassion for others, expressionism, organizational skills, and logic. Until I stopped focusing on what I lacked and started focusing on what I had, I could not optimally apply my gifts for the kingdom.

Starting from elementary school and continuing into the workplace, we are constantly told to focus on improving things that we don't do well. Positive reinforcement for things we are good at comes and goes, but negative reinforcement is almost always a constant. And it's not just in schools or the workplace—it's everywhere. For example, every year thirty NFL teams vie to win the Super Bowl, but only one can win it. Meanwhile, in the off-season most of the other twenty-nine teams become pre-occupied with revamping their weaknesses. But a few teams decide not to dwell on their weaknesses, but on *optimizing* their strengths. A couple years ago the Baltimore Ravens committed their off-season to making their good defense great. In the season that followed, their previously nondescript offense showed no significant improvement, and ultimately settled into being . . . an updated version of a nondescript offense. But the strength of the team-defense—was *phenomenal.* In fact, their defense was so good that they won the Super Bowl almost in spite of their anemic offense.

That is the approach we ought to take with our God-given talents: Recognize and acknowledge them. Develop them. Optimize them. And *apply* them with purpose and vigor.

Being a Good Steward of Money

Just as our time and talents are to be used to steward forth the Truth of Jesus Christ, so is our money. The Bible is filled with Scriptures that speak to the significance of giving. Nearly all either directly or indirectly allude to four important principles:

1. Those who give freely are blessed.
2. The Lord loves a cheerful giver.
3. Giving with ulterior motives or without sincerity is looked upon unfavorably by God.
4. Our gifts are intended to place God first in our lives.

The following verses are but a few of many that reinforce these four points:

1. Those who give freely are blessed.

One man gives freely, yet gains even more; another withholds unduly, but comes to poverty. A generous man will prosper; he who refreshes others will himself be refreshed.

(*Proverbs 11:24–25*)

2. The Lord loves a cheerful giver.

Each man should give what he has decided in his heart to give, not reluctantly or under compulsion, for God loves a cheerful giver.
(2 Corinthians 9:7)

3. Giving with ulterior motives or without sincerity is looked upon unfavorably by God

Be careful not to do your 'acts of righteousness' before men, to be seen by them. If you do, you will have no reward from your Father in heaven.
(Matthew 6:1)

4. Our gifts are intended to place God first in our lives.

"Sacrifice thank offerings to God, fulfill your vows to the Most High, and call upon me in the day of trouble; I will deliver you, and you will honor me."
(Psalm 50:14–15)

Combining these four Biblical principles allows us to create a credible aggregate statement for giving:

Give freely to God from the heart, for in doing so you honor Him.

Do you give to the Lord freely? Do you give without guilt and with a pure heart? And is your giving sufficient such that God takes precedence over everything else in your life?

Learn from My Mistakes

We were a typical young couple. Married right out of college, neither of us commanded a hefty salary, but our combined income allowed us to purchase a small starter home a few years after marrying. We went to church but didn't think much about tithing—it just wasn't that important to us—*"We'll get ahead, then we'll tithe later; besides, our time is valuable too, and we're giving a lot of it to the church."*

A short time later we moved to Illinois, where we purchased a moderate three-bedroom home. Pam worked as a self-employed Interior Designer while I worked as a Buyer. Again, we attended church but found ourselves tight on money, and decided to give less than a full tithe in parallel with donating considerable time and talent to the church. We did not recognize it at the time, but a clear pattern was emerging.

Our next move took us to St. Joseph, Michigan where, again, we were initially tight on money. Except during this time we didn't even attend a church. We were drained from donating so much time to the church in Illinois, and believed that a temporary hiatus from church would be the best thing for us. In retrospect, and in reality, we dictated the situation on our terms, which were opposite of God's will.

While in St. Joseph, some rather interesting developments began taking shape. First, we began to accrue some debt, slowly at first and then rather quickly. Pam was not working full-time, and we had a rash of unforeseen expenses come our way, along with two car payments. Secondly, after years of trying to have children, Pam became pregnant—with twins. We made the difficult decision to have Pam be a stay-at-home mother. We believed that to be God's will, and our belief thereof has never diminished.

A short while later, we heeded God's call to move to Holland, Michigan. This move was absolutely illogical when viewed from an earthly perspective. I accepted a cut in pay along with a lesser position, yet we knew we had to make the move because God's pull was undeniable.

By the time we settled in Holland we were seriously in debt. Too many moves without recovering home equity; a significant cut in pay; a plethora of unforeseen expenses; mismanagement of income and expenses; and, most significantly, a failure to put God first led to us looking deep within to ascertain what went wrong and where we needed to go from there.

Until recently, even when I did put my time and talent to work for the kingdom, it was, in essence, for my benefit. Youth Leader, Sunday School Superintendent, Bible Study Leader, Treasurer—all were done to ease a sense of guilt over not tithing. When looked at against the Biblical aggregate statement given earlier—to *"Give freely to God from the heart, for in doing so you honor Him"*—I failed miserably. My giving wasn't done freely or from the heart, and it most definitely didn't honor God.

When we started attending Beechwood, God began to restore my heart. I had accepted Jesus as Lord and Savior many years before, but I was never very good at consistently living for Him. But during the past few years, as I've developed a strong desire to not only know Christ but serve Him, I have learned much about what it means to be a Christian steward.

The Bible tells us that we reap what we sow. Pam and I are painfully aware of that truth. Only within the past few weeks have we started to give a full tithe to the church. In the "better late than never" category, I tell you in truth that *everything* we give is now—finally-given freely and from the heart.

I believe that when it comes to giving to the Lord, our attitude is much more important than what we actually give. Learn from my mistakes: regardless of your situation, do not allow guilt to separate you from Jesus' love. *Whatever* you give, whether it's one dollar or a million dollars, is not to be given out of guilt but out of love and desire:

> *For if the willingness is there, the gift is acceptable according to what one has, not according to what he does not have.*
>
> *(2 Corinthians 8:12)*

It took me many years to realize that Jesus does not desire our money, He desires *us*. Our "gifts," which are God's to begin with, are merely a means for drawing us closer to His healing presence. And that is cause for celebration!

Of Burdens and Privileges

During the first day of classes in my junior year of High School, my Speech Teacher told us that *"what you get out of this class will directly reflect what you put into it."* I had heard other teachers express similar sentiments, but she said it with considerably more conviction. Thus I uncharacteristically took her words to heart and brought energy and enthusiasm to the class. And as the school year progressed, her words rang true. I felt a sense of quiet satisfaction from knowing that my efforts were solid and my attitude sincere. Nevertheless, despite affirming her words firsthand, I never quite adopted them.

Fast-forward some thirteen years. Happily married for five years and recently relocated to Illinois, life was good. And from a spiritual standpoint, it was better than good. Pam and I joined a vibrant church in our community and quickly became active members. When asked to be on the church consistory, we agreed with no hesitation. When asked to help form and lead a young adults Bible Study, we agreed with no hesitation. And when asked to be our Church Treasurer, I . . . hesitated.

In my mind, being on consistory and leading a Bible Study group were privileges, but being a Church Treasurer would be a burden. But in the end, though I never even bothered to pray for discernment, I decided to fill the need. I figured that as we weren't able to fully tithe the church, donating more time would help make up the difference.

Predictably, my attitude soon became me. I didn't enjoy being Church Treasurer. It took around ten hours each week, and it felt thankless. Instead of seeing it as a privilege (as any opportunity to serve God is) I saw it as a necessary burden. Even worse, deep down I knew that my "burden" was self-inflicted, brought about unnecessarily by *manufactured* guilt. I had taken it upon myself to discount the insurmountable value of grace through Jesus Christ, and in doing so robbed myself of fulfillment and joy from Christian stewardship.

For the past several years I have stopped letting guilt triumph over grace. I know that I am unworthy to receive His grace, yet I accept it freely and thankfully. Thanks be to God!

I have also learned that *everything* we do in service to the kingdom ought to be a source of joy. I have never been as active in His service as I am now, and I have never felt joy and fulfillment as I do now.

"What you get out of this class will directly reflect what you put into it."

Class dismissed. Now comes the fun part.

Transparency

"What you see is what you get."

-Flip Wilson, Comedian

Do you allow people to see the "real" you? Do people *know* what you stand for? Do you consistently lay open your heart, mind, and soul for others to see? If you can answer "yes" to each of these questions, then you might consider skipping this chapter and proceeding to the next one. But before you do, there's just one more question: If you asked everybody who you regularly interact with—extended family, friends, co-workers, neighbors, etc.—what they felt you were *most* passionate about, would they answer as one?

When contemplated honestly and insightfully, few people can answer "yes" to the last question. In truth, being transparent presents an enormous challenge. Our universal desire for acceptance and affirmation often leads to outward suppression of our innermost beliefs, rendering the very fiber of our being—what we stand for—open to speculation.

Some claim to be transparent insofar as they don't deny their convictions. While commendable, this assertion in itself does not *necessarily* equate to genuine transparency. It is not uncommon for people to lapse into a false sense of security, often accompanied by self-righteousness, when insulating themselves from others whose viewpoints are opposite their own. This is basic human nature: we all gravitate instinctively toward like-minded people, making it much easier to live according to our convictions. And indeed, Christians *need* to be surrounded and lifted up by other Christians. But if we restrict ourselves to revealing our beliefs only to like-minded people, then our self-proclaimed transparency is selective in nature. If we are to make disciples of *all people,* as Jesus calls us to do, then we must be transparent to all people. Transparency in a Christian sense entails that we not only never deny our convictions, but that we consistently *embody* them, regardless of what situation we're in or with whom we're interacting. Not denying our beliefs is important, but embodying our beliefs for all to see is true transparency. And though transparency in itself doesn't equate to godliness, it is definitely an element thereof.

Alignment Leads To Transparency

At first glance, *alignment* and *transparency* may appear to be virtually identical. But when looking beneath the surface, several key distinctions can be made.

First and foremost, alignment *leads to* transparency, but transparency does not lead to alignment. Alignment is a methodical *process*—a check-and-balance—for ensuring that thoughts, words, and actions consistently correlate with foundational beliefs. This process is essential for regularly assessing whether we're successfully living according to our beliefs, and what to focus on if we're not. Such an assessment should also include how we're doing in comparison with our personal quest. And it goes without saying that both our foundational beliefs and personal quest must be in clear support of God's Word. This process, when executed regularly and with integrity, is a key step toward abiding in Jesus. It produces a sort of moral compass that nudges us back to the path of righteousness when we invariably stray off course.

Transparency, on the other hand, relies not on a process or checklist, but on instinct and intuition. To be sustainable, transparency must be deeply ingrained, such that we *instinctively* exemplify what lies within, and *intuitively* know when we're not. People who are consistently transparent are those for whom living in truth is as natural as breathing. For them, transparency is not a cognizant effort, it's a way of life. But getting to that point doesn't come easy, nor is there any guarantee against backsliding. And that's where alignment once again enters the picture.

Merely *wishing* to be transparent—to live outwardly in perfect harmony with what lies inside—is typically wishful thinking. We may *think* that we can live transparently by simply willing ourselves to do so, but without an objective tool to assess how we're actually doing, we are likely to fail. And lest we forget, failure is not always characterized by *knowingly* coming up short versus a standard; oftentimes, it's what we *don't* know that causes us to fail. The underlying reason that I am such a proponent for systemic self-governance is that history has proven time and time again that our habits eventually, and essentially, become us. And that being the case, shouldn't our habits—our instinctive actions—reflect what we believe?

In May 1999, the state of Michigan changed the law mandating seat belt usage from "secondary" to "primary." Under the old law, the only time that a driver could be ticketed for not wearing a seat belt was when there was an associated moving violation. The new law, however, empowers police officers to issue tickets to people not wearing seat belts regardless of whether or not they've also committed a moving violation. The state's "click it or ticket" campaign that accompanied the new law worked: Michigan reported that seat belt usage rates rose from 70.1% in 1999 to 82.3% for 2001. Drivers who had never bothered putting on a seat belt in the past were forced to change their ways in order to avoid getting ticketed. Such an adjustment was no doubt inconvenient and challenging initially, yet highly attainable for those who *purposefully* and *methodically* reminded themselves to buckle up. It is quite likely that some people went so far as to leave themselves notes in their car reminding them to buckle up before driving. And it's equally likely that those who took such an approach found that their notes quickly gave way to ingrained habit and instinct. Whereas at one time they had to be methodical in order to buckle up, later they did it with nary a thought.

We become our habits. Alignment *systematically* moves us toward living according to our beliefs, which in turn leads to transparency being second nature.

The balance of this chapter focuses on the importance, challenges, and rewards of placing our heart squarely on our sleeve.

Is Transparency Really Important?

Many people claim to not care less about how others perceive them. In his signature song "*My Way*," Frank Sinatra sang of having lived life on his terms, which for him was a source of great pride. But if everybody lived according to his or her own "way," truth would no longer be seen as absolute or governing, but rather as whatever people wanted to make it; *My way may not be your way, but who's wrong if everybody's right?*

Unfortunately, this scenario is not rhetorical. Pervasive individualism has led to a greater western society that embraces pluralism: the belief that "reality" is comprised of a plurality of entities. Many people no longer view God as the source of absolute Truth, and fewer still view Jesus as *the Way*. Even some Christian churches now subscribe to this point-of-view. Indeed, "truth" is believed in many circles to be whatever each individual designates it to be.

What we are faced with at this time is a massive shortage of people who seek to live authentically. Most are quite content to find a safe harbor in our pluralistic society. And those harbors are everywhere to be found; specific groups cater to nearly every conceivable special interest. Yet even as more people than ever go off in search of a desirable, safe harbor, God's Word remains constant and, eternally speaking, the only truly *safe* harbor available. It is more imperative than ever that, in a world where "anything goes" and "truth" is ever changing, Christians lead by example and *outwardly* live according to God's Word.

Why do you suppose that so many people are exploring faiths and interests other than Christianity? It is basically a given that anyone who has experienced sustained spiritual fulfillment is not inclined to shop for other alternatives. And since *active* Christians claim to be genuinely fulfilled, one has to wonder why so many people who are spiritually "on the fence" seem to view Christianity with a degree of mistrust and, perhaps, disdain.

I am convinced that we ourselves are partially responsible for this situation. God's Word teaches us everything we need to know about how to live in godliness, but we are often so reckless in living according to His Word that we inadvertently discredit our faith in the process. We can (and must) take comfort knowing that grace is extended to all who confess Jesus Christ as Lord and Savior, but it does not give us a license to be aloof, smug, or indifferent to those who haven't yet discovered the Truth of Jesus Christ.

If we are to ever fill the Great Commission, as our Lord calls us to do, then we must take an honest, reflective look at the core of our being, essentially becoming transparent *to ourselves.* Doing so is the only way that we can truly provide honest answers to the difficult yet fundamental questions that surround our faith in Jesus: *What is it that I am called to do? What does it mean to be a Christian? Should I be content in knowing that my salvation is assured, even as I fail to bring others to Christ?*

When we take a long look in the mirror of our souls, most of us are forced to acknowledge that we are not doing enough to outwardly reflect our faith. Sadly, this lies in stark contrast to many followers of Islam, the second largest (and arguably fastest growing) religion in the world. *Generally* speaking, the average Muslim appears to be convicted in their faith such that he or she willingly lives subservient to it. To the Muslim, religious rules and regulations serve a higher purpose. And for many people who are spiritually undecided but searching earnestly for a source of spiritual fulfillment, Islam is attractive; its order and structure lie opposite to the boundless individual freedom that comes with societal pluralism. Indeed, because we are "wired" to seek order in the midst of chaos, nearly anyone who seeks a higher purpose in life will, at some point in time, gravitate toward order and structure. Most Christians would correctly point out that Islamic "order and structure" has been mandated by men and leads merely to compliance. Most would further point out that *Christian* "order and structure" comes directly from God's Word and leads not to compliance, but to sustained fulfillment and *eternal life.* But realistically, if a person doesn't yet know real Truth, then they must ascertain truth on their own; and regardless of what we know to be factual, if we fail to actively embody our convictions, non-believers will gravitate toward a more appealing, safer harbor.

How do others see you? Can they clearly see that you are so convicted in faith, and have such strong love for the Lord, that you visibly, outwardly reflect what's in your heart?

They certainly ought to. Knowing that your acceptance of Jesus Christ as Lord and Savior has assured you of eternal life ought to be all the reason you need to outwardly reflect your beliefs! You have been given the most precious gift imaginable: salvation. Share your gift with others. If you know that Jesus Christ is *the Way*, then you owe it to others to bring them to the same knowledge. Our Lord teaches us not to conceal our faith but to reveal it:

"And I say to you, everyone who confesses Me before men, the Son of Man will confess him also before the angels of God; but he who denies Me before men will be denied before the angels of God."

(Luke 12:8–9)

There is too much at stake to *not* heed Jesus' words. According to a "Status of Global Mission 1997" study by Justin D. Long, the number of active Christians—that is, Christians who are committed and active in the Great Commission—is around 759 million. Yet the study estimates the *total* number of Christians in the world to be just shy of 2 billion. When factoring in that the world's population is estimated to be around 6 billion, it is rather apparent that we Christians *must* make our presence felt. We account for around one-third of the world's population, yet most of us are not actively engaged in what we are called to do. How will the other 4 billion people come to know Truth?

Many people are searching—knowingly or unknowingly—for some semblance of truth and meaning in a world dominated by deception and frivolity. According to Adherents.com, a web site devoted to tracking religious movements and demographics across the globe, there are currently over 4,200 religions, churches, denominations, religious bodies, faith groups, tribes, cultures, movements, ultimate concerns, etc. throughout the world.

Yet even though there are a lot of faith options on the menu these days, our Lord calls us to bring all people to just one—the Truth:

"Go therefore and make disciples of all the nations, baptizing them in the name of the Father and the Son and the Holy Spirit . . ."

(Matthew 28:19)

Every Christian must determine how much time and effort to expend carrying out the Great Commission. The playing field is decidedly not level—we all face different constraints and limitations, and have been gifted with unique skills and abilities. Nevertheless, in spite of our differences, our common focus should never be on why we *can't* bring others to Christ, but on how we *can*. And never underestimate that even when not *purposefully* bringing Truth to others, if what we say, do, and think are synchronous with what we believe in our hearts, and if what we believe in our hearts is that Jesus *is Lord*, then we actively bring others toward Truth. Indeed, the best way to ensure that non-believers don't continue to grope their way through darkness is to light the path for them. Jesus is *the* safe harbor that all people must find, and His disciples must point the way. Let our words and actions correlate perfectly with our beliefs such that we never give others a legitimate *basis* to speculate about what we believe, for the manifestation thereof ought to be unmistakable.

And let us remember that to believe in Jesus is to love Jesus, and that to truly love our Lord we must also love one another. Is there any better way to love than to consistently embody the *source* of love?

The title of this section asked whether transparency is important. Clearly, it is. But beyond mere importance, transparency is *essential*.

Rewards Come Through Transparency

When others casually ask how you're doing, does your reply tend to be quick and automatic? Perhaps you answer something like this: *"Fine. How about yourself?"*

Even on really bad days, when nothing seems to go right, our common tendency when asked how we are doing is to say that we're fine. We may occasionally regret not being as forthright with people as we should be, but most of us consider our "programmed" responses to be neither *intentionally* deceitful nor flat out lies. But what does Scripture say about such an approach?

> *Better is a poor man who walks in his integrity than he who is perverse in speech and is a fool.*
>
> *(Proverbs 19:1)*

Proverbs 19:1 teaches us to consider integrity essential for godly living. A synonym for *integrity* is *honesty;* Merriam-Webster's on-line dictionary defines *honesty* as "adherence to the facts." Armed with this information, one can only conclude that *any* untruth is a lie. Even little lies, the sort that we often don't even recognize or acknowledge, restrict us from living transparently, and therefore keep us from realizing genuine spiritual fulfillment.

Think back to when you were a child. Can you recall a time when you told a "little" lie that led to a full-blown crisis?

I certainly can—on many occasions! A typical scenario in the house I grew up in went like this:

Dad: "Which one of you kids threw a pool table ball through the downstairs paneling?"
Sister Denise: "Not me."
Brother Tom: "Not me."
Yours truly: "Umm . . . uhh . . . umm . . . not me."
Dad: "Well if nobody is willing to tell the truth, then you're all grounded until somebody does!"

What an awful, sinking feeling to know that you have backed yourself into a corner! Telling the truth right up front would have been difficult but tolerable, but having to confess after initially lying is much worse, not to mention extremely embarrassing. My father always told us that he could tolerate a lot of things, but lying was not one of them. And I knew that, yet I still lied. Why?

Uncertainty . . . rationalization . . . *lying.* It's that simple. When anticipating an undesirable reaction to telling the truth, we instinctively begin to feel less certain about what we ought to do. Even though we know that we should be truthful, if we let uncertainty hang around long enough, the probability of rationalizing our pending lie as a viable option is dramatically increased.

This sequence of events is not limited to children—adults routinely fall into it as well. A manager gives an underachieving subordinate a favorable review because he doesn't wish to deal with the subordinate's negative reaction. A husband calls his wife to tell her that he will be working late, then makes a beeline for the local sports bar. A mother tells her children that she's "too tired" to take them to the park, when in fact she simply wants to stay home. Even little lies have significant consequences. In order for a person to be trusted, he must first be *trustworthy;* and after a person has lied, trustworthiness is difficult to regain.

For anyone with a conscience, living with lies is like being imprisoned. Until we repent and live in integrity (truth), we cannot be fully liberated from the chains that bind us. Some of the most miserable people on earth are those who are hiding something. How does one escape from imprisonment?

". . . and you will know the truth, and the truth will make you free."
(John 8:32)

Transparency

Living transparently is all about living truthfully. No facades. No hidden agendas. No skeletons in the closet. *What you see is what you get.*

And what you "get" when living in truth is liberation. The shackles come off and we are no longer slaves to uncertainty and rationalization. Genuine freedom comes about through transparency, and transparency is all about living according to the truth of one's convictions.

Beyond personal liberation after being freed of lies, transparency greatly enhances one's ability to love others. Think of it this way: if we are *not* living transparently, we are living hypocritically. There is little gray area; either we are living according to truth or we are living according to lies. And without a doubt, our ability to love others is very much contingent on how we ourselves live. When teaching a child about the dangers of smoking cigarettes, a father who himself is a smoker has considerably less credibility than a father who doesn't smoke; what's more, the father who smokes *knows* deep down that what he says is not completely credible. But the father who doesn't smoke is able to parlay his concerns to his son or daughter in absolutely credible fashion.

The example above is not intended in any way to indict smokers, but rather to illustrate how the *purity* of conveying a simple message is greatly enhanced when we live according to the words we impart. When we are liberated from lies and deception, hypocrisy is replaced with transparency, which is essential for loving others:

> *Let love be without hypocrisy. Abhor what is evil; cling to what is good.*
> *(Romans 12:9)*

I would be greatly remiss if I failed to mention that the most significant reward for living transparently is persecution for the sake of righteousness. We *honor* our Lord when we exemplify our faith in Him. But more than that, we invariably draw closer to Jesus when we make our faith in Him transparent to others. Even during difficult circumstances, we are abundantly blessed when persecuted for having spoken or acted on behalf of Jesus' saving Truth:

> *"Blessed are those who have been persecuted for the sake of righteousness, for theirs is the kingdom of heaven. Blessed are you when people insult you and persecute you, and falsely say all kinds of evil against you*

because of Me. Rejoice and be glad, for your reward in heaven is great; for in the same way they persecuted the prophets who were before you."
(Matthew 5:10–12)

Recognizing and Dealing with Challenges to Transparency

It was mentioned earlier that uncertainty leads to rationalization, which in turn leads to lying. This scenario is all too common, and easy to fall prey to; I would venture to say that we *all* succumb to lies much more often than we realize or care to acknowledge. Indeed, how are we to overcome the hypocrisy that comes through lies and deception?

The first step is the most important of all: acknowledging our fallibility. I am convinced that what keeps most Christians from living transparently are inadvertent lapses into a sort of spiritual stupor wherein the reality of being fallible is greatly obscured. We must *vigilantly* bear in mind that *nobody* is immune from temptation, deception, and lies. The sooner we ingrain that fact in our minds the better, for it has led to many Christians losing sight of right and wrong. Regular study of God's Word is the single best way to remain properly grounded in Truth, followed in short order by active participation in church, fellowship, and other Christian endeavors that help to keep us humble and properly oriented toward godliness.

After acknowledging that we are fallible, it is important to recognize that we *will* fall. Fallibility is not theory—it is reality. The only variables are *how* and *when*—not *if*. And even though vigilance will help considerably, there will inevitably be times when we will fail to outwardly embody what lies within our hearts.

That's where repentance and redemption enter the picture. Jesus' death on the cross and ascension into heaven provides us with grace such that we can overcome our sins.

It is important to remember that we can always rely on grace to pull us through. When we get down on ourselves, all we need to do is ask Jesus for forgiveness and redemption. The Lord never forsakes us, and counts us as worthy even when we don't:

"Are not five sparrows sold for two cents? Yet not one of them is forgotten before God. Indeed, the very hairs of your head are all numbered. Do not fear; you are

more valuable than many sparrows. And I say to you, everyone who confesses Me before men, the Son of Man will confess him also before the angels of God."
(*Luke 12:6–8*)

Transparency is difficult, yet its rewards are infinite and eternal. Seek alignment between thoughts, words, and deeds versus your innermost beliefs, and you will soon live transparently without even being cognizant of it. And when you fall off the path of righteousness, as you invariably will, seek forgiveness and restoration from the Lord, for His purpose is clear:

"I have come as Light into the world, so that everyone who believes in Me will not remain in darkness."
(*John 12:46*)

Choose Light.

Courage before Transparency

The prospect of arriving a few minutes late for my appointment didn't bother me; after all, I was about to spend two full days with a Leadership "coach," taking part in something called a Leadership "summit." Indeed, I could definitely afford to be late for this one.

I didn't know what to expect; I was told to go to a place called *Courageous Leadership, Inc.*, where I would spend two days with a guy with a funny name who would help me to find my "authentic self." This held only slightly more appeal than getting a root canal.

After arriving, I exchanged pleasantries with CLI president and founder (and leadership coach) Lamont Moon (yes, the guy with the funny name). Lamont explained that for the summit to be of value I would need to be completely honest and open. My thoughtless reply to his comments effectively captured a 37-year history of *claiming* to live transparently: "Of course," I said, "I'm here to gain the maximum benefit from whatever it is we're here to do. I won't hold back."

Less than thirty minutes later, I began to feel considerably less confident. Lamont had told me that to grow into the person I *could* be, I would have to surface and grapple with what lay deep within. But I didn't anticipate exploring the absolute depth of my love for self and other loved ones. Or talking openly about key events that profoundly affected me. Or being taken to task for not looking Lamont in the eye when addressing a key point (how could I have anticipated his reaction when I myself was unaware I was hiding something?).

The Leadership Summit, combined with a year of personal coaching afterwards, was a watershed moment for me. I learned much about myself, including many things that I *needed* (and need) to deal with in order to be all that God created me to be. What did I learn? That I allowed personal insecurity to paralyze me on occasion; that I denied myself fulfillment that comes through embracing and employing God-given talents; that "leadership" is so much more than most of us think it is; and that *genuine* transparency is not selective, it is all-inclusive.

My life was forever altered On February 12–13, 2001. Lamont and his associate Ty helped bring the "real" me to the surface and to consistently embody what I most ardently believe. In other words, they taught me what it meant to live transparently. Am I a better leader? Yes! But more importantly, I'm a better disciple.

One final note: while this book was written because I chose to heed God's will, I must also tell you that without God first leading me to Lamont, not one word would have made its way to these pages.

Uniqueness

Although *uniqueness* is a necessary ingredient for optimal spiritual fulfillment, it may appear, at least on the surface, to actually *oppose* godliness. And as *any* opposition to godliness precludes genuine spiritual fulfillment, prior to espousing the value of uniqueness it is necessary to make a *case* for uniqueness—to show that uniqueness is a contributor, rather than an inhibitor, to genuine spiritual fulfillment.

Biblical Uniqueness Leads to Spiritual Fulfillment

Uniqueness merely for the sake of uniqueness holds no value. But when a strong desire for godliness leads a person to become truly unique—authentically unique—there is significant (and eternal) value. Indeed, as godliness must always govern uniqueness, we shall begin our "case" for uniqueness by focusing first on godliness.

There are numerous passages in Scripture indicating that we are to strive for godliness. While the notion of striving for godliness may appear to be elementary (perhaps even rudimentary), for sold-out, convicted Christians it is downright *radical*. Other religions pay homage to distant, abstract gods, effectively limiting them from *embodying* anything *except* conceptualism, but Christians worship the Son of God, who is One with the Father, and who is absolutely concrete. Simply put, God has gifted us with the perfect role model:

His only begotten Son, who was perfect in every way, even in humanity. Thus, as the godliness we are to strive for has already been modeled by Jesus, all we have to do is strive to live as Jesus did, for His earthly life *is* the very definition of godliness. The "WWJD" (What Would Jesus Do?) bracelets that became popular a few years ago effectively capture that godliness, contrary to being ambiguous, is absolutely *specific,* and can serve as a spiritual filter to help ensure that what we think, do, and say embodies our discipleship in Jesus Christ. While both the Old Testament and New Testament Scriptures *teach* us how to live, Jesus *demonstrates* how to live. Furthermore, when you ask Jesus for help to live as He did, He will strengthen your faith, commitment, and resolve as never before. Rededicate yourself to godliness each day by asking Jesus for forgiveness and inner strength; and emulate Jesus—study and learn how He extended grace and humbly served others; how He interacted with all people (even those who were shunned by society); and how He always sought to do God's will. While none of us can ever live a pure life as our Lord did, we can (and must) strive to live according to His example.

Having now established that Scripture would have us strive for godliness, and that Jesus is the Living Model for our pursuit thereof, the next consideration for arguing that uniqueness is essential for godliness (and by extension genuine spiritual fulfillment), is the authenticity of Scripture itself. This is a difficult task in that deeply rooted *faith,* by and in itself, is requisite for maintaining an absolute and unwavering belief in the authenticity of Scripture. If a person claims to believe in Jesus, yet is not *completely convicted* in his belief, then he is certain—often unknowingly—to question the legitimacy of Scripture. He will *inevitably* subscribe only to Bible verses that he naturally agrees with, while either discarding or disregarding verses that he disagrees with. His faith in Scripture is similar to the faith I place in my present employer: although I disagree with our top management on a few specific issues, in general I am very much in concurrence with how our leaders are managing our company. I have faith in my employer . . . but it's not absolute. And while I can (and should) take a cautious *long-term* approach to my employer, I cannot afford to take the same approach with my faith. It is okay for me to develop and grow in faith, but it must be accompanied by a continuous evolution toward being convicted in it, essentially bringing my faith to an immovable state (which is precisely where it's been for the past several years). The primary basis for my belief in the authenticity of Scripture is its infallibility. God's Word is indisputable, indispensable, and perfectly logical. Indeed, to believe in anything *other* than Scripture as the source of absolute Truth is to place subjectivity ahead of objectivity, and frivolity ahead of logic. There are thousands of factual Christian books that dedicate hundreds of pages to *effectively* debunking evolution, naturalism, and other manmade religions and theories, yet none are as effective as Scripture itself. The Word—God's Word—is pure, and when we allow its purity to consume us, it becomes us.

Thus, it is only proper to allow Scripture itself to formulate the remainder of the argument for its authenticity. God calls us to live "*not by bread alone,*" but "*by everything that proceeds out of the mouth of the Lord*" (ref. Deuteronomy 8:3). And as "*all scripture is inspired by God*" (ref. 2 Timothy 3:16), it becomes clear that godliness and an unwavering belief in the authenticity of Scripture go hand-in-hand. And finally, as Scripture *is* God's Word (the word "*inspired*" literally means "*God-breathed*"), and as God calls us to be godly, we must live according to the *totality* of Scripture.

I believe that we can now comfortably claim that godliness—striving to live as Jesus did—requires one to willingly be *governed* by its Source. Not influenced by its Source—governed by its Source. Having advanced our case to this point, we can now return to the core issue of whether *uniqueness* is a contributor or inhibitor to spiritual fulfillment; or, to ask the same question in a slightly different manner, "is uniqueness *ungodly?*"

Our answer depends on whether we approach the question from a human perspective, or from a Biblical perspective. The prevailing point-of-view held by secular society is that uniqueness is tied *strictly* to individuality, and that individuality is essentially freedom. This point-of-view could not be further from the truth! I am absolutely convinced that there is a *direct* relationship between *ungoverned* (by God) individual freedom, and individual and societal deterioration. In fact, in terms of societal deterioration, I would go so far as to claim that, excluding "natural" disasters and the like, *all* of the problems that plague us as a greater society are borne out of individualism (selfishness). Sexual "freedom" has led to rampant divorce and legalized abortion, and, in general, the "nuclear" family being an endangered species. Spiritual "freedom" has led us to celebrate personal *enlightenment* while minimizing the importance of the Christian Church (*who needs a church if I'm a church unto myself?*). And intellectual "freedom" has led to our schools teaching Darwin's fatally flawed theory of evolution—as opposed to creationism, which is the only *logical* answer for the origins of both humankind and the world we occupy. When we place our will ahead of God's, the result is predictable and unavoidable: decay.

Uniqueness from a Biblical perspective differs dramatically with uniqueness from a human perspective. Biblical uniqueness produces not decay, but personal and spiritual *growth*. There is nothing more fulfilling—and nothing more unique—than striving to become what God created you for. Those who strive for such a prize are few in number yet voluminous in impact, and are in fact the *only* unique people in the world. Did you catch that? People who submit their will to God's will—in totality, and in absolute faith—seek to become what God created them for, making them the *only* unique people in the world. Their brand of uniqueness runs absolutely counter to what the world considers "unique," which is precisely why Christians who are actively engaged in the Great Commission are the only people who can legitimately claim to be unique.

Don't believe me yet? Listen to the definitions for *uniqueness,* as given by Merriam-Webster: *"Being the only one"*; *"Being without a like or equal"*; *"Distinctively characteristic"*; *"Unusual."*

Now take note of the uncanny similarities between Webster's definition for uniqueness, and God's Word:

> *"Say to the Israelites, 'You must observe my Sabbaths. This will be a sign between me and you for the generations to come, so you may know that I am the Lord, who sets you apart as holy."*
>
> *(Deuteronomy 31:13)*

> *"You are to be holy to me because I, the Lord, am holy, and I have set you apart from the nations to be my own."*
>
> *(Leviticus 20:26)*

> *"In this way you are to set the Levites apart from the other Israelites, and the Levites will be mine."*
>
> *(Numbers 8:14)*

> *At that time the Lord set apart the tribe of Levi to carry the Ark of the Covenant of the Lord, to stand before the Lord to minister and to pronounce blessings in his name, as they still do today.*
>
> *(Deuteronomy 10:8)*

"They are not of the world, even as I am not of it. Sanctify them by the truth; your word is truth."

(John 17:16–17)

Shall I go on? There are forty-three verses in Scripture where the words "set apart" are used! Moreover, the Greek word for *sanctify* is "*Hagiazo*," which means "*dedicated to God, consecrated to God, set apart for God—Exclusively His, pure, sinless or upright.*" In other words, when Jesus asks God to sanctify His followers (Ref John 17:17), He is asking God to set them apart *as His own*.

To live for God is to be set apart by God. This simple yet profound fact extends well beyond uniqueness and into a whole new stratosphere. Yet that is precisely the difference between being "unique" in an earthly sense, and being unique in a Biblical sense. How feeble minded we are when seeing uniqueness as the rest of the world does! In the absence of godliness, there is nothing unique about a person covered head to toe with tattoos, or living alone in the mountains, or running a Fortune 500 company, or even methodically attending church each Sunday. But when godliness is at the core—that is, when a person has unabashed love for and unwavering faith in the Lord, and consistently strives to live according to what God has decreed—then she has been set apart by God.

In contrast to how the world views uniqueness, the truth is that *anybody* who purposefully places their will ahead of God's is not unique, but a *conformist*. Rock-and-roll "rebels" who reject God's Word are not rebellious, they are conformists. "New age" thinkers who reject God's Word are not intellectual or open-minded, they are conformists and closed-minded. "Driven" executives who reject God's Word are driven only by selfish ambition, not by a meaningful higher purpose. They too are conformists. And "faithful" people who attend church but fail to embody the Source of *The Church* are not faithful to Christ, they are faithful to religion. They too are conformists, for just as Jesus admonished the Pharisees for being "religious" and hypocritical at the same time, so too are those who revel in religious tradition while lacking passion for Jesus. The bottom line is that anyone who sees "uniqueness" through the eyes of the world is a conformist. Unless you are Biblically unique—set apart by God—you are not unique.

We Must Choose Which Standard to Live By

We must decide between worldly "uniqueness" (conformance), and Biblical uniqueness (to be set apart by God). We cannot have it both ways—we are either for Jesus, or we are against Him.

> *And do not be conformed to this world, but be transformed by the renewing of your mind, so that you may prove what the will of God is, that which is good and acceptable and perfect.*
>
> *(Romans 12:2)*

Even those of us who have conscientiously submitted our will to Jesus struggle with the "either-or" nature of uniqueness. In truth, although Scripture paints uniqueness in black and white "colors" (either you belong to Jesus or you belong to the world), we do our best to inject some gray into the picture. I believe that the majority of Christians have, knowingly or unknowingly, adopted *both* interpretations of uniqueness, *believing* in God's Word while not willing to be *governed* by it. To clarify, "passive" Christians are much more comfortable thinking of Scripture as a set of *guidelines* than as the Source of absolute Truth. Yet because the world and the kingdom are diametrically opposed (until Jesus returns), there cannot be multiple standards for uniqueness. There can be only one standard, that which is given in Scripture.

Allow me to illustrate *why* Christians struggle with this. Imagine that you have just turned five years old and are preparing to enter Kindergarten. Far from dreading the prospect of thirteen years of arduous study, you are unabashedly excited at what lies ahead. And so you show up for the first day of school, eagerly anticipating what comes next, when your teacher begins passing out a rather large book to each student. Your excitement quickly gives way to bewilderment as your teacher tells you that everything you need to learn in life is contained in this one book. You think, *"How can that be? There must be some kind of mistake. I may not know a lot of things yet, but I know this much: there are, umm—what's that word?—Oh yeah, <u>millions</u>, yes millions, of books to read, so if this one book gives me all the answers, then why do we need all these other books?"* And so you must make a decision: do you obey your teacher and study the book that you have been given, or do you satisfy your intellectual curiosity by reading all of the other books?

This illustration may be a bit elementary (pun intended), but I believe it closely parallels the choice made by Adam and Eve. Throughout the history of humankind, we have repeatedly demonstrated that we prefer what we want to what God wants for us. Indeed, our strong tendency is to act on curiosity, even when it is unhealthy. For that reason, and to whatever extent possible, we need to draw the line between healthy intellectual pursuits and an unhealthy indulgence in false teachings. Be careful to not stray far from Truth.

Incidentally, prior to solidifying your faith in Jesus Christ, it is perfectly natural, and not unhealthy, to search for truth. And it is not easy for us to accept that Truth is found within one Book. Our sinful, selfish human nature is to either reject the Bible as Truth, or, more commonly for many Christians, to see it not as *the* Source of Truth, but as *a* source of truth. There is a world of difference between the two perspectives—viewing the Bible as the Source of absolute Truth is to see the world with clarity; viewing the Bible as a source of truth is to replace or supplement God's Word with what we want. It is a never-ending struggle, even for the most ardent believers, to accept that Biblical Truth and worldly interpretations of "truth" are in opposition.

A Higher Purpose

For sports fans like myself, the 2001 major league baseball season was a memorable one. The Arizona Diamondbacks edged the New York Yankees in a thrilling seven-game series; Sammy Sosa hit over sixty homeruns for the third year in a row (an unprecedented feat); and Barry Bonds shattered the single season record for homeruns by hitting 73 "dingers." But I believe that the most remarkable achievement during the 2001 baseball season came not from the World Series winner, nor from any individual player, but from the Seattle Mariners. By winning 116 games, the Mariners tied a record held previously by the 1906 Chicago Cubs for most wins in a single season. It was an achievement of epic proportions, one that if viewed objectively easily eclipses the significance of the plethora of homeruns by Sammy Sosa and Barry Bonds. Baseball has seen an upward trend in homeruns for many years, and while both Sosa and Bonds deserve much credit for their on-field accomplishments, when viewed in the context of statistical trends, their exploits are not all that surprising. While recognizing that the number of games played was only 152 in 1906, the fact remains that since 1961 when baseball went to a 162-game schedule, no team had won as many as 116 games. Even when viewing the Mariners accomplishment strictly in the context of the past forty years, the fact is that *no team* had won that many games, while over a thousand teams (by single season) had a chance to do so. Unique? Indeed!

Why do I bring this up? Because most fans associate the Mariners 2001 season with failure as opposed to success. After winning 116 games during the regular season, the Mariners lost to the Yankees in the second round of the playoffs. And in our culture, when it comes to sports, unless you're the last team left standing, you're branded as a loser. Yet even that doesn't tell the whole story. Barry Bonds, playing on a team that failed to make the playoffs, was the most celebrated player in all of baseball last year, because he set an *individual* record while playing a team sport. (To his credit, Bonds didn't ask to be placed on a pedestal, but he had no choice).

Can you see how flawed our thinking is in comparison to what Scripture teaches us? Our tendency is to celebrate individuals, in all walks of life, while quickly discarding larger groups that quietly excel, even though they may come up short at times. In this case, a team that overcame the loss of high-profile superstars Randy Johnson and Alex Rodriguez did something that no other team had ever accomplished, yet were actually ridiculed by some for not winning the World Series.

The same thing happens to those who strive for godliness. Even after a long, sustained period of living for Jesus, when we stumble (as we inevitably will), we will be criticized by others, including some within the church. We may be labeled as hypocrites, closed-minded, elitists, and worse. Yet it is through one another—through the *team* of Christians that we are a part of—that we can best deal with such adversity. Just as every member of the 2001 Seattle Mariners was unique simply for being part of something more important than themselves as individuals, so are we unique when we understand that being a contributing member of the Church of Jesus Christ *sets us apart.* We may be criticized at times, but we must remain steadfast in our commitment to other Christians, and to living according to what Scripture teaches us.

Neither uniqueness nor greatness is about individual accomplishments—both are about becoming the person God made you to be so that you can optimally contribute to bringing Truth to all people in all nations.

On Pentecost during the first days of the Church, a large international, intercultural group of Believers came together. They came from Parthians, Medes, Elamites, Mesopotamia, Judea, Cappadocia, Pontus, Asia, Phrygia, Pamphylia, Egypt, parts of Libya near Cyrene, and Rome. There were both Jews and converts to Judaism, Cretans and Arabs. Their uniqueness did not lie in their individuality, but in the fact that they were willing to *set aside* individuality for a higher cause, even as some ridiculed them for doing so:

All of them were filled with the Holy Spirit and began to speak in other tongues as the Spirit enabled them. When they heard this sound, a crowd came together in bewilderment, because each one heard them speaking in his own language. Amazed and perplexed, they asked one another, "What does this mean?" Some, however, made fun of them and said, "They have had too much wine."

(Acts 2:4, 6, 12–13).

Uniqueness = Authenticity

Former professional basketball player A.C. Green is truly a unique person. By living each day for Christ in an environment where temptation, hero worship, and self-centricity normally prevail, Green stands apart. The "A.C." in his name stands for *"Abstinence Committed"* . . . A.C. Green is a virgin.

A 38-year old virgin? A 38-year old virgin who recently retired after playing sixteen seasons in the NBA? *Yes.* When Green accepted Jesus Christ as his personal Lord and Savior, he did so with *absolute* acceptance. He could not, in good conscience, circumvent God's Word and God's will by taking a thoughtless, spiritless approach to sex. Indeed, while Green does not lead a life of abstinence simply for the sake thereof (he strongly desires to marry and have children), he is an inspiration to people everywhere, and particularly to young people who feel pressured by the world around them into having premarital sex. Where does A.C. Green find the strength to avoid acting on sexual desires and temptation?

Through believing in the totality of Scripture, and through having the conviction to live according to it. Green has no choice but to deny himself, for doing otherwise would detract from *authenticity* through living for Jesus Christ.

One of Merriam-Webster's definitions for *authentic* is *"Conforming to an original so as to reproduce essential features."* As "authenticity" applies to Christianity, its definition is absolutely straightforward: *conform to Christ in order to reproduce His essence.*

In December 1999, *Sports Illustrated* sent columnist Rick Reilly to do a piece on A.C. Green. Green admitted to feeling sexual temptation, but also said that Christian friends help keep him accountable to godliness. More than that, for many years Green has set aside the first part of his day to be spent in quiet time with God. And Green doesn't simply read the Word, he seeks to *memorize* it; after all, it is easier to live by the Word if it's etched upon your mind. But that's not all Green has done; he has made a binding promise to God, one that continually sustains and protects him against temptation. Green explained his vow of abstinence to Reilly:

> *"I promised God this, and I'm not going to break it. I love myself and my future wife too much to just waste it."*

Jesus experienced worldly temptation yet never sinned due to unwavering and absolute trust in the Father, enhanced by understanding and memorizing Scripture, and by unflinchingly fulfilling His destiny (God's will): self-sacrifice in order to save all others.

As being unique is to be authentic, and as an authentic Christian is one who conforms to Christ in order to reproduce His essence, it is apparent that A.C. Green qualifies as unique. Green feels temptation just like everyone else does, but denies himself through the help of fellow Christians, daily quiet time with God wherein he memorizes Scripture, and a promise to God. And Green has abundant love for self and others. By making the decision to emulate Christ, A.C. Green has successfully reproduced Christ-like qualities within his own being. And that is unique!

Becoming Unique

The secret to developing into a truly unique person is to surrender your will to Jesus. There are no new age theories or concepts to learn, no advanced technologies to leverage, and no independent, personal "statements" to make that will lead you to uniqueness. The *only* path to uniqueness is to submit your will, in its entirety, to Jesus.

> *But we have this treasure in earthenware vessels to show that this all-surpassing greatness of the power will be of God and not from ourselves.*
> (*2 Corinthians 4:7*)

The "treasure" that Paul refers to is our Lord Jesus Christ. When we make Him the center of our lives, great things will happen. Not through what we do, but through what He does within us. If you desire uniqueness, then choose authenticity: choose Jesus.

Night and Day

When I was sixteen years old, I began working in a restaurant as a Dishwasher. The restaurant had only recently opened, and all the employees were expeditiously learning how to do their jobs. Well, all except one: our chef, Roy.

Roy was experienced, confident, arrogant, and, oftentimes, abusive. I knew I didn't like Roy as soon as I met him, and I wondered what made him so bitter. But I never bothered to ask him.

One Monday, seemingly out of the clear blue, Roy walked into work a changed man. He told anyone and everyone within earshot that he had been "saved" during the previous weekend. All day long, Roy stated—loudly at times—that he had seen the light, and that he was reborn as a disciple of Jesus Christ. I heard later that Roy had somehow been coerced into attending a prayer meeting, and that he had been overwhelmed by the folly of his ways, and the free offer of salvation through Jesus Christ.

Most of the employees initially welcomed the "new" Roy. Aside from perpetually smiling, humming hymns, and giving glory to God, Roy was now approachable, amiable, and helpful. He was noticeably different, and a whole lot easier to like.

But what happened next was inevitable. When it became apparent that Roy had permanently nailed *all* of his old self to the cross, he was quickly scorned and ridiculed by most employees. They would talk about how the "old" Roy was short-tempered and mean-spirited, but at least the old Roy could appreciate dirty jokes and petty gossip. And they would derisively point out that all the new Roy did was sing hymns and praise God, and that he was no longer one of "them." Yes, they had desired that Roy change for the better, but this was not what they had in mind.

Yet in the face of persecution, Roy never wavered, drawing strength from Scripture:

"That is why, for Christ's sake, I delight in weaknesses, in insults, in hardships, in persecutions, in difficulties. For when I am weak, then I am strong."

(2 Corinthians 12:10)

At that time in my life, I was a neutral Christian. And while I didn't join others in mocking Roy, I didn't seek him out either. If I had, it wouldn't have taken me as long to discover what Roy already knew:

Uniqueness = Authenticity = Godliness = Fulfillment = Eternal life.

Venturousness

A Parable: Fear, Faith, and a Mountain

There was an honorable man who on his thirty-eighth birthday took stock of his life. The man realized that he had been blessed, for he was happily married with two wonderful children, financially stable, and highly appreciative of the finer things in life, namely peace, tranquility, and fulfillment. Beyond his earthly blessings, the man was assured *eternal life,* for many years before it had been offered to him in exchange for . . . for nothing! It was free, and it was binding, and all the man did was choose to accept the Gift.

The man recalled how in the years following his initial acceptance of the Gift, he often failed to properly acknowledge the Giver of the Gift. Indeed, the man had everything he needed to remain thankful and joyous, yet became very complacent very quickly.

And in truth, the man had good *reason* to feel complacent, for his earthly life was good and his eternal life assured. Still, the man felt that something was missing, though he wasn't sure what. The man believed this to be rather odd, considering that over the previous three years he had come to know and appreciate the Giver of the Gift as never before, developing an increasingly fulfilling personal relationship with Him. But even as the man felt a heightened sense of spiritual fulfillment, he could not shake the feeling that, perhaps, fulfillment could be even greater if only he could uncover what was missing in his life.

In the months that followed, the man continued to wonder why, during a time in life when he was truly able to appreciate his good fortune, something would be missing. The man needed to know—he *had* to know—and thus began pursuing the only option that would enable him to discover what was missing in his life. And so he began to visit the Giver of the Gift with even greater regularity and purpose.

Thus it happened, after visiting the Giver of the Gift for many months, that the man finally discovered what was missing in his life. *He needed a mountain to climb!* This simple fact was abundantly clear to him after he had ascertained it, yet it had never dawned on him until he *actively* sought out the Giver of the Gift. Yes, he would climb a mountain, and finally, once-and-for-all, he would replace complacency with an even deeper sense of fulfillment than he had already experienced. Hardly able to contain himself, the man felt ready to begin climbing.

With great enthusiasm, the man visited the Giver of the Gift and told Him about his amazing discovery. The Giver of the Gift knowingly smiled, then told the man exactly which mountain he was to climb.

Contemplating the journey that lay ahead, the man was nearly bursting with anticipation. But anticipation quickly gave way to doubt, for as he moved closer and closer to the mountain, the man realized that he could not possibly climb it. The man was so daunted by the size of the mountain that he could not take the first step.

Within a few weeks the man began to doubt whether the Giver of the Gift had really intended for him to climb that *particular* mountain. Exasperated, the man approached the Giver of the Gift, saying "My Lord, You convinced me that I could climb this mountain, but as I moved closer to it, I have found it to be too large. Perhaps my mountain lies elsewhere?"

The Giver of the Gift replied, "My son, I have already revealed to you the mountain you are to climb. All that awaits is for you to take the first step."

Instinctively—and impatiently—the man answered, "Lord, this *cannot* be my mountain. I will know the mountain I am to climb when I see it, and this is not it. I . . . I can't quite explain *how* I'll know which mountain I am to climb—I'll just know. But one thing I am absolutely certain of is that this mountain is not intended for me."

The Giver of the Gift quickly responded, saying "My beloved child, I feel your frustration and it saddens me. But remember this: When I gave you eternal life, I asked nothing in return. Even now, I ask nothing in return. Yet I am offering you miraculous joy and fulfillment, if only you will have faith in Me. I have already shown you the mountain you are to climb, but I cannot take the first step for you, nor can I make you take it. Only you can decide to place absolute faith in Me. Truly, I tell you, My Word is My Bond; just as I promised you eternal life, so do I now promise you, if only you will take the first step, that I will carry you up your mountain. My son, you have nothing to fear yet fear consumes you. Yes, even now fear is preventing you from climbing your mountain."

The man was more befuddled than ever: *Fear is preventing me from climbing my mountain?*

The man had no choice but to inquire further: "My Lord, how can you tell me to take the first step when You know that I lack proper knowledge and tools to climb a mountain such as this? Can you not see that I am ill equipped? I have never climbed a mountain even half this size, and if I attempt to climb this mountain I will most certainly—and quickly—fall over the edge!"

Ever patiently, The Giver of the Gift told the man, "Beloved child, again I tell you, if you take the first step I will carry you the rest of the way. Yet you are right to say that you lack the knowledge and tools to climb this mountain. Still, I tell you the truth, it is not a lack of knowledge or tools that prevents you from climbing the mountain; it is fear that holds you back. Why do you continue to consume yourself with the size of the mountain rather than the beauty of the mountain?"

Upon hearing this, the man was momentarily speechless. After a few moments, he gathered his thoughts, saying, "My Lord, I do not understand how You can tell me to appreciate the beauty of the mountain when I can scarcely see it! The enormity of the mountain eclipses any 'beauty' it might contain! Lord, You must see how big this mountain is? How can I even begin to . . . to . . ."

Unable to complete his question, the man let out a heavy sigh. Several deep breaths followed as he contemplated the second most important decision of his life. Finally, after what felt like an eternity to him, the man once again addressed the Giver of the Gift:

"Okay. Okay. I will take the first step up the mountain. You have told me which mountain I am to climb, and climb it I shall. I am not exactly sure what will happen after the first step, but I know that You will be there for me, just as You have promised."

The man took yet another deep breath, then slowly, slowly, placed his right foot above his left. He had taken the first step! Immediately, he felt an undeniable sense of relief intertwined with renewed purpose; *I can do this . . . I can <u>do</u> this!* And at that moment, as the man looked up the mountain to see what lie ahead, he made the most incredible discovery of his life:

The mountain appeared to be—no, it was most definitely—shrinking!

With his eyes stinging from effervescent tears of joy, the man attempted to make sense of what he had just witnessed. Yet he could not, for he had previously seen the mountain with his own eyes, and it was not scaleable.

Knowing that the answer could only come from the Giver of the Gift, the man went to Him, asking, "How did You make the mountain shrink after I first stepped foot on it? Is that what You meant when You said You would carry me?"

The Giver of the Gift smiled gently and replied, "My son, I did not make the mountain shrink; you did. All mountains are merely footstools to Me. But as for you, when you replaced fear with faith, you saw the mountain as it truly is. I told you that fear is what held you back, and I tell you now that what overcomes fear is faith, and that faith comes about through obedience, prayer, and the study of My Word. Yes, I will carry you up this mountain, just as I have carried you up other mountains you never knew existed. But be on guard, for if you try to climb the mountain without Me, the mountain will once again be insurmountable; however, if your belief in Me is unwavering, then I will soon reward your faith by giving you even bigger mountains to climb in My Name. Truly I tell you that faith overcomes all, even converting human weakness to godly strength."

The man let the words sink in: *Fear is what held you back . . . Faith overcomes all . . . Human weakness becomes godly strength . . .*

Then the man opened up the Book given to him by the Giver of the Gift. He felt his heart race as he read from the Book:

> *"I tell you the truth, if you have faith as small as a mustard seed, you can say to this mountain, 'Move from here to there' and it will move. Nothing will be impossible for you."*
>
> *(Matthew 17:20b)*

Looking up to admire the beauty of the night sky, the man could not help but notice that the mountain had vanished.

Small Steps

For over four decades, Bil Keane has faithfully cartooned *"The Family Circus."* Beyond appearing in over 1,500 newspapers globally, making it the largest syndicated comic in the world, *The Family Circus* has been a source of laughter and smiles ever since its inception. Much of the cartoon's appeal stems from its simple, idealistic depiction of family life in America.

My favorite *"Family Circus"* comics are the ones in which Bil Keane is on "vacation," and his comic strip son Billy fills in. Oftentimes, little Billy will trace his steps while tromping all over the neighborhood, wandering here, there and everywhere, yet somehow finding his way home.

From a spiritual perspective, when we absolutely know where we reside—in Jesus—we too can venture into new and wonderful directions. Yet we are wise to understand that spiritual maturity is a major determinant for how far we ought to venture. Just as Billy knew that he was prepared to journey to the outer limits of his neighborhood, but not beyond them, so must we discern appropriate boundaries for our spiritual ventures. And our boundaries must be established not out of timidity, but boldness balanced by wisdom and prayer.

Even as the extent and scope of our spiritual ventures are determined in large part by spiritual maturity, faith is the essential ingredient for spiritual venturousness. And in order to experience optimal spiritual fulfillment, Christians must continually grow in faith such that, *in proportion to spiritual maturity,* they regularly venture into new territory for Christ. Too many Christians wait for a sort of personal epiphany to occur before venturing into new spiritual territory, and most of those who wait never venture into new territory, preventing them from experiencing optimal spiritual fulfillment.

Billy's approach lies in contrast, and is much more conducive to developing genuine, sustainable spiritual fulfillment. Rather than waiting (and waiting . . . and waiting . . .) for the "right" time to be venturous, Billy explored new ground, which prepared him to venture further and further out over the course of time into more uncharted territory. Billy experienced immense joy by taking small steps in new places, and those small steps readied him for increasingly significant journeys in his future.

I realize that comparing a fictional cartoon character to a real life spiritual journey is, to say the least, a stretch; but I believe that we can borrow from Billy's approach to venturousness.

When venturing into new territory for Christ, take small steps at first, knowing that the size of your steps will increase over time in proportion to your faith. Understand that the size of your steps is not what matters most; that you take *a* step is what really counts. Jesus will carry you up your spiritual mountains, provided that you believe He will:

But when he asks, he must believe and not doubt, because he who doubts is like a wave of the sea, blown and tossed by the wind.
(James 1:6)

Don't let doubt keep you from climbing, and moving, mountains. When you venture into uncharted territory, spiritual fulfillment will take hold of you and far surpass even your loftiest expectations.

Uncharted Territory

Just as uniqueness for the sake of uniqueness has nothing to do with genuine fulfillment, neither does venturousness merely for the sake of venturousness. Both must be a subset of something much greater, namely godliness. But while Biblical uniqueness equates *directly* to authenticity (godliness), Biblical venturousness is about *elevating* one's godliness to higher levels. Indeed, venturousness entails moving from understanding God's Word, to appreciating God's Word, to acting in accordance with God's Word, and finally, after allowing faith to supplant fear and uncertainty, to venturing into uncharted territory as a committed, convicted disciple of Jesus Christ.

For those who have ascertained Truth, venturousness is an important, progressive, and logical step toward abiding in Christ. And while recognizing that each person's spiritual journey is unique, and that there is no universal timetable for spiritual maturity, the fact is that anyone who abides in Christ has invested much time and effort to grow in Christ. Growth in Christ includes, but is not limited to, developing strong knowledge of Scripture, regular prayer, discernment of your unique purpose, consistently placing the needs of others ahead of self, and, overall, living according to God's Word. Some Christians experience quick and dramatic spiritual growth after initially accepting Christ, while others take significantly longer to grow spiritually. I myself am part of the latter group.

My spiritual journey has been marked by occasional waywardness, producing sporadic, intermittent Christian growth and maturity. In fact, only recently have I *consistently* become venturous for Christ. And while I have advanced considerably in my spiritual journey—residing, at least in my opinion, somewhere between being lovingly obedient to God and fully understanding my unique purpose—I recognize that I am still not *perpetually* in step with Jesus. I also recognize that to truly abide in Jesus I must be *increasingly* venturous for Him. Finally, as I believe my quest is to *Help bring forth God's kingdom*, I must acknowledge that it is only through increasingly venturing into uncharted territory that I can effectively fulfill my quest.

As you may have ascertained, I am the man in the "parable" that opened this chapter. For me, writing this book was akin to climbing a spiritual mountain, and on my own I could not manage to even take the first step. But after I placed absolute faith in Jesus—that is, after I let Jesus carry me up my mountain—the book began, in a very real sense, to write itself.

What mountains have you contemplated climbing? I urge you—I implore you—to prayerfully discern a mountain to climb. Take solace in knowing that when you let Jesus carry you, your mountains are reduced to molehills. But be vigilant in maintaining faith in the Lord, for doing otherwise will cause you to see the mountain through your own eyes, rather than through the Lord's:

> *But Jesus immediately said to them: "Take courage! It is I. Don't be afraid." "Lord, if it's you," Peter replied, "tell me to come to you on the water." "Come," he said. Then Peter got down out of the boat, walked on the water and came toward Jesus. But when he saw the wind, he was afraid and, beginning to sink, cried out, "Lord, save me!" Immediately Jesus*

reached out his hand and caught him. "You of little faith," he said, "why did you doubt?"

(Matthew 14:27–31)

Preparation Meets Opportunity

Former University of Texas football Coach Darrel Royal was once quoted as saying, *"Luck is what happens when preparation meets opportunity."* Coach Royal knew that without proper preparation, his team would not optimally capitalize on its opportunities.

The same principal is true when it comes to spiritual venturousness. It is utter foolishness to venture into a significant endeavor, spiritual or otherwise, with little or no preparation. This assertion may appear to contradict my earlier statement that "faith is the essential ingredient for spiritual venturousness," but in truth preparation does not compete with faith, it strengthens faith.

While we are not to set aside spiritual venturousness until we feel "comfortable"—it is *never* comfortable venturing into uncharted territory—we are to parallel our spiritual ventures with purposeful, continual spiritual preparation. This preparation involves growing in faith and knowledge through the study and application of God's Word, along with regular prayer, fellowship with other believers, and obedience borne out of desire to serve the Lord. And though we will never be completely prepared in any one of these areas, our mindset must be that our level of effectiveness when venturing into new spiritual territory is very much dependent on our level of preparedness.

Jesus demonstrated that spiritual preparedness is requisite for spiritual effectiveness:

They left that place and passed through Galilee. Jesus did not want anyone to know where they were, because he was teaching his disciples.

(Mark 9:30–31a)

Our Lord knew that He had to properly equip His disciples prior to sending them out as *"sheep amongst wolves"(ref. Matthew 10:16)*. And not only did Jesus teach the disciples about what it meant to follow Him, but when He did send them out, He sent them out in pairs:

> *Then Jesus went around teaching from village to village. Calling the Twelve to him, he sent them out two by two and gave them authority over evil spirits.*
>
> *(Mark 6:7)*

Taking small steps in parallel with continual preparation leads directly to increasing the boundaries of our spiritual "territory." In the case of the first Christian disciples, their initial steps, however small they may have been, when combined with the teaching received from the Lord, enabled them to take giant strides later, giving birth to the Church of Jesus Christ.

The Relativity of Venturousness

> *"Salvation is found in no one else, for there is no other name under heaven given to men by which we must be saved."*
>
> *(Acts 4:12)*

When you accepted Jesus Christ as your Lord and Savior, you were freed from bondage and gifted with salvation. Indeed, salvation through Jesus Christ is the only fixed (absolute) point-of-reference that all professed Christians share. Beyond that, as we have all been gifted with unique minds, talents and gifts, our viewpoint as it regards our spiritual journey is uniquely our own.

For example, my definition of a spiritual "mountain" is very likely to differ from yours. To illustrate the point, beyond writing this book I believe that my last six spiritual mountains, shown chronologically from most distant to most recent, are as follows:

- Setting aside quiet time in the morning to spend alone with God.
- Being a puppeteer for "Caraway Street" (children's program at church).
- Coordinating/planning our Tuesday morning men's Bible study.
- Becoming a Care Elder.
- Participating in several dramas at church.
- Volunteering as a Kids Hope Mentor.

Perhaps upon looking over my list, your immediate thought is that my so-called mountains aren't mountains at all, they're more like anthills! Or, perhaps, you may consider my mountains to be of a very tall sort. Regardless, your point-of-view emanates directly from your point-of-reference, and in truth, the only point-of-reference that matters when it comes to my spiritual mountains is mine!

For me, each of the mountains listed required me to be spiritually venturous, for at their onset each represented uncharted territory to me. For example, while many Christians have set aside quiet time for Jesus since their youth, I didn't do so until a few years ago; thus, as my point-of-reference is uniquely mine, setting aside daily quiet time with the Lord was, for me, venturous.

There is no absolute scale for venturousness. At face value, my self-proclaimed venturousness pales in contrast with those who have sacrificed everything to become missionaries, or who on a daily basis face hostility and/or persecution while bringing the Good News to others. And while their mountains are very tall indeed, when seen through their own eyes—from their own unique point-of-reference—they likely appear to be much smaller than how I see them. Spiritual maturity, combined with discernment of one's unique spiritual gifts and purpose in life, gives each individual a unique point-of-reference.

In fact, I would dare say that for some reading these words, the very act of reading a Christian book on spiritual fulfillment represents venturing into uncharted territory!

Amazingly, we are not required to venture into uncharted territory in order to have eternal life. The old adage *"Nothing ventured, nothing gained"* does not apply to salvation, for when we confess Jesus Christ as our Lord and Savior we gain eternal life without having done anything to earn it. But for your own benefit (optimal spiritual fulfillment), and out of reverence to God, I urge you to find a mountain to climb. And I especially urge you to allow Jesus to carry you up your mountain.

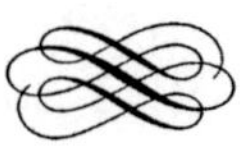

Deep Water

Allow me to preface this story by quickly telling you about my dear friends Keith and Christine. Our friendship spans over twenty years, and Pam and I feel immensely blessed to have such a wonderful, loving relationship with Keith, Christine, and their extended family.

Keith has always had a mixture of venturousness, passion, and talent. Just prior to marrying Christine, Keith began working for a pool company, quickly becoming proficient at tiling and coping.

Never content to be average, Keith dedicated himself to being the best. He worked long hours and treated customers like royalty. Predictably, within a few years Keith started his own company and, after considerable sacrifice, carved out a successful, sustainable business, one that specializes in top-quality, high-end work.

A few days ago I asked Keith how business was going so far this summer. What he told me spoke volumes about what it means to boldly (yet safely and purposefully) venture into deep water.

In typical understated manner, Keith mentioned that he had been asked by the manager of a well-known entertainer to build a custom pool. Knowing that the potential client's lifestyle was very much opposite his own, Keith wrestled with whether to accept or decline the job. After praying for discernment, Keith ultimately agreed to do the job, assuring his client that he would be absolutely straightforward with him, for his word was his bond.

During the course of the job, Keith never betrayed his Christian beliefs; his faith in the Lord was transparent and unbending. And as the job progressed, Keith developed an increasingly strong relationship with his client! He didn't force his beliefs upon his client, but he didn't suppress them either; indeed, rather than merely speak his beliefs, Keith embodied his beliefs.

While the rest of the story has yet to be determined, the reality is that the likelihood of instantly converting a "successful" (by worldly standards) non-believer to the Truth of Jesus Christ is not great. Yet with Jesus anything is possible, and the spark that Keith has started may well turn into a flame in due time.

Interestingly, there was a time in Keith's life when he himself was vulnerable to the trappings of stardom. But that was a long time ago, and things have changed. These days, Keith is as venturous as ever, but his ventures serve a higher purpose. He is God's disciple.

Worship

"God is spirit, and his worshipers must worship in spirit and in truth."
(John 4:24)

A.W Tozer is widely considered to be one of the most influential Christians of the twentieth century. Before going home to be with His Lord in 1963, Tozer wrote more than forty books, served as Pastor for several churches, and earnestly, relentlessly pursued God. Tozer experienced intense joy when worshipping the Lord, something he did often and with great zeal. Yet it pained Tozer to witness the Christian Church fail to worship in absolute spirit and truth, and thus he spoke out, saying "*Worship is the missing jewel in modern evangelicalism. We're organized; we work; we have our agendas. We have almost everything, but there's one thing that the churches, even the gospel churches, do not have: that is the ability to worship. We are not cultivating the art of worship.*"

I believe that Mr. Tozer's concerns are valid even today. In spite of continual and mounting challenges coupled with erosion in the ranks of active members, the Christian Church maintains adequate resources, yet, in many cases, an inadequate approach to worship. Why is proper worship so important? Because worshipping God—*exalting* God—is a direct reflection of our love for God; serves as a gateway to Jesus; is instrumental for bringing about wholeness; and, of great importance, is the most significant commandment given to us by the Lord:

"'Love the Lord your God with all your heart and with all your soul and with all your mind.' This is the first and greatest commandment."
(Matthew 22:37–38)

When coupling John 4:24 with Matthew 22:37–38, Jesus' words make clear that we are to worship in spirit and truth, and with all of our heart, soul, and mind, *out of* deep, steadfast love for God.

Jesus' words speak to the purpose and process of worship, providing clarity for the greater Christian church as well as for each and every Christian. Indeed, the church must gear its efforts toward *enabling* its members to experience the fullness of Christ through a Biblical, spiritual, heartfelt, soulful, and intellectual worship experience, while each individual must pour themselves into worship such that their love for the Almighty flows forth from every fiber of their being.

A.W. Tozer did not allow the misgivings he had toward the church to prevent him from giving his all to God. Tozer knew the importance of worship well and had no desire to deprive himself of one of God's greatest gifts. Tozer also understood that the foundation of worship is expressing heartfelt gratitude and love to the Savior, and that the "church" isn't bricks and mortar, but people united in a quest to glorify and serve Christ.

Love for the Lord = Worship for the Lord

Regardless of circumstances, we experience an undeniable sense of purpose, accompanied by deep joy, when we place Jesus at the center of our lives. Moreover, through humbly and regularly acknowledging that we have been gifted with eternal life simply by accepting Jesus as our Lord and Savior, we are properly positioned for genuine, chronic spiritual fulfillment. Are those not sufficient reasons to love the Lord our God with every fiber of our being? The answer can only be a resounding "yes," which leads to a rather fundamental question:

Does your worship for the Lord adequately reflect your love for the Lord?

Ruminate on the question before jumping ahead too quickly, for it is a question worthy of rumination:

Does your worship for the Lord adequately reflect your love for the Lord?

Worship

In the chapter on *Love,* I touched briefly on the importance of outward expressions of our love for others. The same principle applies to worshipping God, only at a significantly deeper level. We *must* worship God in order to be made whole, for failure to do so leaves us hopelessly and woefully incomplete. Each of us has been born into sin, and each of us continues to sin during our lifetime. No person, with the exception of our Lord Jesus Christ, has lived even one day devoid of sin. And as we are born broken and digress into further disrepair over the course of time, we are absolutely reliant on the grace of Jesus Christ to be made whole. Only by truly acknowledging our broken state are we sufficiently positioned for wholeness. Confessing Jesus as Lord and Savior is necessary, life changing, and eternal, yet it is only through *worshipping* the Lord in spirit and truth—out of love—and with all of our heart, soul, and mind, that we find wholeness: fulfillment. Yes, we are saved through accepting Jesus Christ, but to gain the maximum benefit of salvation we must perpetually live in communion with salvation's source—Jesus. Anything less is akin to accepting the rarest and most precious gift imaginable, but inexplicably not opening it until some later date. Why wait for heaven when Jesus offers you a glimpse of it now?

Just as relationships are damaged when love is assumed but rarely (if ever) demonstrated, so is our relationship with the Lord damaged when we fail to worship Him in accordance with our love for Him. And make no mistake: when our relationship with God is less than ideal, it is always our fault, for our fickle, sinful nature is the only variable in our relationship with God, and stands in stark contrast to our Redeemer's fixed, ever-loving nature.

It is a fallacy to believe that since God already knows what lies in our hearts, worship is not necessary. Granted, this sort of outlook does contain a degree of truth—God does know what lies in our hearts and does not require our worship for validation—but to focus solely on those aspects is to overlook that the beneficiary of worship is not God, it's us!

Understand that God's command to love Him with all of our heart, soul, and mind is not given out of self-indulgence, but *unfathomable* love. God is perfect and His dominion eternally secure, yet His love for us runs so deep that He died at our hands so that we might gain eternal life. In spite of the fact that we are hardly deserving of His gift, God strongly desires for us to live eternally with Him, and to have deep joy and genuine fulfillment during all of our days. But God's desire for us can only come about if we attempt, however feebly, to reciprocate the love He bestows upon us. When we worship in truth and spirit, and with all of our heart, soul, and mind, we shift our focus from ourselves to our Lord. And by moving our focus to Jesus, we immerse ourselves into His healing presence, experiencing a taste of heaven on earth. It is during those rare and precious moments, in those times when we are freed from our own bondage, that we see Truth as it really is. Words cannot begin to describe such purity.

Our love for God and our worship for God are to be one and the same. If you truly love the Lord, you will naturally and joyfully praise Him *with all of your heart and with all of your soul and with all of your mind*. Let your worship reflect your love, and lead you directly to Jesus Christ.

Mathematics

Let us dispel the common misconception that a favorable scenario is one in which a person receives something equally proportionate to what he has given. In truth—and in all aspects of life—we *rarely* desire to receive the equivalent of what we have put forth, for doing so provides little incentive to put forth anything of value in the first place! Indeed, our inherent approach to life is to attempt to gain more than we give.

We see evidence of this fact in the stock market, where during times of prosperity people aggressively invest their money in the hope of increasing wealth, but where during hard times—times in which the market fails to return wealth—the amount of money transacted dries up. After all, why would anyone desire to trade money merely for the sake thereof? We *invest* our money with the intention of increasing our wealth.

Regardless of whether we recognize (or acknowledge) our inherent desire to gain more than we give, we all, to varying degrees, routinely engage in the approach. People attend college in return for a secure, prosperous future. People give gifts out of reverence and/or love, yet benefit themselves through personal satisfaction derived from the act of giving itself. Many people will drive out of their way to go shopping so that they can pay less and/or receive better quality goods in exchange for their dollar. And many people volunteer—with pure intentions—to help others less fortunate, and derive great benefit themselves through improved life balance and clearer perspective.

The list could go on and on, but the point is simply that our human tendency, knowingly or unknowingly, is to seek and expect a higher return against what we initially "invest." This is true even when the benefits derived from our investment are not especially tangible, as was the case in two of the examples cited above, in which personal satisfaction was derived from giving a gift, and life balance and perspective derived from volunteering. In fact, as we move toward godliness, we find that intangible benefits are much more enticing than tangible benefits. Hence, when managed correctly, our inherent, persistent desire to receive more than we give can actually produce powerful and rewarding win-win scenarios. During those times when we purposefully invest in others for their benefit, we replace (to some extent) inherent selfishness with Christian godliness. And when purposely placing others ahead of ourselves, we become the principal beneficiaries, for godliness leads directly (and expeditiously) to genuine, sustainable fulfillment.

Fully knowledgeable of man's sinful nature, God in His infinite goodness seeks to bring us closer to Him through, in a very real sense, *catering* to our nature.

Think of it this way: In our broken state we are consumed with little more than our earthly, short-term well being, even as God is wholly consumed with our eternal well-being. But God cannot force us to accept His Truth, thus He makes us an offer that any shrewd investor cannot pass up: Eternal life in exchange for our will, i.e. the receipt of something that holds indescribable, positive value for something of abhorrent, *negative* value. The "trade" is rather one-sided, given that we surrender absolute bondage while receiving absolute freedom.

I believe that it is important for us to acknowledge that when initially accepting Jesus as Lord and Savior, our underlying motive is simply to secure something of great value. In the infancy of our relationship with Jesus, we are overcome with an incredible sense of relief at knowing that our eternal destination is secure. Yes, we passionately glorify and honor our Lord, but mostly because of what we have been gifted with. To clarify the point, ask yourself this question: *If you were provided sufficient knowledge of the greatness of God, yet were led to believe that there was no such thing as heaven, would you bother worshipping God?*

Your answer—and my answer—is "no"; giving freely without receiving something of significant value is simply not in our nature. Indeed, if we are guilty of initially accepting Christ with an ulterior motive, then we are only guilty of reflecting our very nature. Just as Adam and Eve were not content with their lot in life, neither are we. *That* we all seek greener pastures is not open for debate, but *where* we seek greener pastures certainly is. We can obtain a temporary, variable measure of happiness from the world, or we can obtain eternal, fixed joy and fulfillment from Jesus Christ.

Thankfully, when "investing" in matters of the Spirit, we *always* receive far more than we contribute. In truth, there is no mathematical equation (at least in an earthly sense) that can reconcile the "transaction" of salvation. Try as we might, we must acknowledge that as the numerator (eternal life) is infinity, and as the denominator (our will) is less than zero, our salvation does not compute. Yet for reasons that we cannot possibly fathom, God gifts us with salvation.

Increasing Rewards through Increasing Your Investment

> *He went to Nazareth, where he had been brought up, and on the Sabbath day he went into the synagogue, as was his custom. And he stood up to read. The scroll of the prophet Isaiah was handed to him. Unrolling it, he found the place where it is written: "The Spirit of the Lord is on me, because he has anointed me to preach good news to the poor. He has sent me to proclaim freedom for the prisoners and recovery of sight for the blind, to release the oppressed, to proclaim the year of the Lord's favor." Then he rolled up the scroll, gave it back to the attendant and sat down. The eyes of everyone in the synagogue were fastened on him, and he began by saying to them, "Today this scripture is fulfilled in your hearing."*
>
> *(Luke 4:16–21)*

As evidenced by the words "*that was his custom,*" God's only begotten Son considered being at Synagogue to be of great importance. Possessing knowledge and insight that religious leaders could scarcely imagine, Jesus nevertheless attended and contributed to worship.

Just as Jesus actively contributed to worship, so must we. Too many Christians take a passive approach to worship, robbing themselves of experiencing its many splendors. Worship is *not* to be treated like a spectator sport! In fact, God's Word clearly directs us to actively participate:

> *Instead, speaking the truth in love, we will in all things grow up into him who is the Head, that is, Christ. From him the whole body, joined and held*

together by every supporting ligament, grows and builds itself up in love, as each part does its work.

(Ephesians 4:15–16)

The strength of the Christian church depends on us. Jesus is the basis for the Church—the Head of the Church—but we make up the Body of the Church. And as any highly functioning Body requires all of its parts to work in synchronicity, as members of the Body of Christ we must complement each other through cooperation, kindness, love, obedience, and, when appropriate, discipline. (Note: *Any* discipline must be considered prayerfully, must be godly in nature, must be administered lovingly, and must serve to redirect a person toward Jesus).

It is through our combined, cumulative efforts that we successfully bring about a nurturing, enriching worship experience for each individual and, by extension, for the Body as a whole.

Are you getting involved? There are plenty of opportunities at each and every Christian church to *actively* contribute. Whether your spiritual gifts lie in administration, evangelism, exhortation, hospitality, intercession, knowledge, leadership, music, preaching, teaching, writing, or anything in between, there is a *need* for you to put your God-given spiritual gifts to use on behalf of the kingdom.

While the spiritual gifts listed above do not constitute a full listing, one can easily see that many are of the "behind the scenes" variety. This is an essential point because many Christians mistakenly believe that if they are not preaching, teaching, singing, or playing an instrument, they are not contributing. Even worse, many fail to use their gifts at all due to convincing themselves that their contributions are not essential. On the contrary, Scripture makes clear that *everyone* is called to contribute to the Church:

Just as each of us has one body with many members, and these members do not all have the same function, so in Christ we who are many form one body, and each member belongs to all the others. We have different gifts, according to the grace given us. If a man's gift is prophesying, let him use it in proportion to his faith. If it is serving, let him serve; if it is teaching, let him teach; if it is encouraging, let him encourage; if it is contributing to the needs of others, let him give generously; if it is leadership, let him govern diligently; if it is showing mercy, let him do it cheerfully.

(Romans 12:4–8)

Increase your rewards derived from worship by increasing your investment. Get involved with your church—I can guarantee that your "spiritual portfolio" will never look better!

All Paths Must Converge

While there are vast differences between churches regarding how to worship, our common goal must always be to bring glory to God. Regardless of whether we kneel, sit, or stand; regardless of whether we sing ancient hymns with an antique organ, or modern praise songs with a 10-piece band; regardless of whether we pray with emotional, outward expression, or with reflective, introspective silence; regardless of all these things and more, we must always be focused on giving thanks and praise to our Lord Jesus Christ. We ought never to forget that while our means will always vary, as Christians our worship must center on *glorifying* our Savior.

Can we agree on that much?

Therefore do not let anyone judge you by what you eat or drink, or with regard to a religious festival, a New Moon celebration or a Sabbath day. These are a shadow of the things that were to come; the reality, however, is found in Christ.

(Colossians 2:16–17)

It is not my place to editorialize on what I *think* worship ought to entail. I have my opinions on the subject (as we all do), but I am hardly qualified to advise anyone on how to worship God. Indeed, only Scripture can give us answers, and what we glean from God's Word is that we are to focus our worship squarely on Jesus Christ. Jesus is the Head of our collective Church, and as such is worthy of our praise. Worship the Lord your God with spirit and truth, and with all of your heart, mind, and soul. And *do not* go through the motions of following rules and traditions without properly understanding and *appreciating* what those rules and traditions stand for:

The Lord says: "These people come near to me with their mouth and honor me with their lips, but their hearts are far from me. Their worship of me is made up only of rules taught by men."

(Isaiah 29:13)

When we sing our songs, let us sing joyfully to the Lord. When we pray our prayers, let us pray in earnest to the Lord. When we greet one another, let us extend our greeting in the name of Christ. Everything we do is to be done in Christ.

Only God Is Worthy of Worship

For there is one God and one mediator between God and men, the man Christ Jesus . . .

(1 Timothy 2:5)

There are many people who I admire deeply; in fact, the chapter following this one is dedicated to just such a person. But there is a vast difference between how I view people I admire versus how I view my Savior. The difference is best expressed through simply stating that the qualities I most admire in people are those which are godly in nature. I admire those who are able to emulate, in limited fashion, our Lord Jesus Christ. Yet I clearly recognize that anyone who emulates the Lord does so with imperfection—with sin in his heart—and thus is worthy only of admiration, not worship. In comparison to God, Jesus and the Holy Spirit, which are perfectly unified as One in Divine Nature and Purpose, and which are the very *definition* of goodness and love, even the most godly person falls well short of being worthy of worship.

As you read this, you may be thinking, *"No kidding! Tell me something that I don't already know!"* But in truth, this is an important lesson for us to learn, for history has shown repeatedly that people, under given circumstances, will worship almost anybody and anything. Though astute and intelligent, many of the German people fell prey to Adolf Hitler's powers of persuasion. In America, many people are consumed with the accumulation of wealth and possessions, and/or attaining a position of status. As for Christians, we too are vulnerable, as evidenced by the many people who routinely place church leaders (ministers, priests, etc.) on a pedestal, oftentimes, and usually unintentionally, shifting their focus from Jesus to a person who is merely an ambassador for Jesus. Taking nothing away from those who are called to ministry, the fact is that they too are sinful beings, and while absolutely worthy of respect and admiration, they are absolutely unworthy of being worshipped.

I believe that there are two keys for avoiding inappropriate worship of people and/or material pursuits.

The first key is to recognize and acknowledge that we are all vulnerable to unknowingly elevating people and/or materialism to a status equivalent to, or even greater, than what we afford Jesus. It is easy to lapse into being a lukewarm follower of Jesus while passionately following men. When I was a child and became interested in sports, I considered professional athletes to be worthy of praise and adoration. When I was a teenager and discovered rock-and-roll, I considered certain musicians to be worthy of praise and adoration. And in my single days, I often considered certain (i.e., attractive) females to be worthy of praise and adoration.

Did I ever actually *worship* anyone other than God? No . . . yes. While I never intentionally worshipped anyone or anything of the world, I often, and with little thought, placed a disproportionate amount of adoration and attention on individuals, which by extension shifted my focus, slowly but surely, from God to the world. Any time we take a stronger interest in things of the world than we do in God, we severely handicap our ability to properly *worship* only God:

Do not love the world or anything in the world. If anyone loves the world, the love of the Father is not in him.

(1 John 2:15)

The second key to avoiding inappropriate worship of people and/or material pursuits is to *purposefully and continuously* worship Jesus.

When you think of worshipping the Lord, what instinctively comes to your mind? If you are like most people, you probably think immediately of worshipping God in church. And while church is essential for maintaining a healthy spiritual condition, we ought to be worshipping our Lord constantly, in all places and at all times. I am not suggesting that you break out in song while sitting in your next business meeting, but that you offer up thanks and praise to God throughout the day. Regardless of whether your prayers are silent or vocal, pray!

Too many Christians view worship as an isolated event that takes place on Sunday morning. In truth, this viewpoint is not at all conducive to *abiding* in Jesus! If we are to maintain a proper Christian focus—one that consistently places Jesus at the center of our lives—then we must worship Him accordingly. And that means not compartmentalizing Jesus as "a Sunday thing." Jesus is available to us every minute of every day, but it is up to us to call on Him.

Indeed, a surefire way to be subservient to Christ, and not subservient to the world, is to live as the Psalmist lived, knowing that perpetual worship leads to perpetual joy and spiritual fulfillment:

> *I will extol the Lord at all times; his praise will always be on my lips.*
> *(Psalm 34:1)*

From The Outside In

Within a few weeks of moving to Holland, Pam and I began scouting the area for churches. We both desired to rekindle our fire for the Lord, and believed that finding a church that would cater to our mutual desire was of great importance. One Saturday I noticed an ad in the local newspaper for an outdoor service at Beechwood Church. I showed the ad to Pam, and we agreed to attend the service.

Upon arriving the next morning, we quickly detected a rather noticeable "buzz" in the air. The Holy Spirit's presence was unmistakable! Smiles and handshakes were in abundance, and everywhere we looked we saw casually dressed people occupying lawn chairs. Many people spread blankets out for their children to play on. Pam and I guessed that the celebratory atmosphere at Beechwood was likely similar to the atmosphere that accompanied Jesus' sermons.

Feeling immediately connected, we found the worship service to be heartfelt, Biblical, and challenging. And the feeling of worshipping in a perfectly *natural* Sanctuary surrounded by grass and trees, and filled with fellow Believers, was undeniably powerful. Afterwards we enjoyed fresh donuts, hot coffee, snow cones, and fellowship.

After a few more visits to Beechwood, we knew that we had found our home. Still, in the end, what convinced us to join Beechwood was not outdoor worship (even though it remains an absolute highlight of our summer months). Nor did we join Beechwood on account of its gifted, godly Pastor (who has since left the church, and has been replaced with another gifted, godly Pastor). Nor did we join Beechwood based on the prospect of a beautiful, expanded *indoor* Sanctuary (which was in the planning stages then and has since been completed). Nor did we join Beechwood because of the diverse, melodic music from our choirs and musicians. While all of these factored into our decision, by and in themselves they did not entice us to join Beechwood.

What ultimately convinced us to join the Beechwood family was, and is, a clear, visible, and fixed focus on Jesus Christ as the Head of our Church. Pam, Spencer, Trevor, and I are an active part of a congregation that worships our Lord with spirit and truth, and with heart, soul, and mind.

Eventually, trees rot, people pass away, and buildings fall into disrepair. But if the Body of our Church continues to properly focus on the Head of our Church, then we are certain to persevere for many, many years. God Bless the Church of Jesus Christ. God Bless Beechwood.

Xanderism

(Leaving a Legacy)

While the intent of this chapter is to convey the importance of leaving a legacy, the means of conveying that message are distinctively different in comparison with every other chapter in *Alphabet Soup*. Xanderism focuses on one man—my father—whose "simple" life had a profound, lasting impact on many people, and which serves as a viable model for living in a manner that naturally brings forth a rich, positive, lasting legacy.

What is it that makes my father's life worthy of study? Only this: my father is greater than anyone alive. I am emboldened in making this claim by basing it entirely on truth and Truth. Along with many others, I can well testify to my father's acceptance and unwavering commitment to Jesus Christ as his Lord and Savior. Many years prior to his death, my father had nailed his sinful nature to the cross by accepting and living for Jesus. That is truth. As for *Truth,* Scripture tells us that anyone who confesses Jesus as Lord and Savior inherits eternal life in heaven, and anyone who lives in heaven is greater than anyone who presently walks the earth:

> *"For God so loved the world that he gave his only Son, so that everyone who believes in him will not perish but have eternal life."*
>
> *(John 3:16)*

"I tell you the truth: Among those born of women there has not risen anyone greater than John the Baptist; yet he who is least in the kingdom of heaven is greater than he."

(*Matthew 11:11*)

Lest I lose your interest and/or accreditation, allow me to explain what this chapter is *not* about. Xanderism is not a detailed, chronological history of my father's life. Nor is it an attempt to frame my dad as a sort of universal role model for Christianity. Nor is it intended to glorify my dad (only Jesus is worthy of glorification). And finally, while acknowledging that I purposefully focus on my dad's positive rather than negative traits, Xanderism is not intended to suggest whatsoever that *any* viable role model (with the notable exception of *the* Role Model, Jesus Christ) is without fault. Yes, my dad is greater than anyone who lives among us, but only because he now dwells eternally with the Lord in heaven.

Having sufficiently covered what this chapter is not about, allow me to briefly elaborate on what it *is* about. While exceedingly brief and invariably flawed—it is, after all, written from a naturally biased point-of-view—this glimpse of my father's life is appropriate for reinforcing the importance of living life in a manner that enables others to learn from, to be influenced by, and to spiritually grow due to *your* living example. Xanderism focuses on the compounding effect that our words and actions have on other people, particularly within the context of the many roles we occupy in life (child, sibling, spouse, parent, grandparent, friend, Christian, et al).

As you read what follows, I strongly encourage you to reflect on the legacy that, even today, you are leaving for those around you. When you are gone, how will people remember you? For better or worse, your life—your legacy—will shape others to a greater extent than you might think.

As I would be remiss for having failed to explain the origins of the "Xander" portion of Xanderism, I will now impart that it is a nickname given affectionately to my father by my mother, and is short for my father's first name, Alexander.

Merriam-Webster's on-line Collegiate Dictionary defines *"Ism"* as *"A distinctive doctrine, cause, or theory."* Focusing solely on the "cause" aspect of *Ism*, one of Merriam-Webster's definitions for *"Cause"* is *"A person or thing that is the occasion of an action or state; especially: an agent that brings something about."*

With help from Merriam-Webster, we can now define *Xanderism* as *"Bringing something about in others by living life according to a cause(s)."* The "something" we bring about is absolutely tied into the cause(s) we are committed to, and the extent to which we live according to what we believe.

A Good Son, a Good Brother

By virtue of being the oldest of eight children, my father had no choice but to set *some type* of example for his siblings! Though as a youth he got into a fair amount of mischief, dad's likable, devoted, kind, venturous, and honest nature proved to be infectious to his family and friends.

From the moment he arrived in America (from Malta) at nine years old, my father viewed the country as his playground. Naturally gifted with a quick wit and an easy smile, dad quickly made a lot of friends and began to influence those around him at an early age. He often used humor as a way to gain acceptance, and, as kids are wont to do, as a means of both getting into trouble and out of trouble! As a child, dad was someone other children gravitated to. They liked him because he was *likable*. (Thus it is no surprise that children continued to gravitate toward my father for the rest of his days; his easy going, fun loving nature was rather contagious, particularly for youngsters.)

Strongly devoted to his parents and siblings, dad didn't stray far from where his heart lied. Helping at home was expected and, with all those brothers and sisters, necessary. And as dedication was important to my dad, it was no surprise that when he met and fell in love with my mother while in High School, they were married a few years later and stayed faithfully and happily married until he passed away at age sixty. Dad was unwavering in his devotion to people he loved.

I believe that my dad first learned the art of kindness from his mother. My grandmother could be as stern as anyone, yet everything she said and did was out of care and concern for others, and love for her Lord. Taking his cue from his mother, my dad also had a knack for showing compassion to people. Whether it was the clerk at the store, the man at the junkyard, or the neighbor down the street, my father was kind to others.

Always venturous, dad thrived after coming to America. For him, the land of opportunity was exactly that. I don't think he ever forgot where he came from, or the blessings he received throughout his life. His brothers and sisters have never forgotten their roots or blessings either, which I believe reflects, ever so slightly, their oldest brother's influence.

What follows next is an unaltered autobiography that my father wrote for school when he was ten years old. The autobiography was written over fifty years ago, but remains timeless in its depiction of a ten-year old boy arriving in a place that had only previously existed in dreams. It captures the essence of my father's early years perfectly. Youthful exuberance and bravado are on full display, but if you look closer you will detect several qualities—likability, devotion, kindness, venturousness, and honesty—that I believe defined my father's youth, and helped form the foundation of his character as he moved into adulthood.

MY AUTOBIOGRAPHY

My name is Alex Gafa and I think my life is quite an interesting one.

I was born in Malta during the Second World War on October eighth, nineteen hundred thirty-nine. It was very hard for my mother to get milk and I sometimes had to go without it. Since my Dad was in the Navy for eight years he did not recognize me when he got home.

It may seem strange to you how I got to talking English so fast. Well, when I was small and getting my talking age my mother taught me how to speak English. So that is how I can pronounce my words so well.

In 1948 we started off for Canada in a boat named the "Rodnick." Since the boat was so slow it took us two weeks to get across the Atlantic Ocean and to the harbor in Brooklyn. The tall buildings and the big ships made me so excited that I almost fell overboard.

From Brooklyn we took a train to Montreal, and from there we took another train to Windsor, Canada.

While we were living in Windsor we were introduced to a strange American custom. It was the practice of begging on Halloween, which was the day we arrived there. Some children with funny masks came and begged for candy. We did not know who they were and we children were afraid. My sister and brother started to cry but I just stood there staring at them.

One day my Dad was talking about the United States and its wonderful jobs. We decided to go there. We bought everything new, including a new house and car.

I go to Lincoln school and have a lot of new friends.

I like the United States very much. There is just one thing I like better about Malta and that is the weather.

A Good Husband

Husbands, love your wives, just as Christ loved the church and gave himself up for her.

(*Ephesians 5:25*)

It is not an exaggeration to surmise that had he been called to do so, my father would have willingly, unhesitatingly, laid down his life out of love for my mother. Just as a dedicated soldier is willing to lay down his life for country or cause, and just as our Lord laid down His life out of unspeakable love for all humanity, my father would have done so out of love for his bride. Amazingly, dad's love for my mother never peaked; it continued to escalate day after day, month after month, and year after year, seemingly limitless and unending. And unlike so many people who pledge lifelong love for another but fail to live accordingly, my parents actually made good on their pledge. Mom and dad not only never wavered in their commitment to one another, they became *increasingly* enamored with one another. Their love grew ever deeper, ever wider, and ever truer. "*The two shall become one*" was continuously exemplified by my parents.

The love my mom and dad had for each other was always reciprocal, never one-sided. Neither "kept score." And like all marriages, theirs had its share of arguments and disagreements, yet unlike most marriages the *foundation* of their union was a parallel commitment to each other and to Jesus Christ, through which the long-term outcome of the marriage was never in question. When a husband and wife jointly fix their eyes on Jesus, by extension they fix their eyes on enabling one another to be in discipleship for Jesus. My parents lived according to this simple yet profound truth, and it served them well.

As you have probably already gathered, I cannot bring myself to comment on my father's legacy as a husband without giving equal time to my mother. Mom and dad were as close to inseparable as could be imagined. Where there was Al, there was Angie; where there was Angie, there was Al. They vowed to love one another *"In sickness and in health, until death do us part,"* and that is exactly what they did. From the time they were High School sweethearts until the day my father died, their vows became more and more intrinsic, such that eventually the words were no longer "just" words but a perfectly ingrained, perfectly *natural* part of their very being.

As for longevity, in truth the nearly forty years of wedded bliss they shared cannot be properly gauged when viewed quantitatively. Their time together (and for that matter, any couple's time together) can only be accurately assessed when considered *qualitatively.* As people have no control over dying, it becomes imperative that we invest ourselves fully into living. The duration of my parents marriage was a variable only in the sense that it was a given that the marriage would end not by choice, but by natural cause. Mom and dad could have been married for sixty years or sixty days, but the quality of their marriage renders the duration thereof as a secondary consideration, for when one looks back on time it is not to remember time itself but to remember what took place in time. And what took place for Alex and Angie Gafa between 1960 and 2000 was special.

I could continue to extol my parents' marriage and, more pertinent to this chapter and the book to which it belongs, my father's legacy as a husband, but in the interest of accuracy I will let my mother finish the task for me.

What follows is a letter from my mother to my father written twenty-two months *after* his death. Mom wrote the letter out of love, loneliness, and a very real need to reconnect with her beloved. Her letter was not originally intended for public consumption, but after explaining the intent of the *Xanderism* chapter, she (and I) felt comfortable printing it. The poignancy, beauty, and honesty in her letter bear powerful testimony to my dad's legacy as a faithful, loving, nurturing husband. Mom's letter speaks to its subject in ways that I cannot, and provides firsthand evidence of both the beauty of deep love, and the pain that inevitably accompanies deep love when a spouse passes away. For me, my mother's heartfelt letter indirectly, yet resolutely, answers the question, *"Is it better to have loved and lost than to have never loved?"*

Yes, it *is* better to have loved and lost than to have never loved-provided that the love shared between two people is rooted in mutual acceptance and love for the source of love, Jesus Christ. My parents are separated only for the moment, for they have assured themselves of a blissful, eternal reunion with one another and their Savior. And that is cause for celebration.

Here is my mother's letter:

Dearest Angel,

Looking at our picture hanging in the dining room prompted me to a sad, sick feeling. You were already so frail and looking poorly.

I can honestly say I remember that day well. We had our pictures taken at a Dave Roberts studio and our appointment was at noon.

When I think of it, I believe you cooperated for this picture taking session all for me. It wasn't your style to spend that kind of money and go through the bother of being so picky with the selection of our clothing. I believe even at that time you knew I was having this done to remember "us" together. You weren't feeling especially well that day and we had each brought two different outfits for different poses.

Afterwards, we went to Friar Tuck's for lunch and you ordered a chicken pot pie and must have eaten all of two bites and told me you didn't feel hungry. I faintly remember getting a sickened feeling that I must have gotten these pictures taken just on time. They were taken in March of 1999 and you died a bit less than a year later.

Al, it's nearly Christmas day and I miss you more than words could ever say. We were about as close to one another as anyone I could imagine. Even though I'm doing okay, I still feel like half of me is gone and I really don't think that feeling is ever going to leave me.

I never realized just how special you were until your passing. Obviously, good people are sometimes taken for granted.

I can't help but wonder what you're doing, but someday I'll see you again in whatever way God wants. I look forward to that day; having a grand reunion with our Lord and Savior and all of my loved ones who have gone before me.

Bye for today,

I love you darling,

Angie

A Good Father (and Grandfather)

My dad was not a perfect father in the fairy-tale 'Ward Cleaver' mold, but he was absolutely real. As a father, dad had some very real shortcomings—he wasn't the world's greatest listener, he occasionally displayed a quick temper, and at times he was overly consumed with his own interests—yet he worked hard to overcome those obstacles, and in fact *grew* into a wonderful father.

Dad turned twenty-two when my brother Tom was born, was twenty-three when I arrived on the scene, and was not yet twenty-five when my sister Denise was born! I am amazed that my parents kept it together after having three kids in less than a four-year span, but keep it together they most certainly did. Dad set aside any aspirations of college (though he did take some night classes later) in exchange for supporting his family by working earnestly and diligently. He started as a Clerk for the City of Warren, Michigan, and steadily, over a period of many years, rose through the ranks until reaching the position of Civil Engineering Manager for the city. This was quite a feat for someone with a High School education and a young (and growing) family to support. There were many valid reasons for me to look up to my father, not the least of which was his strong work ethic. My dad worked hard for what he got, and I believe that his lifelong commitment to hard work is a central part of his legacy as a man and as a father. Children benefit enormously when they are able to witness firsthand the challenges, sacrifices, and benefits that come from working hard, and my father provided that example for his children on a daily basis.

Even as dad worked hard, he made a point to spend ample, quality time with us. I have many fond memories of being with my dad while I was growing up, but in the interest of space and of sticking close to the subject matter, I will share but a few.

Most of my earliest memories of my father revolve around sports. We would go to Detroit Tiger, Red Wing, or Piston games, and would always end up devouring a burger and a milkshake at the local Big Boy afterwards. More often than not, it would only be the two of us, making our time together extra special. Dad felt that one-on-one time with his children was important. His example inspired me to take a like approach with my sons.

Dad always had an easy, humorous nature about him. In our early years, dad would often place Tom, Denise, and I on top of our refrigerator just to watch us laugh from the bottom of our bellies. In my teen years, he would give me a playful whack on the head, prompting me to ask "why?," to which he would invariably answer, "That was for the next time you get out of line." Yes, playfulness was a priority for my father, evidenced further by the many *mock* threats he made to administer a "blasting" to one of his children, threats that were always met with laughter, thus serving their intended purpose.

My dad was not a heavy conversationalist by nature, but his actions always spoke louder than words anyway. There were many evenings—and nights—when he would be outside in our unheated garage working on getting *my* car to run. He knew that I was incapable of properly fixing junky old cars, so he did it for me, and never once complained about it.

When I was around ten years old, my dad bought me a tabletop hockey game. We created an imaginary league, and for quite a while we would play against each other almost every evening. He could have won every game, and in fact did win most games, but he let me win just often enough to keep me coming back for more. And at the end of every game, a "fight" would break out on the "ice," with players from both sides aggressively twirling around, back and forth and side to side, beating each other up mercilessly while dad and I laughed ourselves into convulsions.

My dad was there for me in tough times too. Just a few months after graduating from college, I took a job selling copy machines. While on the road one day in Detroit, I inadvertently made an illegal right-hand turn at a stoplight and, sure enough, was pulled over by a police officer. My situation worsened when I went for my license and realized it wasn't there—I had left it in my gym bag the night before—and worsened even more when the officer could not (would not) release me without proper identification. Hence, after calling home so that mom or dad could come and vouch for my identity, I spent the next hour or so in a holding cell in Detroit. When dad came to pick me up, he laid into the officer at the desk with all the "energy" he could muster. I was angry and embarrassed over being put into a jail cell for a traffic violation and failure to carry a drivers license, but knowing that my father went to bat for me like he did alleviated my frustration just a bit.

Whether it was playing pool, tossing a baseball in the backyard, running to the hardware store, or watching the *Three Stooges*, time spent with my father was always time well spent. He was a wonderful, devoted, loving father, increasingly so over the course of time.

I am convinced that to see the true nature of a man, one must wait until the man becomes a grandfather. My dad was a loving father, but he was an even more loving (and doting) grandfather. He regularly lavished love and affection on Elissa, Lauren, Trevor, Spencer, Kiran, and Karis, and in return received only a plethora of hugs, kisses, and smiles. He had learned the art of fatherhood well, and applied what he had learned to become the world's best grandfather. Ever since the day Elissa was born, my father was at his happiest when in the company of his precious grandchildren. All were treated like royalty. Dad would read stories, play hide-and-go-seek, chaperone each to special places like movies, sporting events, or the zoo, and even built a swing set in his backyard with each of their handprints etched in the cement underneath.

Through uninhibited adoration and abundant love, my father demonstrated godliness to his children and grandchildren. In fact, dad taught his children *how* to impart godly love to their children. He had grown into a great father, and by the time he became a grandfather he was second to none.

Dad's rich legacy as a father and grandfather will stand the test of time. My dad may be gone from this earth, but his legacy is very much alive in the hearts and minds of those he loved, and those who loved him.

A Good Friend

My father made many, many friends over the course of his life. I could recount endless tales of his dedication and commitment to them, but my preference is to focus on what I know best: my own experience as his friend.

One of life's great pleasures occurs when the relationship between a child and parent shifts from being autocratic in nature, wherein the parent is primarily (and necessarily) an authority figure, to being democratic in nature, wherein child and parent are equal, and wherein mutual friendship supplants any semblance of hierarchy. Though neither father nor child ever loses the distinctiveness of their role relative to the other, as time passes by, and as their relationship passes through inevitable highs and lows, they either drift further apart or come closer together. In my relationship with my father, I did both: shortly after marrying Pam, we moved out of state, making the physical distance between my father and I prohibitive to regular visits; yet while we drifted apart physically, we became much closer emotionally. It has been said that prolonged absence allows people to develop a deeper appreciation for others, and I believe that this is especially true when it comes to appreciating parents.

When I was younger I took our time together for granted, but as the years rolled by and I saw my father less and less, I cherished our relationship more and more. Dad was still "dad," but mostly he was a dear, trusted friend, one who I loved talking to and being with.

When we played golf, as we typically did once or twice a year, it wasn't golfing that made our time special, it was rekindling our friendship *while* golfing. When we fraternized over sports or politics, the subject matter in itself didn't provide pleasure, but our camaraderie certainly did. And when we talked about life's weightier issues, as we did on rare occasions, whether or not we agreed was not nearly as important as knowing that we could disagree amiably, and without threat to our friendship.

As mentioned previously, from my father's standpoint, words weren't nearly as important as actions, and *written* words weren't as important as spoken words. Thus, when I received a thank you note in 1999 following dad's surgery for removing several cancerous tumors from his liver, it became a rather cherished possession for me. The note is brief and to the point, yet powerful in its reinforcement of dad's legacy as a father, and as a friend. Here it is:

Dear Mike and Pam,

Mike, you have always made us proud to be our son and our latest ordeal is no exception. Thanks for being there with mom along with Tom and Denise as she had to carry herself through my surgery; it at least made the waiting and apprehension bearable.

I know you were there at my side after surgery but my mind was so muddled. I don't even know if I said anything to you.

I know it was a long way to travel and Pam was stuck with the twins, and I realize it was a hardship to both of you.

I thank the Lord that everyday brings more healing and I am not too far away from a complete recovery.
Thanks again to both of you for your kindness, concern, and prayers.

Hug the boys for me.

Love,

Dad

A Good Disciple

I have saved the best part of my father's legacy for last. Dad's spiritual journey was not terribly dramatic, but it certainly was interesting, and absolutely convicting.

Born into Catholicism, as a youth my father faithfully attended church on Sunday and Catechism during the week. Moreover, dad went to a Catholic High School. In his early years, my father developed foundational understanding, knowledge, and faith in the Holy Trinity.

But over time, dad's commitment to his faith began to wane. While still a Believer, he began skipping church on a regular basis. I recall many Sunday mornings during my childhood when my father would adamantly insist that his family attend church while he buried himself in other tasks. What my father was experiencing at that time was a form of spiritual bankruptcy. He was always a good man who lived according to high morals and ethics, but goodness without *higher purpose* brings about neither salvation nor fulfillment. Dad sensed that his spiritual life was lacking, a fact compounded by the church we attended at that time offering little in the way of intellectual challenges, heartfelt praise for Jesus, or spiritual introspection. (Please note: neither my father's spiritual journey nor my words to that effect are intended as a negative commentary or indictment against Catholicism. A spiritless church does not equate to a spiritless *Church*; i.e., an individual church is merely a component of the greater Church, and in truth all religions struggle with individual churches that are out of touch with the Doctrine(s) intended to govern them. My firm belief, based on God's Holy Word, is simply that *all* Christian churches, regardless of self-titled "religion," must never fail to make Christ the Head of the Church, and must never stray from Scripture as its governing source.)

In contrast to my father's withdrawal from the church, my mother began immersing herself in a "charismatic" movement within the church. Eventually she began attending a non-denominational, highly contemporary Church, and shortly thereafter convinced my father to accompany her. Soon his spiritual fire began to burn again, and as his love for the Lord began to flow stronger than ever, my father was reborn in the Spirit, and vowed to live the remainder of his days in discipleship to his Lord and Savior.

The "start-stop-start-stop" spiritual cycle that so many of us go through was finally over for my dad. His commitment to his Savior would never again fail to be embodied through his words, thoughts, and actions. He quickly became transparent in his beliefs, and his faith defined his existence. Finally, he had unmistakable purpose; there was no question that Alex Gafa was a disciple of Jesus Christ.

Dad would pour through the Word, volunteer at church, and speak passionately and openly about his faith. One could not help but be influenced by dad's love and reverence for His Redeemer.

Although I could fill a multitude of pages detailing additional highlights of my father's wonderful journey to and with Jesus Christ, I will instead close this section with brevity and succinctness by simply reminding you, once again, that my father is greater than anyone who lives among us. His legacy is eternal.

What will your legacy be?

He Did the Best with What He Had

For many years my father played competitive softball. Dad's position was third base, where his athleticism and grace served him well. It is not an exaggeration to claim that my dad was the rare player who could actually turn games around through his glove work—he was that good in the field. At the plate, however, he was—on a good day—merely average. As a singles hitter with speed (in baseball lingo, a table setter), dad was not the first choice to be at the plate in a crucial situation. Knowing this full well, dad worked hard to improve, or at least maintain, his hitting stroke.

Nonetheless, in spite of his best efforts, dad's limitations at the plate often got the best of him. Once, in a tight game, dad did the unthinkable: he struck out . . . swinging! Strikeouts are rare in softball, yet, under the right circumstances, strikeouts can be a terrific source for light-hearted teasing.

So it was that a few days later dad came home after practice lugging something that looked suspiciously like a baseball bat, except that it was full of large holes. It resembled a piece of Swiss cheese contorted into the shape of a bat! Dad grinned from ear to ear as he read the bat's inscription: *"To Al Gafa—He did the best with what he had."*

The "holy" bat hung on our basement wall for many years. Even after realizing many successes throughout his softball career, dad always seemed to cherish that bat more than other memorabilia he had acquired.

I think I know why. *"He did the best with what he had"* is a perfect summation of my father's life. As a son, as a brother, as a husband, as a father, as a grandfather, as a friend, as a disciple of Jesus Christ—my dad did the best with what he had. Sometimes it was a little, sometimes it was a lot, but always it was enough.

My son Trevor's middle name is *Xander.* God willing, someday Trevor Xander will understand why his middle name, though unusual, is so very meaningful. Someday he will truly understand his grandfather's legacy.

Youthfulness

Perhaps when you glanced at the title of this chapter you assumed it to be a celebration of youth; I assure you, it is not! *Youthfulness* does not celebrate youth itself, but rather its healthy characteristics: unassuming humility, unabashed love, and undoubting faith. These characteristics are universal in nature and Biblical in scope, yet inevitably are severely diminished over time as we become increasingly indoctrinated in the ways of the world. Regrettably, the transition between the relative purity of unknowing youth and the absolute impurity of worldliness takes place all too soon. Nonetheless, although all people lose their healthy youthful nature at some point, all have the opportunity to gain it back later. Reclaiming youth is impossible, but reclaiming youthfulness is not. And for the sake of gaining *optimal* spiritual fulfillment, we must do exactly that.

Within the context of both this book and *The Book*, youthfulness is a viable attribute *only* when it encompasses healthy characteristics of youth while completely discarding unhealthy characteristics of youth. And it is important to understand that adopting healthy youthful characteristics is not intended as a sort of inane effort to rediscover lost youth, but as a purposeful decision to live in accordance with God's Word.

Youthful Characteristics: A Mixed Blessing

Before delving into healthy characteristics of youth, it is appropriate to first identify youth's unhealthy characteristics.

The verses that follow allude to selfish rebellion, reckless and/or thoughtless choices, uncontrollable desires, and an inability to discern fact from fiction as being unhealthy characteristics that accompany youth:

> *Forgive the rebellious sins of my youth; look instead through the eyes of your unfailing love, for you are merciful, O Lord.*
>
> (Psalm 25:7)

> *So banish grief and pain, but remember that youth, with a whole life before it, still faces the threat of meaninglessness.*
>
> (Ecclesiastes 11:10)

> *Run from anything that stimulates youthful lust.*
>
> (2 Timothy 2:22 a)

> *Then we will no longer be like children, forever changing our minds about what we believe because someone has told us something different or because someone has cleverly lied to us and made the lie sound like truth.*
>
> (Ephesians 4:14)

Selfish rebellion, reckless and/or thoughtless choices, uncontrollable desires, and an inability to discern fact from fiction—all are childish in nature and all lie in opposition to the healthy qualities of youth that Scripture espouses.

At the opposite end of the spectrum, the verses below define *healthy* characteristics of youth, and, more importantly, the value that our Lord places on *Biblical* youthfulness:

> *About that time the disciples came to Jesus and asked, "Which of us is greatest in the Kingdom of Heaven?" Jesus called a small child over to him and put the child among them. Then he said, "I assure you, unless you turn from your sins and become as little children, you will never get into the Kingdom of Heaven. Therefore, anyone who becomes as humble as this little child is the greatest in the Kingdom of Heaven."*
>
> (Matthew 18:1–4)

Youthfulness

One day some parents brought their children to Jesus so that he could touch them and bless them, but the disciples told them not to bother him. But when Jesus saw what was happening, he was very displeased with his disciples. He said to them, "Let the children come to me. Don't stop them! For the Kingdom of God belongs to such as these. I assure you, anyone who doesn't have their kind of faith will never get into the Kingdom of God."

(Mark 10:13–16)

Unassuming humility, unabashed love, and undoubting faith are characteristics of youth that we are to emulate.

Note that Jesus does not call us to become childish, but childlike. The words may look the same and sound the same, but in connotation they are radically different. To be childish is to surrender to pointless rebellion, desire, and curiosity while lacking in maturity, insight, and logic. To be *childlike* is to have unassuming humility, unabashed love, and undoubting faith, which in combination produce a greater sense of innocence and a renewed ability to once again be awed by that which is awesome. (Lest there be any doubt, the value of being awed should not be underestimated. As children we are constantly in awe of people, places, and things, which brings about a passion for life; but as we gain knowledge and information, our ability to be awed is lessened, and often leads to stoicism and hard-heartedness.)

To further differentiate childishness from childlikeness, bear in mind that children act childishly because it is a perfectly natural state of being for them, but that when adults act childishly it is a perfectly *unnatural* state of being. Indeed, while there is no absolute standard for socially acceptable behavior, it is fair to state that, as people get older, unhealthy characteristics of youth are *increasingly* frowned upon. There may be societal pockets that find such behavior acceptable, but greater society generally looks down on those who are rebellious simply for the sake thereof, or act on uncontrolled desires, or blindly indulge in curiosities (many of which are inevitably destructive). To be sure, in varying degrees all people engage in *unhealthy* youthful behavior, yet most manage to control it somewhat by steadily gaining maturity, insight, and logic. Given that developing control over unhealthy youthful tendencies is a lifelong endeavor, it is to be expected that young people will at times act in a manner unbecoming "acceptable" behavior. But adults who consistently give in to pointless rebellion, desire, or curiosity have failed to replace their childish nature with adult maturity, and thus are deemed, appropriately, as childish.

So as not to confuse the issue, it must be noted that our *inherent* nature contains a mixture of both healthy and unhealthy characteristics. While unassuming humility, unabashed love, and undoubting faith come naturally to children, so too does the propensity to sin. All people are born into sin, and as evidenced by repeated displays—*by adults*—of temper tantrums, possessiveness, pettiness and selfishness, nobody *completely* loses what they inherit. Thus it is essential to acknowledge our shortcomings for what they are and willingly accept the grace offered by Jesus Christ.

Given that worldly paradigms generally lie in stark contrast to the absolute Truth of God's Word, it is crucial that we become ever cognizant of the sizable chasm between worldliness and godliness. Think of the integral lessons you learned while growing up, and perhaps of the "lessons" you absorb even today. Does an influx of *worldly* knowledge move you closer to God? Absolutely not! Yet, unfortunately, the vast majority of what we learn has much to do with the world and little to do with God.

To become godly we must parallel discarding much of what the world teaches us with developing a personal relationship with the source of godliness, Jesus Christ. To do otherwise is to deny oneself spiritual fulfillment, for while worldliness brings natural erosion to the *relatively* innocuous childlike qualities we start out with, godliness *restores* those qualities, and thus properly positions us for fulfillment.

Of Knowledge and Wisdom

In many respects, we are living in an unprecedented age. Technological, scientific, medical, industrial, educational, and financial breakthroughs seem to take place every day. Yet though we possess more worldly knowledge than ever before, most of us are woefully lacking in wisdom. Even worse is that many people actually mistake knowledge *for* wisdom.

Worldly knowledge is readily available, but Biblical *wisdom*—the only "wisdom" truly worthy of being labeled as such—comes only through living for Jesus Christ. Some of the most knowledgeable people in the world are some of the most unfulfilled people in the world, and some of the least knowledgeable people in the world are some of the most fulfilled people in the world. That is not to suggest that knowledge is unimportant (Scripture makes clear that it is vitally important), but that *in itself* it holds little value. The world tends to equate knowledge with credibility, and credibility with wisdom. But while knowledge in itself *positions* us to be credible, it does not ensure that our credibility is viable. Let us not forget that when Jesus admonished the Pharisees, as He did on several occasions, it was not because they lacked knowledge but because they were enslaved to it. Scripture makes clear that knowledge is not an end in itself, but a vital *component* of wisdom, which comes only through the Lord:

> *For the LORD gives wisdom, and from his mouth come knowledge and understanding. For wisdom will enter your heart, and knowledge will be pleasant to your soul.*
>
> *(Proverbs 2:6, 10)*

On our own (in the absence of Christ), we mistake knowledge for wisdom; but when we live for Jesus, the godly knowledge we accrue serves as an essential supplement for godly wisdom.

Unlearning

To reclaim our youthful inheritance we must be reborn as a child of Jesus Christ:

> *In reply Jesus declared, "I tell you the truth, no one can see the kingdom of God unless he is born again."*
>
> *(John 3:3)*

When we accept Jesus as our Lord and Savior, we are properly positioned to reclaim our youthful inheritance. Yet as Scripture teaches that we must become as little children to gain the kingdom of heaven (ref. Mark 10:16), it is imperative that we purposefully *unlearn* much of the worldly knowledge we have acquired.

Make no mistake, unlearning is much more difficult than learning. Our natural inclination is not to qualitatively decrease our worldly knowledge, but to quantitatively increase it.

What do we need to unlearn? That love is selective. That societal harmony comes through mass acceptance. That self-worth is subjective. That truth is whatever we want to make it. That science answers all of life's mysteries. That religiousness is godliness. That inner-strength is enough to overcome anything. That knowledge is wisdom. That some people are more important than others. That happiness and joy are the same thing. That youthfulness is frivolousness.

Living for Jesus positions us to shed the many false worldly paradigms we have acquired over our lifetime. If you subscribe to the Good News of Jesus Christ, then why deny yourself the fullness of its power?

At one time you were unassumingly humble, unabashedly loving, and unwaveringly faithful. Selectively unlearning what the world teaches is a vital step for reclaiming your inheritance. Worldly knowledge gives way to Biblical wisdom as God's Truth is revealed. To embrace wisdom is to embrace your inner child:

> *Then Jesus prayed this prayer: "O father, Lord of heaven and earth, thank you for hiding the truth from those who think themselves so wise and clever, and for revealing it to the childlike."*
>
> *(Matthew 11:25)*

It's time to take back what the world has robbed you of. Don't wait.

Who's Teaching Who?

As the old adage "children are to be seen but not heard" implies, there are many who believe that kids have little or nothing to offer adults. Indeed, such an outlook is understandable given that knowledge resides with those who are older and wiser, and that before one can be a contributing member of society one must first learn the ways of the world. Yet while this philosophy is not necessarily incorrect, it is incomplete.

Adults often fail to account for the fact that many characteristics of youth are absolutely healthy (and *Biblical*), and that the best role models for healthy youthfulness are children. Contrary to children having nothing to offer adults, children have much to offer adults, if only we are willing to learn from them.

I received a valuable lesson in youthfulness a few years back when I volunteered to facilitate a Junior Achievement program to kindergartners at a local elementary school. (Junior Achievement is an international non-profit organization dedicated to educating and inspiring young people about business and economics.)

Eighteen little people excitedly took their spots as I began the first "class." Reading the initial segment of the story "Rico and His Friends," I was instantly captivated by the children. They enthusiastically answered my questions, and even more enthusiastically delighted in the activities I led them through.

When I made my weekly visits over the next four weeks, the children became increasingly enamored with the story and activities, as well as . . . *me.* The feeling was mutual—I had made eighteen new friends.

During my last visit to the class, I gave each child a certificate of completion and a small keepsake. Satisfied that I had taught the children well, I began packing up to head back to work. Then, one by one, the children began hugging me! I was surprised that they had not yet learned that it is not "normal" protocol for students to give hugs to guest teachers . . . yet I reveled in their affection and returned it with gusto.

And that's when it hit me: *These children had taught me more than I had taught them!*

Beyond being intrigued by a simple story; beyond being unmistakably excited as soon as I entered their classroom; beyond clinging to a certificate and bookmark as prized possessions; beyond all that and more, these children were unassumingly humble, unabashedly loving, and unwaveringly trusting.

I learned a valuable lesson from a group of kindergartners, a lesson reinforced during the following two years as I taught Junior Achievement for two more kindergarten classes.

If you desire to be youthful, I highly recommend that you learn from the best.

Zealousness

Few words in the English language evoke a more immediate or pronounced response than the word *zealousness*. Most people are wary of others who are so fervent in their beliefs that they cannot, or will not, consider other viewpoints. Even within the context of Christianity—especially within the context of Christianity—zealousness must be approached with considerable caution and selectivity. Why? Because while anyone who has developed proper understanding and appreciation for salvation through Jesus Christ cannot help but be lovingly zealous in faith, love for Jesus is diametrically opposed to love for the world, thus zealousness for Jesus is considered by many "worldly" people to be undesirable extremism.

Perhaps you believe that contempt displayed toward Christians who are openly zealous for Jesus is not directed at them as much as it is toward zealous behavior in itself. This school of thought assumes that people believe zealousness *of any sort* to be overtly and unhealthily extreme. But a closer look reveals that zealousness *in itself* is not frowned upon nearly as much as we might think it is.

For example, zealousness for physical appearance, zealousness for money, zealousness for career aspirations, and zealousness for a whole host of other earthly pursuits carries significant worldly credibility, particularly in western society. Each and every day thousands of people spend massive amounts of money to "enhance" their appearance, or risk financial security in deference to quickly accumulating wealth, or set aside healthy life balance in favor of climbing the company ladder. Are these people perceived as extremists for their zealousness toward worldly pursuits? Perhaps in some circles they are, but in the eyes of many they are to be commended for living life with passion.

In the context of greater society, when one objectively considers the things that we are *demonstratively* passionate about, one must conclude that "normal" life in America is characterized in large part by unhealthy zealousness. To writ:

- According to the report "Sexuality, Contraception, and the Media," released by the American Academy of Pediatrics Committee on Public Education in January 2001, adolescents will have spent 15,000 hours watching television by the time they graduate, and will view nearly 14,000 sexual references per year. With sexuality ingrained in our minds from our earliest days, should we be surprised by the fact that 27.5 million people in the U.S. visited adult-oriented pornographic Web sites in January 2002? (Based on data from Nielsen/NetRatings, the Internet audience measurement service).

- According to Cardweb.com (the U.S. Payment Card Information Network), the average credit card balance per household with at least one credit card was $8,562 as of September 30, 2001; 1.3 million cardholders declared bankruptcy in 2001.

- According to the American Council on Alcoholism, over 20 million people in the United States have a serious problem with alcohol. Moreover, according to the National Highway Traffic Safety Administration (NHTSA), of the 41,945 total traffic fatalities in 2000, 41 percent (17,380) involved alcohol.

The list could go on and on, but the point has been made sufficiently. And lest you believe that unhealthy zealousness is a western phenomenon, be assured that worldly zealousness, *particularly for false religious beliefs,* is in many respects even more predominant in the east, as evidenced by regular displays of fanatical repression and violence against those whose beliefs don't align with the majority. Regardless of which corner of the world we occupy, zealousness toward anything ungodly is invariably destructive in nature, while zealousness toward anything godly, *when properly founded and channeled,* is invariably constructive. Yet in spite of the apparent black-and-white nature of zealousness, we must be ever cognizant of the fact that Christians who are demonstrably zealous in their love toward Jesus Christ are not seen as commendable in the eyes of many, but rather as condemnable. Whether we like it or not, from the vantage point of mainstream society, zealousness for God is not afforded the same latitude as zealousness for worldly pursuits.

Recognizing this basic truth forces us to make an important decision: we can hide our zeal for the Lord and safely assimilate ourselves into worldliness, or we can be openly, lovingly zealous toward Jesus while inevitably (but not disdainfully) distancing ourselves from those who do not share our fervor.

Before you instinctively choose one option or the other, do not lose sight of the fact that condemnation toward zealous Christians comes not only from non-Christians but from fellow Christians as well. Indeed, it is folly to not acknowledge that Christians who are overt by nature are commonly perceived by Christians who are covert by nature to be lacking in godly humility and authenticity. And it is equally folly to not acknowledge that naturally covert Christians are commonly perceived by naturally overt Christians to be lacking in godly passion and love.

I am sorry to say that when it comes to the "piousness versus zealousness" debate, many Christians are quick to judge others according to their own belief system, in which bias and prejudice are inherent. In fact, and most unfortunately, judging other people is rather prevalent among Christians: Christian denominations judge one another as too conservative, too liberal, too ritualistic, too charismatic, not charismatic enough, too ... whatever, and, within our churches, members judge others according to similar criteria. Who's right when everybody's wrong?

Only Jesus lived without sin, therefore Jesus was the *only* person to have ever loved God with absolute purity. Incredibly, Jesus' perfect love for the Father was paralleled by His perfect love for us, culminated by the unspeakable sacrifice He made on our behalf. Only Jesus is fit to judge what lies within each person, and until that time comes, only Scripture is truly worthy of our individual and collective governance. Yes, for the sake of order and compliance we need governments to create societal standards of conduct and to govern according to those standards, but for the sake of our eternal destiny, what lies within—our morality—must be based on and governed by the Word of God.

There is little question that zealousness is an extremely challenging area for believers. Further compounding the fact that we face the very real prospect of ridicule and/or disdain from others for openly demonstrating faith in Jesus Christ is that we also face the very real prospect of acting in a manner *contrary* to what we believe in. Our dichotomy is this: while properly founded (and channeled) zealousness is invaluable for personal spiritual fulfillment and bringing God's Word to fruition, unfounded and/or improperly channeled zealousness tends to bring about unhealthy isolation, diminished credibility, a subjective belief system, and, potentially, ungodly behavior.

Christians face a great challenge in bringing forth the gospel Truth of Jesus Christ in a manner that neither adds nor subtracts from its purity. Every word we say, every action we take, and, yes, every word we write, ought not to add or subtract from Truth but rather serve to draw others *toward* absolute Truth—God's Word. Even godly people with godly intentions cannot add anything of value to Scripture. What we can do, however, is give our best effort to attract others to God's Word while being careful to not detract from its purity.

The bottom line challenge for Christians is to be lovingly zealous toward Jesus and His teachings, *while* remaining discerning, empathetic, faithful, humble, kind, and loving. If you believe that our challenge is easy, I urge you to consider it carefully, prayerfully, and objectively. Those who have accepted Jesus as their Lord and Savior have been assured the most precious gift imaginable, which is sufficient cause for zealousness toward our Redeemer. But as Scripture calls for us to empathetic, faithful, humble, kind, and, above all, loving, any zealousness we have must never displace those "core" requirements of godliness, and in fact must always be subordinate to them. Regardless of how others may perceive us, if we consistently embody Christian empathy, faith, humility, kindness, and love, then our zealousness toward our Lord, and, for that matter, toward godliness in general, will be perfectly natural.

As Jesus' disciples, we are called to *"go and make disciples of all nations"* (ref. Matthew 28:19). My earlier claim that "zealousness must be approached with considerable caution and selectivity" is based primarily on the risk we bring to fulfilling the great Commission if we place zealousness in front of godliness. The risk is real, for the end result of placing zealousness before godliness is inevitably a perversion of Truth. How do you suppose non-believers will react if we attempt to force our beliefs on them without a willingness to listen to them? How do you suppose non-believers will judge *Christianity* if they observe us displaying more passion toward religious rituals than toward our Lord and Savior? Will non-believers see us as Christ-like if we are demonstrably zealous in faith, yet equally zealous in gossiping about others?

Now is a good time for a reality check. Let us briefly walk through answers to the not so rhetorical questions asked above.

The first question asks how non-believers will react if we attempt to force our beliefs on them without a willingness to listen to what they have to say. The answer to this question is obvious, and has been proven time and time again: people are not receptive to *anything* being forced upon them. As ambassadors for Jesus Christ, we must act according to His Word. *Do not* condone other viewpoints, but be willing to listen to them, for failure to do so diminishes your credibility, and, by association, the credibility of Christianity in the eyes of others. Be zealous *out of love* for Christ, but let your zealousness naturally reflect genuine love for the Lord. And show Christian respect to others by listening to what they have to say!

> *Even a fool is thought wise if he keeps silent, and discerning if he holds his tongue.*
>
> *(Proverbs 17:28)*

The second question asks how non-believers will judge Christianity if they observe us displaying more passion toward religious rituals than toward our Lord and Savior. In this case, regardless of the fact that we do not personally define Christianity but merely represent Christianity, non-believers will view our zealousness toward ritualism as akin to zealousness toward Christianity, and thus will likely consider Christianity to be heartless and pointless. This is a bitter pill to swallow for many, but Scripture tells us that zealousness for religious ritual and law for the sake thereof is not godly, and that the zeal we display for rituals and laws will prevent people from coming to know real Truth:

Then Jesus said to the crowds and to his disciples: "The teachers of the law and the Pharisees sit in Moses' seat. So you must obey them and do everything they tell you. But do not do what they do, for they do not practice what they preach. They tie up heavy loads and put them on men's shoulders, but they themselves are not willing to lift a finger to move them. "Everything they do is done for men to see: They make their phylacteries wide and the tassels on their garments long; they love the place of honor at banquets and the most important seats in the synagogues; they love to be greeted in the marketplaces and to have men call them 'Rabbi.'"

(Matthew 23:1–7)

The third question asks whether non-believers will consider us Christ-like if we are demonstrably zealous in our faith yet equally zealous in gossiping about others. I am sorry to report that the answer to this question is quite frequently *yes*. We cannot escape the fact that non-believers are looking to rationalize *why* they don't believe in Jesus Christ, and that our behavior is ideal fodder for that rationality. Many who are struggling with faith issues and know that we are Christians will associate us with Christ. Just as a child's initial standard for parental performance is not based on what he has read but on his own firsthand observations, so also do many spiritually uncommitted people equate Christianity with the Christians they know firsthand. When it comes to how others view Christianity, we must look deep in the mirror and conclude that demonstrable zealousness for Jesus Christ, when coupled with a propensity to engage in petty gossip and slander of other people, yields only mistrust and disillusionment:

If anyone considers himself religious and yet does not keep a tight rein on his tongue, he deceives himself and his religion is worthless.

(James 1:26)

Do not let any unwholesome talk come out of your mouths, but only what is helpful for building others up according to their needs, that it may benefit those who listen.

(Ephesians 4:29)

To be zealous without compromising godliness is absolutely challenging! Any zealousness we have must not detract from godliness but merely reflect godliness. When zealousness is a perfectly natural byproduct of godliness, it is spiritually rewarding and richly fulfilling.

Zealousness as an Ally

Having spent ample time going through the precarious nature and potential pitfalls of zealousness, it is now appropriate to properly explain why, in spite of its risks, zealousness for Jesus Christ is a powerful ally for bringing forth genuine, sustainable fulfillment in the Lord Jesus.

There are three important truths to Christian zealousness. The first of these truths is that zealousness must *always* be unwaveringly for the gospel Truth of Jesus Christ, never for religiosity. The Apostle Paul knew that the Galatians were committed to Christianity based on their unmistakable zeal toward Christ and their care and compassion for Paul during a serious illness; indeed, the Galatians considered Paul as if he *"were Christ Jesus himself" (ref. Galatians 4:14)*. So what prompted Paul to write an epistle to the Galatians imploring them to denounce religiosity and rediscover Truth? After Paul had initially moved out of Galatia, many Jewish-Christian fanatics moved into the area and claimed that, as descendants of Abraham, they were the only truly qualified ministers of Christ, and thus were able to perform miracles. These men denounced Paul's teachings and steered the Galatians from living for Christ to living for manmade religious laws. Paul's letter to the Galatians makes clear that zealousness for Truth is desirable, but zealousness for falsehood is most certainly not:

> *Those people are zealous to win you over, but for no good. What they want is to alienate you from us, so that you may be zealous for them. It is fine to be zealous, provided the purpose is good, and to be so always and not just when I am with you.*
>
> *(Galatians 4:17–18)*

The second truth of Christian zealousness is that not only is properly founded and channeled zealousness desirable, it is *essential* for godliness. As our God is not one of docility but of passion, and as to aspire to be godly is to aspire to be more like God, we are called to be passionate for Truth and righteousness:

> *The LORD will march out like a mighty man, like a warrior he will stir up his zeal; with a shout he will raise the battle cry and will triumph over his enemies.*
>
> *(Isaiah 42:13)*

Never be lacking in zeal, but keep your spiritual fervor, serving the Lord.
(Romans 12:11)

The third truth of Christian zealousness is that it is instrumental for dealing with persecution. Zealousness in itself is powerfully effective in offsetting lethargy, and zealousness for Christ is *absolute* empowerment. In contrast to the half-hearted approach to faith that many Christians take (leaving them vulnerable to conforming to the standards of the world), genuine zealousness for God is the very manifestation of love for God. And the power of God is enough to overcome anything of this world:

> *For God did not give us a spirit of timidity, but a spirit of power, of love and of self-discipline. So do not be ashamed to testify about our Lord, or ashamed of me his prisoner. But join with me in suffering for the gospel, by the power of God.*
>
> *(2 Timothy 1:7–8)*

Of Zealousness and Fulfillment

Eternal salvation comes through confessing Jesus Christ as Lord and Savior. Genuine, sustainable fulfillment comes through living according to Scripture. If you desire spiritual fulfillment, I urge you to zealously embrace and live according to the "ingredients" listed in this book, all of which are Biblical and essential for optimal fulfillment. I encourage you to:

Zealously seek proper alignment between foundational beliefs and thoughts, words, and actions. Be zealous in doing weekly assessments of how you are doing in each *Alphabet Soup* "ingredient" every week, and focus on making necessary adjustments in order to progress toward sustained spiritual fulfillment.

Zealously seek balance in your life. Based on your unique DNA, find the optimal balance between mental, physical, social, and spiritual activity. Don't suppress emotion; manage emotion.

Zealously seek to be as Christ-like as you possibly can. Understand that the goal of all Christians must be to perpetually abide in Christ, and that a genuine search for truth and meaning will reveal your unique path to achieving that goal.

Zealousness

Zealously seek to be a discerning child of God. Be obedient in prayer and the study of Scripture so that you can properly discern your gifts and how to best carry out God's will.

Zealously seek to consistently be empathetic toward people. Listen to others and respect them as Christ taught us. Seek common ground and avoid the temptation to judge.

Zealously seek to grow in faith. Zealously avoid inadvertently worshipping the "gods" of our world. Let faith in Jesus Christ change uncertainty into boldness.

Zealously seek God's grace. And zealously *cherish* God's grace. Accept His grace willingly and enthusiastically, and extend Christian grace to other people.

Zealously seek to be appropriately humble. Avoid false humility while striving for true humility. Don't be self-limiting or self-serving, but selfless.

Zealously seek to influence others in a positive manner. Do not equate position or status with credibility, yet use your own position for good. Remember that influence has a tremendous exponential effect.

Zealously seek joy. Know that joy in Jesus Christ is eternal while happiness in worldly pursuits is fleeting. Be like Harriet Tubman, who knew that nothing in the world could rob her of joy in her Lord.

Zealously seek to be kind to others. Kindness may not always be reciprocal, but fulfillment is found when we are unfailingly kind to others. Remember that kindness takes many forms, but must always be based out of love.

Zealously seek to love the Lord your God with all of your heart, soul, and mind, and to love others as yourself. Don't keep score of rights and wrongs, but do remember that the love we display toward others is a direct reflection of our love for God.

Zealously seek a healthy, fulfilling marriage. If you are contemplating marriage, or even if you are already married, examine your hearts, minds, and souls to ensure that both you and your partner are emotionally, mentally, and spiritually synchronized. Marriage is all about give-and-take, yet its rewards are incalculable.

Zealously seek intellectual, social, and spiritual nourishment, for doing so is requisite for genuine fulfillment. Nourish others and watch in amazement as they grow in Christ.

Zealously seek optimism by being purposefully grounded in realism. Let the Truth of Jesus Christ and the promise of salvation through Jesus Christ produce *genuine* optimism.

Zealously seek to be prayerful. God wants to hear from you! Let obedience borne out of love and desire for Jesus produce a natural desire to be in communion with Jesus.

Zealously seek to understand and live according to your unique quest. God has a specific plan for you, and if you are open to receiving it you will be blessed in abundance.

Zealously seek to have healthy relationships. Let your relationship with God govern all of your relationships. Be zealous in trying to see people as God sees them, in being hospitable toward others, in settling disputes quickly, in never compromising your belief in God, and in treasuring your family and friends.

Zealously seek to be a good steward for God. Let your time, talent, and money be put to good use for the kingdom of God.

Zealously seek to be transparent. Strive to let others see you as you truly are, not purposefully but naturally. Let your light shine!

Zealously seek to be unique. Understand that "uniqueness" by the world's standards is not unique whatsoever, but that authenticity in Jesus Christ is absolutely unique.

Zealously seek to be venturous. Allow God to carry you up your spiritual mountains and you will be richly blessed!

Zealously seek to worship the Lord in spirit and truth. Let your worship for the Lord properly reflect your love for the Lord. And never fail to recognize Jesus as the Head of the Church.

Zealously seek to leave a legacy. Be godly in all the roles you occupy in life, and do not discount the effect you have on others.

Zealously seek to be appropriately youthful. Be childlike. Let unassuming humility, unabashed love, and undoubting faith become you. Recognize that you will have to unlearn some worldly teachings.

Zealously seek to be appropriately zealous. Never let zealousness for the sake thereof to pull you away from other core elements of godliness. Let zealousness be a natural byproduct of godliness.

Zealously seek the Lord your God; in Him you will be eternally fulfilled.

Sometimes Zealousness Comes in Pairs!

Pastors' Mike and Erin were still completing Seminary when they arrived at Beechwood Church as husband and wife. To say that Mike and Erin were lovingly and faithfully zealous for Jesus Christ would be an understatement, as would to say that Mike and Erin helped carry Beechwood through a difficult time of transition. Indeed, they shepherded our church through a turbulent time period, even as they wondered what role they would have in the church going forward.

After successfully bridging a yearlong gap between one Senior Pastor departing and his replacement coming on board, Mike and Erin began to feel God's subtle call. They had been at Beechwood for around three years and had focused their energies on carrying out God's will, but something told them that God had new plans for them. Thus for several months Mike and Erin prayed for discernment, until finally God revealed His plan: they would co-pastor a small church in upstate New York, a mere twenty minutes from where Mike grew up and where his parents still lived. This was an ideal arrangement if ever there was one, for beyond Mike being able to hop on a John Deere at his dad's farm (which he longed to do), Mike and Erin could split pastoral duties *while* spending equal time raising their two young children. God had a plan for Mike and Erin, and their zealousness toward heeding God's will enabled God's plan to come to fruition.

Since Mike and Erin are two of my favorite people, I was honored when asked to take part in a tribute to them prior to their departure from our church. Representing "Men Working," I was asked to "roast" Mike for a few minutes—out of love and reverence, of course! I chided Mike for inadvertently locking some of us out of the church one morning; for responding to a draft letter I had written by (jokingly) telling me it was too poorly written to send out; and for initially failing to surmise that *he* was the guest of honor at a surprise breakfast. After gently "roasting" Mike, I expressed my deep and heartfelt admiration toward Mike and Erin, particularly for their absolute passion and commitment to their Lord, and to their Lord's Church.

Zealousness takes many forms, but when it is naturally borne out of love for God and love for people, its effect is powerful and undeniable. Pastor Mike and Pastor Erin are living proof of that truth.

Alphabet Soup

Spiritual fulfillment is a gift from God that is second only to salvation. It is right there at your fingertips, just waiting for you to seize it.

The recipe you have been given is based on God's Word. The recipe *works*. Alphabet Soup will lead you toward genuine, sustainable fulfillment. Its ingredients are pure and its flavor rich. And best of all, once you commit to subsisting on a spiritual diet of Alphabet Soup, you will never again experience spiritual starvation; genuine, sustained fulfillment in Jesus Christ will be yours.

Will you choose fulfillment today?

Carpe Diem.

To order additional copies of

Alphabet SOUP

Have your credit card ready and call:

1-877-421-READ (7323)

or please visit our web site at
www.pleasantword.com

Also available at: www.amazon.com

Printed in the United States
27300LVS00001B/268